A RECORD

OF

PSYCHIC EXPERIENCES

BY

GEORGE F. GOERNER

FIRST PRESIDENT

LOS ANGELES SOCIETY FOR ADVANCED PSYCHICAL RESEARCH

LOS ANGELES, CAL.

Copyright © 2013 Read Books Ltd.
This book is copyright and may not be
reproduced or copied in any way without
the express permission of the publisher in writing

British Library Cataloguing-in-Publication Data
A catalogue record for this book is available from the
British Library

Fortune Telling

Fortune telling is the practice of predicting information about a person's life. The scope of fortune telling is in principle identical with the practice of divination, however in practice the two differ substantially. The disparity results from the fact that divination refers to predictions considered part of a religious ritual, invoking deities or spirits, while the term 'fortune-telling' implies a less serious or formal setting, even one of popular culture. In the latter environment, belief in occult workings behind the prediction is less prominent than the concept of suggestion, spiritual or practical advisory or affirmation.

Historically, fortune-telling grew out of the folklorist reception of Renaissance magic, specifically associated with the Romani people. During the nineteenth and twentieth century, methods of divination from non-Western cultures such as the *I Ching* (a classic Chinese text) were also adopted as methods of fortune-telling in Western popular culture. Common methods used for fortune telling in Europe and the Americas include astromancy (by the stars), pendulum reading (by the movements of a suspended object), spirit-board reading (by planchette or talking board), tasseography (reading tea leaves in a cup), cartomancy (fortune telling with cards), tarot reading, and chiromancy (palmistry, reading of the palms).

Tarot reading is one of the more common types of fortune telling, and practitioners are split as to the exact nature of the process. Some claim they are guided by a spiritual force while others believe the cards help them to tap into a collective unconscious or their own creative, brainstorming subconscious. The divinatory meanings of the cards commonly used today are derived mostly from cartomancer Jean-Baptiste Alliette (also known as Etteilla) and Marrie-Anne Lenormand (1776-1843). Their history delves much deeper however and many involved in the occult arts have traced their practice back to ancient Egypt and divine hermetic wisdom. 'Hermeticism' is an especially old and venerated tradition, based primarily upon the writings of Hermes Trismegistus, who greatly influenced Western esoteric tradition during the Renaissance and the Reformation. Its doctrine affirms that a single, true theology exists which is present in all religions, and was given by God to man in antiquity. Despite this long history, the first documented complete tarot deck only dates from fifteenth century Northern Italy.

One of the other most widespread methods for divining the future is astromancy; based on the premise that there is a relationship between astronomical phenomena and events in the human world. Many cultures have attached importance to astronomical events, and the Indians, Chinese, and Mayans developed elaborate systems for predicting terrestrial events from celestial observations. In the West, astrology most often consists of a system of horoscopes purporting to explain aspects of a person's personality and predict future events in their life based on the positions of the sun, moon, and other celestial objects at the time of their birth. Most newspapers and magazines carry predictive columns based on these celestial influences – although it should be noted that no scientific studies have shown support for their accuracy.

Western fortune-tellers typically attempt predictions on matters such as future romantic, financial and childbearing prospects as well as more specific 'character readings.' In contemporary Western culture, it appears that women consult fortune-tellers more than men, and some build substantial, life-long relationships with their 'tellers.' Despite this popularity, there is often extreme opposition against fortune-telling in Christianity, Islam and Judaism based on biblical prohibitions against divination. It is banned in the Book of Micah (5:12) and many civil laws have also forbidden the practice. This has caused discord in the Jewish community especially due to prevalent views on mysticism.

As is evident even from this incredibly brief introduction to the art of fortune telling, it is a branch of human mysticism and belief that has an incredibly long and intriguing history. Over the centuries, and across the globe, some form of 'divination' has always been practiced. We hope that the current reader is inspired by this book to find out more about this fascinating subject.

Foreword

THIS book is not for sale. It will not be found on any bookstand. It has only one excuse for being in print. During the many psychic readings which I have had, and the many "circles" and "seances" which I have attended, friends from "the other side" have asked me to show their loved ones on this side how to reach them and how to communicate with them. These are supplications from those on the spirit side of life anxious to make known their continued existence to friends on the earth plane. They involve so many persons still in the flesh that the only way they can be reached, and convinced, is to distribute the evidence among them in this way. The copies go most entirely to my own personal friends. They know me and have confidence in my sanity and veracity, and when I say that the book cannot be bought at any price they will know that I have no pecuniary gain to expect from its publication. I am trying to carry out an obligation to friends "beyond the veil." Their friends on this side can take advantage of it or not, as they please. That's up to them.

Just a word as to the method of preparing the record: The psychic readings were all given in daylight. These were sometimes written down in full in shorthand at the time of delivery. At other times I merely made sufficient memoranda of the message and wrote it out after leaving the psychic. In the case of dark room seances, immediately after the seance was over I made memoranda of the important points while they were still fresh in my memory; then completed the record from these memoranda after reaching my room or office.

The point I wish to emphasize is that while much of the matter obtained during a period of many months would necessarily have to be omitted because of the immense volume it would make, **there is no matter in the record that was not actually delivered in the psychic reading or the seance room.**

There are some mediums who seem to be unable to keep from injecting their personality into a message, and where the message is not clear to them are inclined to fill it out themselves either from the conscious or sub-conscious mind. There are others who will not deliver anything in a message which does not clearly come to them "from the other side." I have had many readings from psychics and attended many seances where the message lacked the stamp of genuineness. In all such cases I have eliminated the message from the record entirely. I could well afford to do this in view of the fact that no part of this record was originally prepared for the benefit of any one except myself, and I am indifferent to the opinion and criticisms of those who do not care to accept it as authentic.

The Author

THE QUESTION

Is there anything to spiritualism, or spiritism? Yes, there is just that much to it that a weak intellect had better let it alone. Unless you are capable of grasping it in all its profound scientific import, it is something beyond you. Unless your mind has been trained to logical thinking and analysis you will not get very much out of it. For in its fullest unfoldment it involves a study not only of spiritualism and spiritism, but likewise of psychology, biology, chemistry and physics. If you are not equal to the task, if you have no aptitude for these things you will never get more than the skimmings that come to those who dabble in spiritualism as phenomenon—hunters actuated by ignorance, superstition or curiosity.

If you are satisfied that you know it all and are ready to dismiss it as a farce because you have visited a few half-baked "fortune tellers" who "couldn't tell you anything," you probably received all that was coming to you, and those who expect to make a fortune by paying a medium a dollar for a "reading," or expect to receive advice by which they might bend the will of another to their own use, generally reap for their reward a dose of delusion and further skepticism.

If you still feel that you know enough about it to condemn it, you might find some consolation in the fact that the giant intellects of the present generation have spent from ten to forty years in patient, exhaustive, hardheaded, coldblooded scientific investigation and experimental work with the persistent determination either to prove or disprove psychic phenomena and have wound up, in every case that we know of, by accepting it as a proven fact.

In this list of investigators will be found Sir Oliver Lodge, Sir Arthur Conan Doyle, Sir Wm. Crooks, Sir Wm. F. Barrett, of the Royal Academy of Dublin; the late Dr. F. W. H. Myers, Prof. Edmund Gurney, Prof. Podmore, Prof. Henry Sidgewick, of Cambridge University, England; Sir Balfour Stewart, the noted physicist; Sir Arthur Balfour, Dr. Camille Flammarion, famous French astronomer; Dr. Lombroso, the Italian criminologist; Dr. Ochorovics, the Russian savant; the late Lord Brougham Prof. Hereward Carrington, Ph. D.; Dr. James H. Hyslop, of the Columbia University chair in mental and moral philosophy; Dr. Wm. James, psychologist of Harvard University; the late Dr. Isaac Funk, preacher, scientist and man of letters; Dr. Albert Durrant Watson, Canadian astronomer; Prof. Edgar Lucien Larkin, the astronomer in charge of Mt. Lowe Observatory; Dr. Von Schrenk-Notzing; Wm. Dunseath Eton, founder and editor of the Chicago-Record Herald; Dr. Alfred Russell Wallace, British exponent of physical science; the late Rev. W. Stainton Moses, the late Archdeacon Wilberforce of London; the late Archdeacon Colley of London Rev. Dr. Dearmer; Rev. Dr. F. Holmes-Duddon; Rev. Minot J. Savage, D.D.; Rev. Chas. Tweedale, F.R.G.S.; G. Stanley Hall, president of Clark University; Prof. Geo. S. Fullerton, of the University of Pennsylvania; Prof. Edward Pickering, of Harvard College Observatory; Dr. Henry P. Bowditch, of Harvard Medical School and Dr. Chas. S. Minot, of the same school.

This list could be extended almost indefinitely and among them you would find the deepest thinkers of the past and present generation. Every one of them a man of international reputation—a reputation won by brains alone. Each and every one of these scholars has given years to the study and research work of determining the truth or falsity of spiritualism—or spiritism. Have you spent as many hours at it as they have years? If not, then forever hold your peace. It isn't a question of what you **think** about it,—but how much do you **know** about it?

There are puzzles, contradictions and confusions, for which the medium is not always to blame and unless you have gone far enough to understand the conditions which bring about these interferences, better let it alone, because your visit to the medium will be a very perplexing and very unsatisfactory one in most cases. Without this knowledge you cannot assist the medium and you cannot assist "the other side." Neither can you protect yourself against fraud (conscious or unconscious) on the part of the medium or ignorance on your own part.

Let us take, as an instance, predictions on material affairs: My own experience has been that we very seldom get "bad" news from the other side. The messages most invariably seem to be to the effect that "things will come out all right," and "you are going to be much better satisfied with conditions in a few weeks," etc. But as affairs in human life develop this does not turn out to be the case and it seems all very disconcerting and confusing to the novice who understands but little of the psychic law. But in this connection it is necessary to remember two things: First, cheerfulness and hopefulness reign supreme on the "other side," and we are repeatedly exhorted to apply this law to our own life. Secondly, the "other side" very often talks in symbols and telling us "things will be all right in a little while" may have reference to a better condition either mentally or materially in this world, or it may refer entirely to a state of relief from anxiety on the other side in the future state. There is plenty of evidence that this is a fact, and this might well be borne in mind by those who know nothing of the scientific side of this doctrine and still persist in seeking mediums for commercial purposes.

Then, too, there are those who expect more—very much more—than they have any right to receive. There are people who will never get it through them that death does not necessarily make us omniscient, omnipotent or omnipresent. Why should an imperfect human being die tonight and wake up tomorrow as a perfect spirit? Life on the other side is a matter of progression and no one becomes perfect there until he has progressed to perfection. If communicating spirits disagree with one another as to conditions here or on the other side, that is no different from what happens with preachers and statesmen on this side.

Friends frequently ask me to suggest "some good medium" to whom they might go. These people often have nothing at heart except money matters, some trifling domestic affair or a commercial success, which usually means the subjugation of some one else's mind to their own personal gain,—the class who seldom get anything from the other side that is worth while. They must understand that spiritualism, or spiritism, operates under definite psychic laws. It is a deep subject and an endless study and my advice in most cases would be not to touch it unless you are going into it earnestly, studiously and deeply. You will never get very far with it, nor very much out of it, in any other way.

Just a word as to evidence in the following pages: If the reader expects something in the way of sensational phenomena, something that will take him off his feet and make his head swim in wonderment, he will not find it. Evidence of spiritualism, or spiritism, does not come that way. The evidence that counts is the **cumulative** evidence; that is, the fragments of convincing proof which in themselves, singly, one piece at a time, mean apparently so little, but in their cumulative effect, in their sum total, they form a continuos, logical chain of evidence which in time will reveal enough to convince any intelligent, living human of the fact of the continuity of life without a break between this world and the next; will prove the truth of spirit return and communication between souls on both sides of the grave. But if you have not the time, the patience or the money to carry out a logical plan of research work, do not expect any one visit to the medium, to the seance room or the manifestation parlor to furnish you the proof,—**because it would be a very unusual occurrence if you got it that way.**

To those who ask, "Well, suppose it is true, what good can it do us to know it?" there is but this answer: If it means nothing to you to know that death does not end all, that the grave does not mean either temporary or permanent annihilation, and that the "stream of consciousness" continues; that life goes on without a break; that your mother, father, sister, wife and children still live; that they can communicate with you, materialize before you and give intelligent evidence of their continued existence and watchful care over you—if these things mean nothing to you, then you may well ask "What good is it?" But if they do mean anything to you, then the question answers itself.

Those who still persist in trying to account for everything in the way of spirit communication by telepathy or mind-reading need to be told that no phase of psychic phenomena has received more careful study, more scientific investigation and experimentation by the leading thinkers of the day than this feature, and the importance of telepathy has been confined to its logical limits. It can no longer be given the serious consideration conferred upon it by the critic who has no more than a shallow knowledge of its scope.

Another test adopted by crucial investigators is that where a number of different psychics, none of them acquainted with the sitter or his affairs, and none of them likely to come into collusion, will give practically the same communicators, with the proper description of each, and will properly connect up the identities, it may be considered reasonably evidential.

But I repeat that this is a deep study. It takes time, patience and effort to get satisfactory results. In no other way will you get them, and in no other way will you find the answer to the many puzzling questions that will arise; such as, "Why do my friends from the other side not come to me direct instead of through a medium?" "Why do Indian guides and Indian controls persist in injecting themselves into these seances?" "Why are the seances usually held in the dark?" "Why do they need a cabinet?" "Where do the 'spirit clothes' come from?" etc., etc. There is reason for these things and not until you understand the law will you solve the problem.

MATERIALIZATIONS

In May, 1921, a friend and business associate induced me to accompany him to one of the materialization seances being held by Mr. and Mrs. Jonson at their home on Vermont avenue. Los Angeles. I had previously had no experience with phenomena of this character, but went through faith in the integrity and conservatism of my friend; but nevertheless with a feeling that he had overdrawn the demonstration, or at least over estimated its genuineness. I did not fear trickery, deception or fraud, for I was ready to believe that the progressive element of spiritualism had eliminated most of the objectionable class of mediums from public seances.

I, with the rest of the spectators, was given every opportunity to make any investigations or examinations of the premises if I decided to do so. This I declined and was willing to take chances on my judgment of human nature in sizing up the calibre and sincerity of Mr. and Mrs. Jonson, plus the intelligence of the visitors, most of whom had already witnessed many of these materializations.

I sat at this first seance with my eyes riveted on the curtain and clothed in my right mind. I missed nothing that came out, went in, or up or down, despite the fact that the room was fairly dark, one shaded electric light being all that was used—augmented in most instances with greater or less intensity by the luminous character of the "spirits," or materialized forms.

After this evening I attended many of these seances, and have seen more than 200 spirit forms fully materialized. I have seen as many as 28 come into the room in one evening, and as many as half a dozen on the floor at the same time. I have seen them appear as little children, young men and women, aged people—sons, daughters, mothers, fathers and grandparents; have seen them recognized by relatives and identified — guides, controls, Hindoo priests, Indian chiefs, poets, noted soldiers, men of letters and statesmen. I have listened to these spirits converse with friends and relatives; have heard them lecture on morality, the psychology of spiritualism and discourse on the events of the day in our own world. I have heard them sing—men and women—with clear, sweet voices that would reach to the farthest corners of a large auditorium.

On this particular occasion, my first visit, I estimated the number of people in the room and the average contribution in money, and grasped the salient fact that any such thing as importing characters from the outside to duplicate and act the part of some 20 to 28 spirit forms appearing at each seance, two and three times a week, representing both sexes of all ages and nationalities, would have involved an expense way beyond any compensation that it would be possible for the mediums to collect at these seances. **That dismissed the only possible flagrant element of fraud entering into the meeting.**

Following this I determined that there must be more or less authentic literature on the subject, and figured it out in my own mind that the best way to get at the bottom of the study would be to investigate it from its scientific side. I made out a list of the better known investigators purchased many volumes and read them ravenously at the rate of one to three volumes per week. I dug into the reports of the three leading societies for psychical research, viz.: the American Society, the British and the French societies, the reports of the three societies comprising many thousands of pages of evidential matter.

In this reading I was confronted by the bold statement, made by eminent scholars, that there never was a thorough, profound student of note who had investigated the doctrine of spiritism **who did not wind up by accepting it as a proven fact.**

Following is a detail record of a number of these seances. The four records given in the early part of the volume are representative of the meetings that took place, and the results obtained, at the general run of seances as they were conducted by Mr. and Mrs. Jonson prior to the organization of the Society for Advanced Psychical Research. After the organization of this society the results were even more satisfactory, as the members all worked together as a unit for harmonious conditions. They had learned how to hold their minds receptive, open to conviction, free of prejudice and divested of preconceived notions on the subject of spirit return. Most of them are members who have gone far enough to know that the frame of mind has a good deal to do with the results obtained and that harmony is an essential keynote. The previous mixed crowds were excluded and the attendance confined to the permanent membership of the society.

A word regarding the Jonson's: I believe them to be the greatest materializing mediums the world has ever had. This may sound like a big order to take. But it is based upon the fact that I have read many volumes on the physical manifestations of psychic phenomena, and am familiar with the work of all the well-known mediums whose results have been brought before the public. I am familiar with the records of the psychical research societies and the writings of the leading investigators in this avenue. But I know of no other two mediums who have produced, night after night, from two to five times a week, as many materializations within a single evening, and have had as many of them on the floor at one time, as the Jonsons have. These were not merely floating hands and heads, but were fully developed spirit forms that moved about among us in the seance room, distributed and received flowers and chatted with us just as "home folks" might do. I believe it safe to say that fully 75 percent of them were recognized and identified.

The Jonsons are simple, sincere, good-hearted people and their work is genuine. It is done openly and every opportunity for investigation given any one present, and these manifestations take place while both of the mediums are out in the seance room in full view of all the sitters. These people are at present under the study of the Society for Advanced Psychical Research and a record of their work is being compiled for the reports of the society. This is a local affair composed mostly of residents of Los Angeles.

NOTES ON MATERIALIZATION SEANCE

At Residence of Mr. and Mrs. J. B. Jonson, 442 N. Vermont Avenue, Los Angeles, California, Wednesday, May 25th, 1921, 8 O'Clock P. M.

Although this meeting was not called before 8 o'clock, the parlor was half filled at 6.30 and at 7 o'clock all seats were occupied, there being 32 visitors present.

At 8 o'clock the door was locked, the curtains drawn and all lights extinguished, except one red electric light at the far end of the room, which was subdued by a thin sheet of tissue paper in front of the bulb.

Mrs. J. made a brief speech on spiritualism, requested all members to remain in a receptive mood as much as possible, clear their minds of any ill-feeling, "grouch" or discontent in order to bring about a harmonious condition. Suggested that they engage in cheerful conversation if it suited them to do so, when there were no materialized forms on the floor.

She next led in prayer and following this came several hymns. Mr. J. suggested that if any one present wished to look into the cabinet, or had any questions to ask, or any investigations to make, they were to feel at liberty to make them. Two gentlemen went to the cabinet, examined the curtain and the walls and partitions and returned apparently satisfied.

This "cabinet" merely consisted of a curtain drawn in front of the doorway which connected the seance room with the front parlor. Back of the curtains was a box-like room temporarily set up of about one-inch mesh wire with upright corner posts. Within the cabinet was nothing but a large, comfortable arm-chair which Mr. Jonson occupied while in the cabinet.

Outside of the cabinet, in the seance room, was a music box of the orchestral type, and this was set to playing after prayer had been offered.

Mr. J. entered the cabinet, drew the curtains together and took a comfortable seat in the arm chair, where he remained until fully "under control"; that is, in a trance. At times he would continue within the cabinet until the seance was nearly over. At other times he would come outside and take a seat in the seance room with the visitors, remaining there until the end.

Mrs. J., who remained on the outside all the time, in her normal wakeful condition, traced the vibration to the various visitors when their relatives or friends materialized, and very seldom made an error in "getting the right contact."

The first form to appear was one of Mrs. J.'s guides, known as "Viola." We were informed that Viola had been "on the other side" for about 40 years, having left this world at the age of 17. She appeared as a young lady about 17, dressed in white robes, very beautiful heavy hair of a brownish shade, hung in curls about her neck and shoulders. She was luminous enough to be clearly visible to every one in the room. Stepped up to members whom she recognized, conversed with them in whispers, received flowers at their hands. These flowers later dematerialized in our presence,—simply vanished, just where no one could tell. Her favorite song when on the earth plane was "Rock A-Bye Baby," and when the visitors all joined in singing this she danced to the tune, and finally disappeared like a cloud of smoke through the curtains.

There was a lull of about 15 minutes, when "Kitty," the "cabinet worker," poked her head through the curtains and greeted the visitors. "Kitty" is supposed to have been a New York street waif who was frozen to death in a dry goods box in an alleyway. Her work behind the curtain seemed to be in adding strength to the medium, "holding the magnetic contact" within the cabinet until the forms were sufficiently built up to have strength enough to come into the room. Kitty was always a welcome guest to those who were accustomed to visiting the seances. She was full of puns, witty jokes and the slang of the street. Occasionally she would come down the aisle to the center of the room, receiving and distributing flowers and would laugh and joke with the visitors.

Indian chiefs and guides frequently came through the curtain in spirit form, and when this happened, just before their entrance to the seance room, Kitty usually announced that she was going to "stick up some red mud for us in a minute." These Indians were as a rule decked out in native costumes, mocassins, war-bonnets, etc. Their voices were generally stronger than the "pale faces" and were more easily heard.

Mr. P. M. Walkinshaw (the gentleman who introduced me to the seance), had informed me that if any one came for him he wished me to go up to them and get an introduction. Finally, a very sweet-faced, curly-haired little child, apparently about 12 years of age, came through the curtains and Mrs. J. announced that it was "Celia," and said she wished to see Mr. W. I went to the curtain, was introduced to Celia and chatted with her for a moment. She did not shake hands, but held her hand up as if ready to shake, and when I offered to take it she drew back and smiled very naturally.

A lady who had lost a sweetheart after their engagement received a visit from her fiancee; chatted with him, embraced him and laughed and joked pretty much as they might have done in earth life. As he had appeared several times before, he was recognized by most of those present—dressed as during life, with the same appearance and general mannerisms.

Two sisters were visited by their mother, conversed with her, embraced her and kissed her. They discussed their earthly affairs and the names of various friends and relatives who had passed over and been met by the mother on "the other side."

Mr. Melvin Severy who usually had a visit from his wife from the spirit side of life, most invariably went to the seances with a large bouquet of roses. His wife seldom failed to come, received the flowers, smiled in gratitude for them and would disappear through the curtain, or through the floor or the wall and the flowers would dematerialize at the same time she did. He would put his arms around his wife's waist, caress her and talk in affectionate tones, bid her goodnight and she would vanish.

On one occasion, Mr. Hoffman brought a box of chocolate bonbons, held them in his lap and when Kitty appeared told her if she would come for them she could have the bon-bons. She came through the curtains, took the box of bon-bons and when she disappeared the bon-bons dematerialized also. (What became of them?)

One very strong spirit form appeared and announced himself as the late W. T. Stead (who was drowned when the Titanic went down). As these mediums have had these same visits from Stead before we may assume this one to have been genuine in view of the striking characteristics and speech and the identity brought out at later meetings.

Note:—Bear in mind that these visitors from the spirit side invariably represent themselves as a friend or relative of some one in the seance room, and those who are familiar with the work and know how to get positive identification resort to the usual method of asking questions about their earth life, something known only to themselves and the "spirit," and if these answers are satisfactory and corroborate the claims as to the communicator, the evidence may be considered reasonably good. But when these visits are made repeatedly and discussions of various bits of life history check up, the identity may be accepted as sufficient. In most cases the personal resemblance is enough but intelligent people who are accustomed to frequenting seance rooms soon learn how to look for the proof.

On one occasion I was given an introduction to "Kitty," which she acknowledged just as we would expect a young miss on the earth plane to do. I complimented her jokingly, by saying, "You're a sweet little tot; I'd be willing to give you a box of bon bons, too, if you'd come down the aisle to see me." She leaned forward, put her face within six inches of mine, looked me straight in the eyes and asked: "Will you make it a ten pound box?"

Most of these materialized spirits speak in whispers, some of them very audibly, while others utter merely a faint vocal sound, although the voice seems to improve after repeated materializations, and occasionally one will speak with the full strong voice of earth people.

NOTES ON MATERIALIZATION SEANCE

Held at Jonson Residence, Los Angeles, Wednesday, 8 O'Clock P. M., June 8, 1921.

There were about the same members present as at the previous meeting. I went in company with Mr. Walkinshaw, as before, and we were given seats in the front row of chairs, Mrs. J. arranging the sitters so they would sit a lady and gentleman alternately.

The procedure was the same as before; the window curtains were drawn, one 16 C. P. electric light with a red tissue paper shade being all the light in the room. To this would be added such light as each spirit would bring with him or her. In some cases this is a strong luminous effect emanating from the materialized form. It seems that those who have appeared oftenest bring the strongest light; although it sometimes happens that some one who has been on the other side for many years and reached an advanced state of progression, comes with a good radiance, or "aura," the first time.

"Viola," one of Mrs. J.'s guides, was the first to appear, as she usually was. This visitation was always a refreshing one. We all had the feeling that we were in the presence of a young, sweet girlish debutante, full of life, beautiful of face and graceful of figure. One of the regular attendants at the seance, Mr. Severy of Los Angeles, tried an experiment for the purpose of determining whether or not the visitors from "the other side" could read our minds, and concentrated his attention on the fact that he would like to take hold of one of the curls on Viola's head to ascertain if it was in any way different from that of a person on the earth plane. She caught the message at once and requested Mr. S. to step up to the curtain; then said, "If you wish you may place your hand on my head; take one of the curls in your hand." Mr. S. did this and vouched for the genuine, lifelike texture of the hair, and that it was as much a part of the spirit as the hands and head.

Mr. Walkinshaw was called up by Mrs. J. to identify a gentleman whom Mrs. J. thought was for Mr. W. It proved however that Mrs. J. got the writer's vibration through W., as we were close friends and came to the seance together. At any rate, W. went to the curtain and this is what happened:

Mr. W. had never at any time seen my father, nor even a photograph of him. But on going up to the curtain and speaking to the materialized form, he returned to me, saying: "That isn't for me; it's undoubtedly for you, George; that must be your father, because he's just you height and general build and has your face, except that he wears a beard."

I stepped up to the curtain; the figure stood with the curtains parted about halfway, so I could see the figure from the chest up. It was a very perfect image of my father, and I asked the question:
"Are you for me?"

Ans: "Yes, my son; I am your father."

Question: "Well, father, I am very glad to see you; this is very wonderful if it is really father. Can you give me some identification, so I will be sure it is father; you know it has been many years since we met." The answer came:

"Yes, 41 years in April." Now, this was correct, as I was not quite eight years of age when my father passed out and the time given by father could not have been more than a few months off there was no mistake about the month of April. I am confident that no one in Los Angeles had this information but myself. My parents died in Washington, D. C., and no one west of Chicago or south of Seattle would know these details. I asked:

"Who is with you on the other side, father?"

Ans: "Your mother and sister Annie." (Correct). I then said.

"If I had known there was any chance to see you father, I would have come to these meetings long ago."

Ans: "Yes, I brought you here. But I am not strong enough to talk longer tonight; will have to return some other time. Goodnight, son."

With this he gradually diminished in size, getting nearer to the floor; then disappeared entirely.

Next came a Sister of Mercy, giving the name of "Sister Emily." She arose gradually from the floor as a small white light and in about one minute developed to a full-sized woman, clad in the brown robe and white bonnet of the Catholic order. The visitors sang "The Rosary," she knelt in prayer, kissed the rosary which was hung about her neck; then walked over to Mrs. Hoffman, bade her arise, led her by the hand to the center of the room and gave Mrs. H. a magnetic treatment for some trouble of the spine. After this she knelt in prayer again, extended her arms to the visitors, as if to say goodbye, and vanished.

After the seance was over I asked Mrs. H. if there was any help from the magnetic treatment; and she replied that it was just like an electric battery applying the current through her body; stated the help was very marked and lasted for sometime after the treatment.

A spirit guide, known as "Constance," came into the room apparently from no place in particular, and walked directly over to Mr. Hoffman, a candy manufacturer in L. A. Mr. H. took her arm and walked down to the center of the room; she nodded to the visitors on both sides of the aisle, received and gave carnations. Those which she gave to the visitors were in some cases carnations handed to her from the room; others seemed to come from nowhere that anyone could see. Those that were handed to her disappeared, or dematerialized, when she did. Constance was always a strong figure, brought a good light with her and remained most anywhere from two to five minutes at each visit.

These characters were all seen at other seances; that they were genuine there can be no question among those who witnessed them.

There were too many people in the room to say that they were all the victims of any kind of fraud. Among the visitors were physicians, dentists, scholars, men of science, and for the most part an intelligent, educated audience. These were the same character of phenomena that have been witnessed in other parts of the world, investigated by the psychical research societies and incorporated in their records as genuine materializations,—psychic phenomena of a high order.

NOTES ON MATERIALIZATION SEANCE

Held at the Jonson Residence, Los Angeles, Tuesday, 8 O'Clock P. M., June 14, 1921.

A club of twenty members had been organized for the purpose of attending regular seances for physical manifestations. This was known as "The Tuesday Evening Club," and was made up from among those whose heart was in the work and who had gone far enough with it to understand the advantage of regular attendance, punctuality and a quiet, receptive mind, free from antagonizing suggestions.

At any materialization meeting conducted by a well developed medium, capable of producing the phenomenon in its highest phase of development, there will every now and then come some startling manifestation that is simply unexplainable by any known physical laws as we understand them on the earth plane. For instance:

On this particular evening the father of Mr. Hoffman appeared to him in the spirit form, clothed, however (as most of the men are) in garments similar to those worn by him while on the earth. This is presumed to be for the purpose of identification. Mr. and Mrs. H. stood talking with their father, who appeared as solid and substantial as any human being might. Back of Mr. and Mrs. H.'s father stood a young man from the spirit side who had come to greet his former fiancee—a lady well known to all of us in the circle. Suddenly the young man stepped forward and **walked right through** the materialized form of Mr. H.'s father without in the least disturbing him. It was just as if one would step through a framed canvas picture and leave frame and canvas all intact after it. It was an excellent evidence of (spirit) matter passing through matter. Mr. H. (living) asked the young man (spirit) why he did this and received the reply, "Oh, just to show you that it could be done."

On another occasion "Sunshine," one of Mrs. J.'s spirit guides, came into the room, and walked out toward the kitchen motioning as if she intended to pick up a fresh-baked cake from the kitchen table. Mrs. J. remonstrated pleasantly, by saying, "Now, Sunshine, why do you want to do that? You know you don't want to eat it." The answer came, "No, but I just wanted to show you that I could do it."

Came also this evening a Turkish dancer at whom we all marvelled. She was a "wonderful spirit." She had on robes of purest white, with Turkish turban and veil about her head. She was beautifully luminant and apparently heavily charged with electricity. She appeared from the ceiling, touched the floor with her feet and rapidly bounded upward again to the ceiling; then back to the floor, danced a few steps, then disappeared as quickly as she had appeared. And while she was in the room the air fairly snapped with electricity. It just seemed impossible for her to remain on the floor.

If the theory is correct that the more luminous ones are likely to be those who have been on the other side for a long time, it is likely that she had never before appeared on this plane since her passing away, and could perhaps remain longer with succeeding visits.

Note:—For the benefit of those who try to argue that all this could have been performed by means of "trap doors" in the ceiling, the walls and the floor; let me say, that in view of all the circumstances, the facts as we know them, our own intimate knowledge of the mediums and the premises, such a suggestion is too silly to discuss as even the remotest possibility.

My father appeared again on this occasion. I chatted with him quite at length and as a further test once more asked what other members of my family were with him on the other side. He patted me affectionately on the shoulder and answered:

"Your mother and sister Annie are both here with me, and will materialize for you when conditions are right." (Answer correct).

There also came to us a tall, well built, handsome Hindoo priest, with the complexion of the Hindoo and the conventional dress of the priests of ancient days as they have been pictured to us. He gave his name (which I failed to catch) and said he lived on the earth plane during the days of the Pharaohs. He was a well developed, strong, luminous spirit and talked in very good English.

A Mr. Victor Sandor had a visit from his sister, who passed away a few years ago in Hungary. A friend in the audience asked this of Mr. S. as a test: "If your sister, who passed away in Hungary, and now converses with you in English, will converse with you in Hungarian, we would consider it a very good piece of evidential matter." Mr. S. then spoke to her in Hungarian and she talked with him as freely in that tongue as she had done in English.

A retired German physician had a visit from his grandmother from spirit land. He discoursed with her in German and then in English, although he assured us that she had never spoken English when on this earth, and he further informed us that she had appeared to him repeatedly and had given unquestioned identity of herself, with various facts of her life, connecting up all the various members of the family with whom she had lived in Germany.

"Emma", a Scotch lassie from the other side, who appears as a spirit guide to Miss Hayden, of Los Angeles, stepped to the center of the room, took a string of beads from around the neck of Miss H. and said she wished to magnetize them. She dematerialized and the beads dematerialized also. In an hour Emma returned, and placed the beads around Miss H's. neck saying "they will give you strength now."

Here is an incident worth mentioning as a remarkable phenomenon: I did not see this myself, but am personally acquainted with all the visitors who did and am confident that they would have no object in simply manufacturing the story if it were not true. It is something that can be too easily checked up.

On Christmas eve, 1920, Mr. and Mrs. J., with their friends, decorated a Christmas tree, lighted it with small electric lights and placed toys and candies around the bottom of the tree. Mr. J. then became entranced, as usual, and in a few moments three little "kiddies" from spirit land came into the room, greeted all those present, danced around the tree, took the toys and candies, thanked everybody present and disappeared. At their disappearance the toys and candies likewise dematerialized.

But these things are not so impossible to those who have attended materialization meetings enough to know that the seances will often bring some of the most astonishing manifestations imaginable, and if the reader of these few records will delve into the records of the scientific experimenters along this line, and the reports of the psychical sociteies, he will hold nothing impossible.

NOTES ON MATERIALIZATION SEANCE
Held at Residence of Mr. and Mrs. Jonson, Los Angeles, Calif., Tuesday Evening, June 21st, 1921.

This was the night of the Tuesday Evening Club. The members were as a rule all in harmony, understood the nature of the phenomena and had gone beyond the stage of mere curosity. A class of this character will most invariably get better results than a mixed crowd of public phenomenon-hunters, who know nothing of the deeper side of the study and come more than anything else to be amused, or amazed, by sensational manifestations.

Mr. J. was controlled, as usual, by "Gray Feather" and as soon as he had "gone under" came to the center of the room, asked for Mr. S. and told him that he knew he (Mr. S.) was not feeling well and needed treatment. Gray Feather then made a number of passes around Mr. S's. stomach and back; said he was run down and must take better care of himself, use more judgment in what he ate, or "you will soon be over on the other side."

After the meeting I interrogated Mr. S. as to the effects of the treatment and received the same answer Mrs. H. gave; viz.: that it was very much like the effect of a galvanic battery and that he could still feel the electric sparks passing through him.

There was present a Mr. Bullock, of Los Angeles, a medium of considerable talent when controlled by Edgar Allen Poe. Mr B. wrote and recited (without previous preparation) many "inspirational" poems, said to have been dictated to him by Edgar Allen Poe. He is said to have the faculty of standing before an audience and delivering as many as 200 poems, every one of them original, and defies any one to show where they ever heard one of them except through him. On this occasion Edgar Allen Poe appeared fully materialized, looked exactly like photographs which the writer has seen of him, and stepping out before the class, recited a new poem, unknown to anyone else in the room, and left the poem instilled in Mr. B's. memory. B. recited it simultaneously with Poe.

Another character stepped out from behind the curtains and announced that he was Ex-President McKinley. He looked it. He was the exact counterpart in build, facial features and mannerisms to Wm. McKinley. He greeted us with that kindly smile that was so well known to all Americans; wished us Godspeed and said he hoped to return to us again in the future. While he spoke in a whisper, his voice was nevertheless audible and could be heard all over the room.

Here is a piece of evidential matter worth recording: Sitting beside me was a strange lady whom I had never seen at the meetings before. Kitty, the cabinet-worker, called the lady by name and asked, "did you like the sweet peas you found in your room?"

Answer: "Yes, Kitty, thank you so much for placing them there."

Kitty: "Oh, I didn't bring them. Ruby brought them to you."

After the meeting I asked for information as to this occurence and received the explanation that Ruby was the daughter of the lady who sat beside me; that Ruby had passed out just a couple of years before; that the lady stepped out into the yard for some purpose and on her return to the parlor in her home found a flower vase had in the meantime been filled with fresh sweet peas.

Query: Now, as Ruby and Kitty had never known each other on this earth, and as Kitty and the lady beside me had never met before, on either plane, how did Kitty know anything about Ruby or about the sweet peas, unless Kitty and Ruby had met "on the other side" and knew of each other's conduct

A certain retired oil man from Oklahoma has a sister in spirit land who materializes at most every meeting when he attends. The oil man brought with him on one occasion a handsome string of beads and placed them around the neck of his sister when she materialized, and told her to wear them on the other side. After this incident the oil man did not attend another of these seances until two months later. On this latter occasion his sister appeared and placed the string of beads into his hands and thanked him for the use of them. I was present on both occasions.

Those who might take the stand that there was a trick in the work, and that the medium took the beads, should bear in mind that this same materialized form had appeared to all of us at many seances; we have watched her take roses and dematerialize them in our presence, and that when the beads were placed on her they dematerialized in the presence of not less than 20 people, and during the entire manifestation both of the mediums, (Mr. and Mrs. J.) were out in the room with the rest of us and in full appearance during the whole evening.

Mr. Lambert of Los Angeles, a psychic who seems to be making good headway toward materializations, went under control in an adjoining room at the same time Mr. Jonson was under control. This was done as an experiment to see whether the two mediums working together would create a stronger vibration or weaken it. Under this experiment Mr. J.'s results were not as good as usual, while Mr. L.'s were almost negative. After Mr. L. again became normal and took his seat in the seance room with the rest of us his control, "Big Oak," continued to hover about the adjoining room for fully half an hour, in spirit form, and was plainly visible to myself and others who looked through the curtain for a sight of the phenomenon. This was merely a cloudlike, tenuous form of a man, with head, shoulders, body, limbs and facial features clearly defined. When Mr. J. came from under control and his guide, "Gray Feather," left the body "Big Oak" also disappeared.

PSYCHIC READING BY MRS. PEPPER

No. 2 Butman St., Beverly, Mass., 11 O'Clock P. M., March 31st, 1920,
"Jim Fiske" Presumed to be Spirit Control

I was introduced to Mrs. Pepper on this occasion unexpectedly. I had never met her before; she knew nothing of me or my family connections or business affairs and I am confident that she had no way of procuring any advance information.

She talked in a social way for a few moments, then went into what I would consider a partial trance and delivered the following message:

You come here, sir, seeking material aid and guidance. You are concerned in the things of this world—success in business. You have met with some reverses lately and are discouraged. But your discouragements do not last long. You have come through all walks of life; you have seen many ups and downs and have gone through many successes and failures; but never to be cast down for long. No matter how dark things may be today, you soon bob up again smiling and take a fresh start. You can always radiate good cheer and a smiling countenance around you, regardless of the trials you may be experiencing within. (Very good character reading).

You have initiative and fortitude. You understand nature and the forces of nature; you know rocks and minerals and nature's forces within the earth, so that you can talk to people and interest them in the things as you explain them. You are working to find new ore bodies, or new veins beyond—somewhere in the West; but you will be disappointed in the results. There are treatment problems that vex and there will be difficulties about your title and deeds from the government. (Correct).

You will not meet with success in New England. There are too many forces working against you at this time. The time is not favorable to your success here. You will be returning to the West very shortly. Your success is not here. You are being surrounded by friends who will later on be of service to you and of value in your business undertakings but not now, and those who are around you in your present work are not your kind of people. They are small, narrow, exacting. You do not like New England. It is not your country and you are out of your element here. It will do you no good and you will not accomplish what you came for. (Correct).

You must get into other business. It is only through other business that you will bring the present undertaking into success. You have an inventive mind. You have invented things before and you will do so again. I see you working on a machine that has something to do with mining. It is for the interest of mines and you will make a success of it. Go to your room often; sit alone with those who control you from the other side and you will work out the means for connecting up this machine so as to make of it the practical, successful invention that you wish. It is good and you should not neglect it. (Correct).

Keep your own counsel and act more upon your own judgment than upon the suggestions of others. But staying in New England is not best for your health. I hear a hacking, unpleasant cough coming up in the throat. If you remained here it would get into your lungs and you would have rheumatism here. (Correct).

While the big vein which you desire most to reach at this time at your mining properties is not going to be what you hope, you will find a way out. Your friends will continue to look to you and trust to you to see it through. You will find a way out in the end, but it will be a hard pull yet and cost much more than the amount you tried to raise in New England.

I see friends around you trying to help you. There is a woman on the spirit side of life, fair and calm, with a sweet smiling face; very beautiful blue eyes; she stands back of you with one hand on your shoulder; she passes both hands over your brow. The name of Annie comes to me very clearly. She throws flowers about you to show that she is brightening your path. She has helped you over many a difficulty and she will help you over many more. (Very correct description of my sister Annie, deceased).

I also see a man, tall and slender but muscular and strong; a very pleasant look about his mouth; strong white teeth, hair brown with gray, very soft and silky, brushed well back over the forehead. He comes from your mother's side of the family and tries to help you through the mother. (Correct description of an uncle on mother's side, according to the memory of my elder sister, although I had never seen this uncle myself).

I see the mother with a full round face, hair parted right through the middle and wavy. Some one near you has an old-fashioned daguerretype of your mother and I see your mother through this daguerretype. There also comes an uncle from your father's side. These are all trying to help you. Keep your courage. Do not get downhearted. Keep up that smile and as you have overcome your difficulties in the past so you will overcome them in the future. Your best days are still ahead of you. You are worried about protecting your friends; but you will find a way to take care of them. It will not be done as soon as you hoped; but you will save them from loss.

I am told to warn you against what you drink. You will say, "there is nothing they can steal from me." Never mind that,—remember what I tell you and be careful what you drink.

Note:—The daguerretype of my mother was doubtless intended for an old-fashioned photograph then in the possession of my elder sister.

In reference to the patent machine, I suspect the psychic was unconsciously reading my mind, as I did most of my studying on this machine just about this time while I was East and my brain was filled up with it.

The prediction as to the "unpleasant hacking cough coming up in my throat" if I remained in the East, and the rheumatism, is good; as this is what usually happens if I remain for any length of time in the New England climate, although it had not put in its appearance on this trip at the time of Mrs. Pepper's reading.

PSYCHIC READING BY MRS. ESTELLE CONE
Church of the Revelation, Los Angeles, Cal., Sunday Afternoon, July 3rd, 1921, at the "Message Circle."

After reading for two or three others she stood before me and gave the following:

Three parties come to you this afternoon. Your father is in the foreground, or at least he comes with the influence of a father, a man of medium height, about your own general build, with a beard and moustache. (Correct). He stands back of you with his hand on your shoulder. Right at his side and a trifle back of him is a woman on the spirit side of life who comes with the influence of a mother. Then farther back is a young man, tall and slender with hair combed back over the forehead. He is not a relative and comes with a strange influence, as if he needed some assistance. You and he were close friends and business associates. You think of him very often and he comes to greet you and tell you that he is trying to work his way through and build up. He sends you a message of good will and disappears. (Answers the description of a friend who passed out about twenty years ago).

Your father takes my two hands and points them to a small city somewhere east, almost clear across the continent, and there are two men arranging some business papers. You are in a quandary just now as to whether you had better tie to one venture that you are already in, or whether to close the doors and put all your energies to another opportunity which you have been offered. You know what you ought to do but are thinking too much about the criticism that it might bring. (Correct).

You are anxious to protect your friends against loss and the message seems to say that your best course is to close the doors to the present work for the time being until the forces which now hold it back come to you again of their own accord. They will listen to you then, because they are going to need you.

I find you building a piece of machinery out of heavy metal, something that turns around and around, something that you have invented yourself; you are going to use it at these properties and make a name for it.

This seems to be your answer. You are being guided by good influences from the other side and they will point the way as you go along. Follow that light and keep close to your father. You will be leaving the city in about ten days. (Correct). You pass through a small town with a railroad station in it painted yellow with brown trimmings. Then through a small, dilapidated "shack" town. This is the property for which you have been negotiating and that is the way out of your troubles.

Note:—The description of the small town and railroad station painted yellow with brown trimmings, was correct, as was also the "dilapidated shack town", although Mrs. Cone had no information from me or any one else as to where the property was located, the railroad station, etc.; **nor did I know these things myself at the time of this reading.**

PSYCHIC READING GIVEN BY MRS. HATTIE PETTIT

At the Residence of Mr. and Mrs. Walkinshaw, Los Angeles, Cal., July 19th, 1921. Subject, G. F. Goerner.

There were seven members in this circle and after reading for two or three others she gave the following reading for me.

The forces seem to be coming to you very thick tonight, and they come from all directions. There is your father. Then your mother steps back of you with her hand on your shoulder in an effectionate way. A sister comes by the name of Hannah, or Anna; then a tall young man, like a professional man, who might be a brother or a close friend. Kneeling before you is a Nun, or Catholic sister; she is a very good influence and stands very strong for you. She was a friend in school days. (All correct).

Your father says to tell you that there is not a day goes by that he is not with you for some part of the day; that he is helping you and these good forces will keep on multiplying. He seems very much pleased with something you have been doing lately. He likes the way you have taken up psychology and says it will help good influences to work for you. He says tell you that he will materialize for you soon and you will be able to talk with him. He says don't be impatient about it and it will come in time. (Correct. The materialization took place).

Things have not gone just right with you in the past. A great many influences have been working against you. But these are going to improve. The old enterprise you have been in is going to be slow and you will have to do something in the way of a decided change all around before you can get the results you want. It will eventually be all you hoped for, but it will be slow. You are being shown the way and it will unfold before you as you go along. (Correct to date).

You are going into other business soon. I see you leaving the city and then returning. This new venture is going to be way beyond any expectations you now have. I see plenty of water over in this new field and there is where you will get on your feet.

In this new venture there comes a young Indian girl who is familiar with the ground; she is a sort of guide and leads me to this water. Back of you is a tall well built Indian; he is taking you over the rocks and picking into the ground and seems to be working for your interest.

Keep up your studies: it is going to be of great help to you. Be your own counsel. You can always do better "going it alone." You have not been very successful trying to follow others. Depend more upon your own judgment and listen less to the views of other people. You know what you ought to do; just follow the suggestions that come to you from the other side.

There is much more that I could say to you; but better leave it for the present. It will come to you in the quiet hours and you will have no doubt in your mind as to the source of it. You can tie to that.

PSYCHIC READING BY MRS. HATTIE PETTIT
At Her Home, Los Angeles, Saturday Afternoon August 6th, 1921.

Note:—Previous to the meeting with Mrs. Pettit at the Walkinshaw home, on July 19th, 1921, I had no acquaintance with her. I was a stranger to her, and she had no means of procuring any information about me or my affairs, as the W.'s were close friends and business associates of mine and were as anxious as I to ascertain the genuineness of Mrs. Pettit's work.

I reached Mrs. Pettit's at 1.30 P. M., took a seat opposite her while she rambled on about local matters rather incoherently for ten or fifteen minutes without touching upon anything that would be of interest to me. I was beginning to get discouraged and thought it probably one of her "off days," and nothing would come of it.

Finally, she remarked: "A voice says, tell George to speak say something; start the vibration." So I broke in by asking, "What is the outlook for the near future?" The answer came:

"They are beginning to come from all directions—your father, your mother, sister, friends and relatives. You have three business trips ahead of you and there are three bright stars being held over your forehead. These are symbols of success for all three efforts. You are leaving tonight, but you will be in Los Angeles again one week from next Tuesday. The business you are gong on tonight doesn't look good to you; but it will turn out better than you think. You have a much bigger property than present appearances indicate. It will drag a little while longer; but offers will come to you in the next few weeks and new parties will come in and help to finance it. Don't take such a dark view of it. It has been a hard pull, but that is over with. You are told to brush aside the past and forget it; it isn't worth any worry. (Most of this prediction appears to be correct to date).

"Next comes a longer trip. You are going to get some new machinery made and you are going to get your patents allowed. Some one in the east is going to make you an offer for this machine; but you will be guided as to what to do about it. The right suggestion will come at the right time. This is going to be a very good trip for you. I can see a big wheel turning around; then two smaller wheels and a little engine trying it out. You think a great deal of this patent and are told to hold tight and keep it to yourself. (Correct).

"The third trip is one you are trying to avoid. But you will not be able to get out of it. You will have to deal with several elderly men almost across the continent, very near the Atlantic Coast. They don't act very quickly; but when you get east you are going to get it the way you want it and you are going to use this new machine on that property. It is the property where you have a great deal of water, because I see water coming out in great gushes. Your mother says, 'Yes, George, you ought to go.'" (Correct, I did go).

At this point Mrs. Pettit gave several violent shudders, like one taken with a sudden chill; then said:

"A young man comes to you, tall and slender, his hair medium brown, his face clean-shaven. He brings a very strange influence and chills me clear through and says: 'Tell George I have tried so hard to reach him. For heaven's sake, George, do try to help me out. I am in such awful darkness. I didn't mean to take my own life. It was all done so suddenly. I didn't think, and they have kept me in darkness all these years. Oh, George, you don't know what it is! I have tried so hard to get to my father and they won't let me see him because I took my own life. Do give me a good thought every day, as often as you can. That will help and I will repay you many times over. You don't know what it means. But you knew me so well, you are the one to help me out. I tried to get to you the other night. I heard you call my name, but I wasn't strong enough to answer. I couldn't stand up. Oh, George, suicide is an awful crime! I see it all now. You ask, why I did it? If I just say I was afraid of something you will know the rest. I went so quickly. And it was such a useless thing to do. If I had only talked it over with you, you could have prevented it. But it was too late. But, George, do give me a good thought every day. Help me out of this darkness and you will never regret it."

I asked the psychic if he could give his name for identification and the reply came, "Yes, it's Harold; there is no mistake."

She continued, "Your sister comes and brings the name of Hannah, or Anna. She says, 'Tell George I love him dearly and visit him every day; tell him that I have my little boy here with me. Tell him we all know how badly he wants us to come and talk with him and we will all come in time. Tell him to keep up his study in this work and the deeper he gets into it the easier it will be for us to get close to him.'

"A young lady steps beside your sister, tall and slender, not very strong looking, medum complexion, with a narrow face. She smiles and says, 'Tell him I am here too and that I help sister Annie because I came first. Tell him I think of him every day. See if he remembers Emil—or Emma—or Mannie—can't quite catch the name the voice is not very strong."

I suspected the lady to be an old schoolday friend, who was always a close friend of my sister Annie in life, by the name of Minnie DeKover, who left the world through tuberculosis. So I requested the psychic to ask the lady to tell me as an identification by what illness she left the earth and the answer came:

"She puts her hand on her chest and coughs and says she went with lung trouble, the same as brother did, and some of my people way back went with the same trouble. She is a very sweet spirit and seems very fond of you." (Correct).

"Your mother and father are also here and your sister again speaks and says, "We will all come to you soon and you can talk with us. Keep on reading and studying; that helps.'

"Your mother gives this as a test message: She says, she and your father were never separated in life but once, and that was when the waters separated them in Europe and he came home alone and I followed. She says, George wouldn't know this; it was before he was born, but sister Clara told him about it. (Correct).

"The young man still stands very close to you. He just clings right to you and seems loath to leave. He says you can help him and just pleads for you to give him a lift out into the light. He says with your help he can win out because he sometimes sees the light breaking through. He says you won't lose anything by it, keep a good thought for me every day and it will all come back to you.

"Your sister speaks again and says you have a long life ahead of you and you must do all the good you can. You will have plenty of success and can help others a great deal. Keep a good thought for us all and we can get that much nearer to you."

Note:—In explanation of the statement made by Harold, through the psychic, "I tried to get to you the other night," etc.; there appeared in my room at night after I had retired a materialization of this young man. He was seated on the floor, leaning against the chiffoniere in my room, with his knees drawn up to his chest and his hands clasped over his knees. I spoke and asked if it was Harold, and he merely nodded his head weakly as if to say, "Yes."

PSYCHIC READING BY MRS. HATTIE PETTIT

At Her Residence, Los Angeles, Aug. 18th, 1921, Thursday, 10 A. M.

Note:—After the previous reading from Mrs. Pettit, on Aug. 6th, I wrote to a friend in Malden, Mass., whom I knew to be a believer in spiritualism, and asked him to give his good thoughts daily on behalf of my friend Harold and help him out. This party wrote me from Malden under date of Aug. 13th, 1921, that he immediately took it up with a psychic of his acquaintance, who was well able to get results. In his letter he advised that the psychic had already got started on the work and for me to ascertain from Mrs. Pettit if Harold hadn't already begun to feel the effects of the work. So on Thursday, Aug. 18th, I called on Mrs. Pettit and received the reading which follows.

I had also in the meantime got some friends, who believe in these things, to help the work along. They all joined in the effort and the message from Harold will indicate the results.

I informed Mrs. Pettit that I had called on this occasion mainly to find out if she could get any further information from Harold as to how he was progressing on the other side. She answered that he had visited her Saturday morning, August 13th, (the date on which the letter was written from Malden) and requested her to tell George that he was making good headway. Bear in mind, that Mrs. Pettit knew nothing of my correspondence east and nothing of my efforts in any other direction in behalf of Harold.

She closed her eyes, as if in a half trance, and said:

"Harold is here now and says to tell George that I got his good thoughts and quick results from his friends. I have been with father. Grandmother is also with me and my little brother, too. I am out in the light and am going to be all right now. Tell him I am going to forget the past. I want George to know how much I appreciate what he has done, and thank the little girl that plays the piano. I have been east and west with his friends and they have all done such wonderful work. Tell him I am going to be with him many times from now on, and he will hear from me often. Everything is all right now. He says he got the message from the East along with the rest of them. Tell George he was mistaken about mother. Mother is still on the earth plane. It is grandmother that is here with me."

She continued: "Standing right back of you, with his hand on your chair, is a tall, stout gentleman with a moustache and goatee and heavy iron gray hair. He says, 'I know George.' He then spreads out some pictures he has been drawing and shows them to you for identification. Some are architectural drawings and some are cartoons in water colors. He says you and he were good friends and still are. He wants you to recognize him."

I asked Mrs. Pettit if he could give me an initial of his name as identification, and she replied: "He puts a big letter T up before you." I replied, "That must be Mr. Thomas," and the answer came: "Yes, it's Jim," and he seems so pleased that you recognize him. He says tell you that his wife and son John are both with him and that they are all your friends. He says John is going to help you in your mining work, and you are going to have Jim with you often now."

(Note:—This was Mr. Jas. Thomas, an old friend, who passed out in Denver. He was strong on architectural and mechanical drawings and water color cartoons. At the time of this message I did not know that his wife had passed over and presumed that she was still alive. But under date of October 29th, 1921—more than two months after the message—I received confirmation of Mrs. Thomas' death).

"Another gentleman comes into the circle and shows me a big cork shoe, with a high cork heel and sole and says he was an old schoolmate of yours. I asked for an identifying initial and the reply came, his first name is Ed and he holds up a letter S., and says he has been on the other side many years. (Recognized as Ed Stelligener, an old schoolday friend, who passed out from hip disease about 25 years ago. He had a broken hip from childhood, one limb being considerably shorter than the other and he always wore a very high cork sole and heel).

"A little redheaded boy comes up before you. He stands back in a shy way, as if he only knew you but a very short while. He has very fair skin and lots of freckles—just a little waif somewhere, and he says you helped him out once in life. (Cannot recall the lad).

"Your mother, sister and father are also here. Your father says pay some delicate little attention to your sister Clara between now and next spring, and help to cheer her up, because she is not going to be with you long. Too much strong medicine has aggravated her trouble. They operated for tumor when her great trouble was really cancer of the stomach. She will be with us sometime before spring and we will all meet her on this side. She will linger along for a while; then have a great deal of suffering for a few days and then pass away. I could have helped her if she had talked with me two years ago." (Correct, sister Clara passed out Sept. 28th, 1921).

I asked Mrs. Pettit if my friend Minnie DeKover was present. She tried for a moment to get an answer, but nothing came. Finally, when she was about to give it up, she said: "There is a big letter M comes right up in front of you, and a voice says: 'Yes, I am Minnie; I heard you call. Tell George I am with him every day'.

"Your father again speaks and says, I woke him up in the mountains the other night for a purpose. He knows. Tell him he has nothing to fear for his health. His only weak point is a little gastritis now and then, but I am taking care of that. Tell him whenever it comes, just press hard on his chest at the sternum plate, and take a few deep breaths. But it isn't going to be anything serious." (My father was a physician and surgeon in life).

(Note:—In explanation of my father's reference to waking me up in the mountains for a purpose; I had retired while over at my mining camp about 9 o'clock at night. A little past eleven o'clock I was awakened by the voice of my father, telling me to "turn on the light." At the same time I had a clear vision of my father standing, materialized, at my bedside. I turned on the electric light in my cabin and saw a large centipede, some five or six inches long, crawling from the wall to my bedding. I killed the centipede with my boot and returned to bed. The next morning I mentioned the incident to my mine foreman,—several days before returning to Los Angeles and interviewing Mrs. Pettit—and the centipede carcass was still on my boot).

"I see you leaving town again in a few days. The last trip was not a very satisfactory one. But it is just as I told you,—things will drag for a little while yet. They are going to be at their best in about nine months from now.

"The next trip you are making will be up North of here. You are going for the purpose of finding out something definitely about building some new machinery. The trip will be a good one and the machine is going to be all right. You will have some changes to make; but your plans will be improved. Your friend Thomas says he is going to get up some new plans for you up North in the next few days." (Correct; the trip up north referred to San Francisco).

(Note:—This prediction as to Thomas getting up some new plans for me up North, proved to be correct. At any rate, new plans were suggested in a way that indicated that Thomas had a hand in them from the other side and they worked very much to my advantage and saved several hundred dollars in the cost of the machine).

"You are still trying to avoid the long trip back east. But you will make it just the same. No hurry about it. Later in the fall will be better. (Took this trip the following spring).

"Your father pictures you to me as living to a rather old age; but you are not infirm, because I see you moving about rather actively, looking over business papers as a symbol of business and work. You are not going to be dependent upon others, but you can look out for yourself to the end. Your friends on the other side all seem to realize the ups and downs you have had in the past, and all seem anxious to help put it behind you."

(Note:—The suggestions from "the other side" as to my business and material welfare, have always originated from them, as I have never tried to use them for my material gain. Whatever they offer in this way is received with appreciation from me; but it is entirely up to them, as I do not believe that a man has any more right to use "spiritualism" for material gain than he has to attempt to capitalize the "Lord's supper" or any other religious practice).

Harold's recognition of "the little lady that plays the piano", has reference to a young girl who worked very ardently to assist Harold. This was not known to Mrs. Pettit, nor was the phrase applied to her by Harold ever used by me, and I consider that it cannot come under the telepathic hypothesis.

PSYCHIC READING BY MRS. MARIE WALLACE,

President of the Progressive Spiritualist Church, San Francisco, at her apartments, 1219 Fillmore St., August 31st, 1921.

You bring with you the influence of a man raised as a boy in a small country community. (Not correct). There were six children in the family and as a boy you were never very well understood by the rest of them. As you grew older they understood you less, and for some years this caused estrangement and feeling between you and them. But during the past few years this has been overcome and there is now good feeling and love between you and your own folks. You are a long ways from where you were born, a long ways from the rest of your people. The family has always been scattered. (Correct).

Following this came a good deal of small talk on social affairs of no importance or interest to me and I was anxious to get it over with. She asked if I knew John and George and Harry and Frank and Tom, etc.;—every one knows people by these names, and most of us have some one by such names on the spirit side of life. I would have been ready to quit if I had not had a feeling that with a little patience and consideration for the medium she would eventually get around to matters of interest to me, for I know that these disconnected allusions are just as likely to come from "the other side" and should not necessarily be attributed to any weakness of the psychic.

Finally she said: You have received very lately a letter with news of the severe sickness of some one very close to you, like an older sister, and that letter has not been answered. You are told to answer it. But the sick party has improved some since that letter was written and is now resting easier. (Correct).

In business matters you have nothing to worry about. Everything is at a standstill just now. The past has not been very pleasant and you have had to overcome many disappointments and obstacles. There were many times when it seemed that life was not not worth living. But you have gone through the worst that you will experience during your life and there is much more sunshine ahead of you than darkness. There are many spirit forces surrounding you. They come as friends ready to help you and through their influence antagonizing forces are kept in the background.

A very sweet-faced lady steps beside you bringing the influence of a mother. She says tell you that you have not been neglected because you have not felt their presence in the past few days, but they are still very close to you just the same.

Your father also comes and I see him as a man wearing a parted beard, like side whiskers and also a moustache. You are a sensitive yourself if you would pay more attention to it and give it a chance to grow. Your father says he is trying to develop this and wants you to take advantage of it. He gives me the influence of a man who had a wonderful ambition, but did not have the opportunity to accomplish the things he wanted to do, and he is trying to make you understand that he is going to do his work through you.

There also comes a sister and brings a little boy by the hand. Your mother takes one of his hands. This means he is a blood tie—your sister's child, I take it.

Standing back of you is a tall young man. He looks as if he might be a brother, but his face is longer and more narrow. I replied that I had no brother in spirit land and the answer came:

"I am Harry." (Should be Harold). I asked if Harold had gotten out of his darkness and received the answer:

"Yes, I am all right now, many thanks to you and your friends. I owe it all to you. You were the only one who could have done this for me and I knew you would help me if I could just get the message through." He says, "Tell George I will never forget it." Then I asked if he was with his father and the reply came: "I see father often, but have not progressed to where I can be with him all the time; but I am making good headway and getting along all right."

A young lady by the name of Minnie comes as a very sweet spirit and says she wants to give you a test question. She says, "Ask George if he remembers the night we stood in the hallway and wanted to talk but were afraid because we thought some one might hear us." I replied that I remembered it perfectly well and the psychic answered, "she laughs heartily about this as though it was some old sweetheart affair." (Correct).

Another lady steps in with light hair and a very bright, sunny face and fair complexion and wants to know if you remember Lizzie. She says she was a schoolday friend; she poses as an actress and sings and says this will identify her with George. I asked if it was Lizzie Webel and the answer came. "No, Lizzie Webel is still in your world." (Identified as Lizzie Hatcher, an alto singer of school days, who afterwards went on the stage as a chorus girl).

The Lizzie Webel mentioned was a pianist; was never on the stage to my knowledge, but performed a great deal in public and social gatherings. There is some mix-up here, as Lizzie Hatcher was quite a brunette with dark eyes; while Lizzie Webel had light hair and was on the blond type. They were, however, both very close friends at school and it is possible that this may account for the psychic getting the cross vibration.

Mrs. Wallace continued: You are trying to buy something, like a mine or property of that kind, from some parties back east, and I am told to tell you to hold out for the contract you want, because if you don't get it that way you will be handicapped in the future. (Correct).

A young business man by the name of John comes to you with pleasant greetings and with him comes an elderly gentleman who says his name is Tom. (Doubtless intended for Mr. Thomas, who is John's father). I thanked Thomas for the help he had given me in

San Francisco on the mechanical drawings and then asked Mrs. Wallace if it would be necessary for me to go East. She replied,

"Your people on the other side seem to realize that you are trying to avoid this until it is more convenient and it seems that they are doing something to help you out—may be you understand it, I don't. But this man Thomas takes a business paper from his pocket, like a contract with a blue cover, and says: Tell George I am helping him to get these papers in the east the way he wants them." She described Thomas as "a professional type of man, broad, stout, stands very erect and has a heavy sandy-gray beard and moustache. He is very strong and will make a good guide for you." (The description is very good of Mr. Thomas).

She went on: These are all your friends and they are anxious to let you know that they are with you. You will become more psychic and they are bringing about this condition so you will be able to see them and talk to them yourself. You will get messages right along and they are going to be of help to you.

Your father says: "Don't throw off these influences that come from our side; we are your friends and the forces that come to you from here are good. Think only good thoughts and only good can come to you."

Note:—A tentative contract which I sent back east, referred to in this reading, was backed with a blue cover. The final contract which was sent to me from the east reached me a week after this reading and was also backed with a blue cover. Question: Did the psychic see telepathically the blue cover which I sent East, or did she see spiritistically the blue cover whch came from the East, to which Thomas referred, **and which was then en route in the mail?**

PSYCHIC READING BY MRS. SARAH SHRODER
Of the Progressive Spiritualist Church, San Francisco, at Her Apartments, No. 148 Fillmore Street, 11 O'Clock A. M., Sept. 14, 1921.

Mrs. Shroder doesn't seem to have the faculty well developed for calling names of visitors from the other side, or describing faces or personal features; but is strong on proving identity by the pictographic method, going into details as to personal characteristics, mannerisms and incidents of the earth life of the spirit presumed to be communicating.

She is a woman of about 60 years of age, and barring frequent infractions of the rules of grammar, is a very good speaker, uses beautiful descriptive language and speaks with sympathy and a great deal of sincerity.

I made an appointment with her by phone, without giving any name or other information regarding myself or my affairs. As this was my first meeting with Mrs. Shroder I was an entire stranger to her.

I asked if it would disturb her if I took her message down in shorthand and she replied, "Not at all, I wish you would!"

She then began: "You are preparing to leave the city in a few hours. You go south, stop at another city for a few days and then go into the mountains for a few weeks. The work you came to do in San Francisco has met with your approval and you go away satisfied. (Correct). I am told to tell you that your efforts down south will be just as satisfactory and your friends from the other side are going with you.

She continued: "It is easy to read for you because you are strongly psychic yourself; the forces who are with you on the spirit side of life came to you immediately as I sat before you and in just a moment I was well within your vibration. You have studied a great deal on this line and advanced rapidly and you understand the forces necessary to mediumship.

"But you are often asking yourself whether certain messages that come to you in a mysterious way are really from the other side, and whether certain manifestations are all imagination. You are a man who has been for many years without a religion and you are still skeptical about this new change in your own spirit.

"But forces tell me very strongly that they are working with you and for you and that they are going to demonstrate to you that there is no mistake about where these messages come from. You will be writing automatically and I am told to assure you that messages which you now get in your sleeping hours will soon come to you in your waking hours. These forces want to help you get into position with you material affairs so they can use you for good work. This work is being planned for you and it will bring you prosperity, peace and happiness.

"Your mother and father both stand right back of you at this moment and they come with a loving influence and holding out their hands to help you and welcome you.

"A young lady with a very sweet face, round and full, comes with a calm way about her, as if she had led a quiet calm life here and has gone to the other side with that same spirit of harmony and has made good progress in the other world. She moves about in robes of white and is very spiritual. She too holds out her hands to you in welcome and puts her arms about your neck in a loving way. She left this world suddenly and I feel a sharp pain in my side as if the trouble was there. Following this was an operation and then she passed away. She says they did all they could for her, but it was too late; but she says she has no regrets and she can do much more good in her present life. She comes with the influence of a sister. (Correct).

"With her is another lady with a well-developed spiritual life. She stands close by your sister and belongs to the same band. She offers you her hands and says she is with you many times when you don't know it."

I asked Mrs. Shroder if the lady would identify herself, and the reply came: "She puts a hand to her chest, breaths slowly and with a great deal of labor as if from some trouble with the lungs, and she shows me a capital letter M. She is a gentle-voiced woman and speaks in that quiet, gentle way." (Recognized).

A young man comes with the influence of a brother." (Most of them make this mistake). I replied that I had no brother on the other side of life and got the answer: "But you must have been very close friends, because the moment he appeared he seemed to take hold of my chair and just move me over near you as if he wanted to get close to you. He identifies himself by saying, 'He has helped me.' Tell him he don't know how much good he has done and tell him how strange it seems now that I should have gone the way I did. I thought it over for several days and then suddenly decided, 'I will,' and then I went very quickly. Tell him I will be with him often and whenever he needs me. He says you and he did the same work here and will now work together better than ever." (We were both associated with the same companies).

"Then comes an elderly gentleman, a very strong character on earth and a strong spirit; he stands very solid and erect; he walks across the floor in front of you with his head up and his shoulders back and says tell you he is going south with you. He was a man who thought a great deal of his word; his word meant more than anything else in the world to him and he says to tell you that when you get on the other side you will find that character is the only thing that helps a man, and if he doesn't bring it with him he has got to develop it afterwards. He says make your word your bond. I am close to you all the time; when you get in a tight place call for me and I will send out a thought to you. You can depend on this. I will be with you to the end. (Understood).

"These all belong to one band and seem very close to you and they will generally all come together. Farther off and in the background are many more; they are all your friends, mostly friends of your younger days. But their arms are extended to you and they stand for you. You have a great many on the other side and I don't see any unpleasant forces trying to get in."

PSYCHIC READING BY MRS. HATTIE PETTIT

At Her Residence, Los Angeles, Wednesday, September 21st, 1921.

I stated to Mrs. Pettit that I had called for a reading in the hope of getting an explanation of two occurrences that had come to me in the past few days. On Saturday night, just shortly after eleven o'clock, Sept. 17th, I awoke and found a young man sitting in a rocker near the open door in the adjoining room to where I slept (at the home of Dr. E. B. Graham) and a voice said: "We want to talk with you." The figure then disappeared. To be sure that I was awake and that it was no hallucination, I turned on the light and made a memorandum of the time; then returned to bed figuring that some one from the other side wished me to see a psychic so they could deliver a message.

I got this far with the statement when Mrs. Pettit said: "Harold gives his name and says very positively that it was he who called. 'Yes, I was there,' he says, and 'I am going to call often in the future and talk with you. I have a message to get through when I can tell it myself. Thank your friends for the help they all gave me; I shall never forget it. But we are all three coming to you before long. My father is here today to greet you."

I asked who was meant by "all three," and the answer came, "your father, friend Thomas and myself." I asked Harold if he had met my father and he answered, "Yes, we are all three here now; we are helping to develop you so we can get closer to you."

Mrs. Pettit described my father, Mr. Thomas and Harold, as she had before, saying, "Your father says he was up north with you; he is going to the mountains with you from here; we are all going. Tell him he may not think I have much business influence, but I have and can get the right thought here and there where it is needed. George is concerned about some party up north, but it will be all right, and if it is delayed a little don't worry; the next trip is going to be satisfactory. After you return you will not be much in Los Angeles, but will be going back and forth a good deal; next year means a good deal of travel for you; after that you will cross the water."

I asked what it was Harold wanted to talk about and got the reply: "It was friend Thomas who has the message for you." On asking if Mr. Thomas could identify himself further the answer came, "I went with pneumonia after five days; the goitre in my throat aggravated my case. Tell George I want to get in touch with my son Walter. He needs me but I can't reach him. Walter does not believe in spirit return and he don't believe in mediums. Tell him your experience with me; he will believe you when he wouldn't listen to any one else. Tell him how to reach me. Do this for me and I will always appreciate it—you know that." (Name should be Gordon instead of Walter. The rest is correct).

I asked if I did right to repulse the gaunt, bony figure that appeared to me one night in my room at the hotel up north and got the reply. "Yes, you did right; that is the way to get rid of undesirable spirits; take a firm stand and order them out. But he will not come again and you have nothing to fear." (This reply came from my father).

She continued, "Your sister Annie speaks and says, tell George I am always present and it helps me to be with him. I am making good progress here; I have a class of children and I help the strangers when they come over. I am not with father all the time, but see him often. You know he came a long while before I did. (Correct). It is getting easier to reach you; keep up your study; you are advancing rapidly."

"Minnie is here, too, and says if he wants more identification tell him I am here with brother Seth." (Correct).

Your father says during all the years that he failed to get a message through to you he was with you and watched over you. He says you had many hard places to climb, but 'I looked after your health and kept you from any serious accidents all these years.'

"All the time you have been here, there is one lady, tall and slender, with glasses and a large hat. She has not been on the other side very long; she stands in the background and acts as if she wanted to ask a favor of you, but seems afraid that you wouldn't be interested enough to care. She is not yet in the light; things look dark around her as if she was having a hard struggle." I replied, 'I will do anything that I can to help her and anything that is necessary.' The answer came, 'She brightens up now and smiles and says tell him its Cora; he knows what I had to contend with." (Recognized as a lady who lived in El Paso and passed out with pneumonia about four years ago).

"Another lady steps up, young and girlish looking, pretty blue eyes, blond hair, rosy cheeks and fair complexion, and says: 'Tell him it's Cousin Lena.'" I replied that I had no cousin Lena, and she answered, "Sewall—Lena Sewall—she pronounced it very clearly. She sees that you remember her and is much pleased." (This was not a relative, but a girl friend in Virginia whom I called Cousin Lena).

I asked Mrs. Pettit if she could give me any light as to whether my friend ——— was going to pull out of his business difficulties. She answered, "He will if he keeps his health; but it looks like a hard pull yet. He will have some successes and as many setbacks. It will be a miracle if he clears himself entirely. He would be better off if he would counsel with a more conservative head before he acts; he shouldn't be so impulsive. With his presence comes a feeling of great concern and worry. What he needs just now is a helping hand—not censure."

She concluded with: There is such a colony of friends around you, as if you had attended some big school in years gone by and many of those who were in the school have gone to the other side and they have all come to let you know that they are still with you. You surely brought the whole school today; the room is full of them."

PSYCHIC READING BY MRS. HATTIE PETITT
At Her Residence, 236 West 31st Street, Lost Angeles, Saturday, 3.30 P. M.

I made this call upon Mrs. Pettit for the purpose of ascertaining if there would be any message from my sister, Clara, who passed away on Sept. 28th, of this year, but gave the psychic no information as to what was on my mind.

I also went in the hope that my sister Annie would confirm the visit which she made to me on last Wednesday evening, the 12th, and at the same time possibly get confirmation of a visit made by Harold Cook to me in the Patagonia Mountains about two weeks ago.

Mrs. Petitt began: "You always bring a crowd with you whenever you come and they all seem anxious to get very close to you." She then described my father, my sister Annie, Minnie, Harold Cook and Mr. Thomas. I asked if my mother was present and got the reply: "Your father says, whenever I come to you, my son, your mother is always with me and she is with you many times when you don't realize it. Business conditions are a little unsettled as you come to us today; you are again in doubt about the party up north and you are in doubt as to how the way will be opened for an important trip which you must take soon. It will be all right, George, and we are sending out the thoughts where they will help. Just a little uncertainty for a while yet and it will work out better than you think. We can do more for you from this side than you can do from your side. Hold to the thought that it will come out all right and that helps us."

Mrs. Petitt continued: "Your sister Annie brings a very strong influence today. She says she is so pleased that you recognized her when she came to the class the other night. She says she is coming soon again and coming often, and says she will not be the only one that will come to you; we are all coming in time. She says the new work you got into is good for you and will help both you and us wonderfully. Keep that up George."

I asked if I was correct about Harold coming into my room in the mountains and got the reply, "Harold says, I came to you through the vines but I wasn't very strong. But I am improving and will come to you often. You did such good work for me, George, that I can never forget it. Your development helps me and I want so much to get higher. I am getting along all right and forgetting the past; you got so many people to work for me; they helped from your side and this too. I can see them all and I have been to the mediums east and west and am going to them again."

Then came the following message: "All the time you have been here there is an elderly lady who stands very close to your chair; she looks at you bewildered as if she hadn't been on the other side very long and doesn't understand her surroundings yet. She looks at you in a dazed way, and seems too weak to speak." I thought it might open the way for a stronger vibration if she caught my voice, and asked: "Is it my sister Clara?" and got the answer, "She shakes her head yes very feebly." I then said, "We'll have to get father to help her out into the light" and received the answer, "Your father says,

No son, your sister has not been in darkness at all; she is just having a hard time getting her bearings; she can't realize yet that she is still alive. She is earthbound to her children and grandchildren; she loved them so much and she can't understand yet how she can still see them and can't reach them. Your coming here is good for her. We told her you would come and it will help her very much."

I asked the psychic if my sister was able to indentify herself and she answered: "I suffered so much toward the last; every one thought I could live a few months longer; I was blind for three days and kept trying to read George's letters; then I was unconscious and when they all thought I was getting better something just cut my breath from me and I passed out. But, oh, George, it seems so good to see you and hear you talk. Father is helping me and I will soon by myself and be stronger."

Mrs. Petitt then gave an imitation of a person going into a faint and said, "Your sister just sinks away; she is too weak to remain longer; but your father says Clara will come to you often in the future and you will see her and talk with her."

"There comes to you another young lady and I think she has been here before. She wears glasses and gives the name of Cora. She says she is not altogether out in the light but is improving and wants to thank you for it. She says your thoughts reached one of my grandmothers and grandmother is working for me here. She says, George was the only one that was broadminded enough to know what I had to fight against and it has been so good of him to help me on this side · but tell him I'll soon be all right."

"Another lady steps in and says, "Ask George if he remembers Stella W.—she puts up a big letter W and smiles. I replied, "Yes, it must be Stella Wagner—an old schoolday friend." Mrs Pettit said. "She nods her head and says, Yes, he's right—there are so many from school here and they all know you." (This is quite likely to be the case. I attended school where there were about 75 girls and as many boys. I knew them all by first and last name and they all knew me the same way).

Your father again says, "don't go to worrying about business. There are plenty of good forces working for you. Keep up your study and your reading and keep in close touch with this side."

I asked if she would tell my friend Thomas that I had not yet been able to locate his son Walter, and asked if he could tell me Walter's whereabouts and got the answer: "Colorado." I said, "Is it Denver," and the answer came, "locate him through Colorado Springs. Walter is not doing very well and he needs me." (This brings to my mind that Mrs. Thomas had a relative who lived in Colorado Springs, and the instruction to "locate him in Colorado Springs" may mean either that Walter—should be Gordon—is living there, or that I can trace him through Mrs. Thomas' relatives. Can't quite understand the mix-up in Gordon's name, except that names and numbers and dates are often confused through the psychic and there seems no satisfactory way of accounting for it.

In explanation of the visit of my sister Annie; I had attended a psychic development class at which Annie's face appeared and she came within four or five inches of my own face, so that I could see her "clairvoyantly," and I was glad to have her confirm this through Mrs. Pettit.

Harold's reference to "coming through the vines" is very correct. One of the wndows in the room where I slept in the mountains was covered with vines, and his materialization to me on this occasion was through this window.

"PHYSICAL MANIFESTATIONS"

At Seance Given at Home of Mr. and Mrs. Jonson, Los Angeles, 7.30 Friday P. M., October 21st, 1921.

There were nine people present, besides the host and hostess. Mr. J. stretched a black curtain across one corner of the room, leaving about two feet of space between the curtain and the floor and about 4 feet betwen curtain and ceiling.

Next placed behind the curtain a chair, a tambourine, two small silver bells and a fan. Mr. J. invited two guests to sit with him in front of the curtain. Mr. L. and Mrs. R. took seats and the three joined hands. All lights were turned out except one red electric light, which made the room plenty bright enough. Then "things began to happen."

A phonograph in the next room was turned on by Mrs. J. and the "guide" behind the curtain kept time with the music with the tambourine. If a piece was put on the phonograph that displeased him, he groaned and scraped the chair up and down the floor behind the curtain.

Finally hands appeared over the top of the curtain and dropped carnations on the floor—"apports." (Where did they come from?) Next the fan began to move back and forth over the top of the curtain. The bells rang and a hand took hairpins from Mrs. R.'s head. When the hand appeared again I offered my handkerchief. It was taken and in a few minutes it was held over the top of the curtain. I tried to take it but twice it was pulled back. The third time I got one end of it and held on; but it was pulled back with a force too strong for me to resist. Finally, I was allowed to take it, and found it tied in a hard knot.

This kept up for 20 minutes. Then the tambourine was thrown over the curtain next the two bells, the fan and finally the chair came out, but was held up in the air for a moment by one hand until some one stepped up to take it. This ended the cabinet work.

Following this we all took seats around a small kitchen table on which were placed two trumpets—one of tin and the other made of fibre.

Mrs. J. immediately went into a trance and remained that way for more than an hour, under the control of an Indian guide purporting to be "Krocho." Mr. J. occasionally went partially "under," but was normal most of the time.

In less than two minutes the table began to vibrate, move back and forth, and up and down. The trumpets tapped on the table and went up against the ceiling and tapped us all on the head.

My father was one of the first to speak through the trumpet. I recognized the voice—not the voice with which he used to talk on earth, but the voice in which he spoke at the materialization meetings. After the usual greetings, same as folks on earth would use, the following conversation took place between us, his voice of course, amplified by the trumpet:

"Father, can you tell me who it was that paid me the visit in my room last night after I had retired?"

Answer: "Yes, it was Harold."

"I was not sure that I recognized him. He has been to see me so often that I thought I could recognize him readily and was inclined to think it was friend Thomas's son. Harold was not very clear last night."

Answer: "He did the best he could, son. The air where you were was very heavy."

"Do you mean, father, that the atmosphere was too dense?"

Answer: "Yes, you had a heavy fog last night. (Correct). But Harold will come again and you will chat with him and see him clearly. Goodbye, son." With this the trumpet dropped to the table.

Next Harold spoke and said: "George, keep your ears open. I'll have to talk fast. There are so many wating to take the trumpet. I could talk all night if I had a chance; but they won't let me. There they are taking it away now." The trumpet again fell to the table and other voices spoke for an hour or more.

Next "Viola," one of Mrs. J.'s guides, came in, greeted the company and sang for us in a voice that was full and "round" and could have been heard in an auditorium of 500 to 1000 people. The music was really beautiful and the song something unknown to me. I had intended asking afterwards if any of the rest knew what it was, but it slipped my mind after the meeting. She would move around the entire circle, stop for a moment at each person's chair and sing; then pass on to the next chair. This was really well worth listening too.

A lady from "spirit side," presumably a departed sister of Mr. L. (whom we have all seen at the materializations) came in, spoke in a very clear voice to Mr. L. and said she had brought back his string of beads, which he had placed around her neck at one of the materializations three months previously, and dropped the beads into his lap, saying, "this is the first chance I have had to return them, as you have never been here since"—doubtless meaning that he had not attended any materializations.

Next came a male voice, giving the name of Timothy O'Boyle, one of the guides to Mr. Herrick, president of the California State Federation of Spiritualist Churches, and called for questions.

Mr. L. asked the following question:

"Tim, do you have animals on the other side?"

Ans: "Certainly, where does man get the idea that he is the only animal privileged to eternal life?"

Mr. L.: "I wanted to know; because I just had a very fine dog die and I was wondering if that would be the end of him?"

Ans: Depend upon it, my friend, your dog will certainly be on the other side waiting for you."

Mr. L.: "Do they use food over on the other side, Tim?"

Ans: "Yes, but not in the same sense that you do on earth. We have fruits and foods, much more delicious than you know anything about; but our method of eating is only to draw sustenance from them. We have wonderful flowers over her—flowers everywhere."

Mrs. L.: "Tim, how about eating meat; is it good for us?"

Ans: "The less animal meat you eat, the less like an animal you will be. No spiritual body consumes animal flesh. If you must eat meat, let it be sea food; next fowl and last of all animals; they are next door neighbors to humanity."

Goerner asked: "Tim, do we communicate less as we go higher in the next world?"

Ans: "Yes, the higher you go the farther away from earth you are and the more spiritual you become. There are spirit forces who are often sent close to the earth and they help the new-comers to get a right start on this side. Their work is very important and it gives them a chance to communicate with their friends for many years."

Goerner: "Is it a fact that the more we get posted on the doctrine of psychology as it pertains to the hereafter, the quicker we get our bearings and take our place toward progressing on the other side?"

Ans: "Certainly, it's no different from your earth—the better you understand a subject the easier you get along with it."

Goerner: "Tim, is it a fact that the materialized forms that come to us from the spirit side are spirit forms precipitated down to us by thought vibration?"

Ans: "Oh, not at all, friend. The materialized forms are atoms of physical matter taken from each and every one in the circle and brought together by magnetic force. There is no mystery about it, friend."

Goerner: "Tim, would you be able to tell me if my sister Clara has got her bearings and is beginning to understand her new life?"

Ans: "Your father is taking good care of her. They are all together and standing close to you at this moment. You will hear from them all in time."

"Tim" then bade us good night and dropped the trumpet. Mrs. J.'s guide, "Krocho," broke in and said:

"Tell chief at medium's side (meaning Goerner) that he looks a lot brighter than he did five months ago. Things are getting better for him. Keep on trying to be fair and square in business and if you lose by it today it will come back double tomorrow."

I asked: "Do you know my friend Thomas on the other side?"

Ans: "There are so many Thomases I don't know which one you mean."

G: "I mean the friend who drew up the contract back east for me and got up the mechanical drawings for me up north. I just want you to tell him for me that I thank him for his good work and want him to know that I recognized his fine hand in it."

Ans: "That's the right spirit, friend. Do you know how few people are ever thoughtful enough to thank their spirit friends for the service they get They thank the earth friends all right, but they seldom think to thank the spirit friends. You've got the right idea, friend, and it sounds good to hear you come right out in the open with it. Believe it friend, Thomas knows how you feel about it."

Following this came about 15 minutes of lecturing on morality, spiritualism and the after life—too much of it to recall in detail. The voice was not of Mrs. J.'s normal self, and the language was undoubtedly not hers in her waking state.

Note:—The flowers brought in as "apports," we were instructed at a later seance, by one of the spirit guides talking through the trumpet, are really picked by the guides themselves from the gardens outside, most likely in our own neighborhood, and brought by them into the house.

REPORT ON TRUMPET SEANCE

At Residence of Mr. and Mrs. Jonson, Los Angeles, Monday, 8 O'Clock P. M., October 24th, 1921.

There were 13 members present at the seance, including Mr. and Mrs. J. The curtain was drawn before one corner of the room, same as on previous occasion, and strips of paper pasted from the door back of curtain to the door jamb, so that it would have been impossible for any one to have opened the door without destroying the paper strips.

Behind the curtain were a chair, tamborine, small silver table bell, a writing pad and pencil. Two members of the circle were asked to sit in front of the curtain with Mr. J. Mrs. M. and myself (Goerner) took seats, all joining hands so that both hands of all three sitters were held.

Soon we had the usual jingling of the tambourine, ringing of the bell, scuffling of the chair on the floor, etc. Every now and then the guide behind the curtain would lean the paper pad against the shoulder or back of one of the sitters and write something; fold the paper and hand it over the curtain. In this way five sheets were handed out. These we did not examine until the curtain work was over and the lights again turned up.

Toward the end of the cabinet work, Mr. J. went into a partial trance and stated that a very strange influence had taken hold of him —a strange woman who had never been to him before; that she came with the influence of some one who had been ill for a long time and only passed out a short time ago, completely worn out by a hard fight with ill health. I remarked, "It sounds like my sister Clara's condition." At this point sister Clara's head appeared over the top of the curtain; it was plainly seen and described by several in the crowd. I asked if it was Clara and got the answer (Through Mr. J.'s control), "Yes, it's written on the paper."

When the cabinet work was over, among the sheets of paper was one with the name of "John," "Mary" and "Clara." The "Clara" was written with a very good imitation of sister Clara's hand. The "John" I do not just now place, although it resembles somewhat the writing of my sister Lillian's deceased husband. Nor do I place the name "Mary." This was my mother's name, but I cannot fancy her signing herself to her son by her given name.

Clara's name was confirmed at the trumpet seance the same evening. She spoke through "Krocho" (Mrs. J.'s trumpet guide) saying: "Tell George that I will soon talk with him through the trumpet. From now on I will be with him often and am going to watch over him through all the years until he comes to this side. I can tell you, Mr. Goerner chief, Clara was a good woman and you don't need to worry about her. She came well able to move right on to higher things; she is all right now."

I replied: "Ask Clara what she thinks of this new life."

Ans: "It's all very fine, George; it's different from what I expected."

"Were you disappointed?"

Ans: "I was only disappointed at finding myself still alive, instead of being in my grave until judgment day. I didn't die at all, George."

"Clara, you used to think I was a heathen because I didn't believe in any judgment day."

Ans: "I know it, brother, but you were more right about that than I was. Good night, George."

Various other parties then took up the trumpets, both of them being used at the same time on several occasions, the communicators being all either relatives or friends of the sitters. The discussions were confined mostly to personal matters, in which some very good identifications were brought out. My father appeared and talked for about two minutes, and dropped the trumpet with, "Good night and God bless you, my son."

An ex-railroad engineer came in greeting us with an imitation of a locomotive starting into action; then the rumbling of the train, and finally the familiar sounds of a train coming to a stop. He gave his name as Blinn and on being asked what he thought of the pending railroad strike, answered:

"It will prove a fizzle, as it should. It was never intended to go through, and it would be better if it did not." With this he gave an imitation of an engine bell ringing, tooted the whistle and rumbled off.

My schoolday friend, Minnie DeKover, took the trumpet and spoke for several minutes in a very clear, distinct voice, recalled bits of earth life, conditions on the other side and gave some information of sister Annie. I can well imagine that they would be close friends on the other side as they were always very fond of each other here, and both well fitted to take a high place beyond.

A pecular incident took place with the appearance of two Minnies at the same time—one to talk to Mr. and Mrs. L. and one to talk with me—keeping both trumpets going. Krocho afterwards explained this by saying that they both happened to be in the same vibration.

Three singers appeared, two ladies, one singing soprano and one alto; the male voice was a tenor. Sometimes they all sang at once; sometimes the two ladies together and sometimes one at a time. Any one knowing those in the circle would know that not one of them had any such voice as came from "the other side."

"Krocho" is a peculiar mixture of a wild, harum-scarum little Indian girl, who talks incessantly, breaks in frequently when the trumpets are in use, and has a good command of slang and poor grammar. Then, on the other hand, she will often break into sane moral lectures of a very high order, use excellent English and deliver as clean and sweet a talk as ever came from a pulpit. The answer is presumed to be that she herself is controlled by different personalities on the other side.

A lady's husband appeared and talked through the trumpet and spoke of meeting his wife's second husband on the other side; congratulating her on having met such a fine mate for a second choice, and stated that her second husband and he had become very chummy and were looking after her comfort and happiness; advised her that she had made a good wife to both of them and they were both cooperating to give her that peace of mind and serenity of soul to which she was entitled.

Another young lady was interviewed by her cousin, who seemed fully cognizant of the fact that she had just taken a long auto ride across the country from Ohio, and stated that he was on the running board all the way. He commented on the trip, gave the names of all the parties in the car; spoke of their new home in California and even described minutely the manner in which they were decorating their rooms, where each photograph and picture was hung and requested that she give his picture a place next to her. She said:

"Well, it is very close to it." The answer came.

"Yes, but I want to be right next to you; take ———'s picture over to the other side and put mine where she is, so I can be nearer to you." The lady answered:

"All right, I'll make the change tomorrow," and received the reply:

"I'll help you hang it up." (My own impression is that he was on the job and assisted in the hanging.)

Viewing the comments of various scientific writers, as to the objectionable side of these seances. Doubtless it exists; but so far as my own experience has gone, throughout all the seances which I have attended, and all the mediums I have met and had readings from, there has never yet come to me anything but a clean, uplifting, wholesome atmosphere; and while the "human element" is always very much present, the whole tone of the work is hedged about by a great deal of "spirituality" and good influence. To me the answer is, we get mostly what we look for.

NOTES ON TRUMPET SEANCE

At Residence of Mr. and Mrs. Jonson, Los Angeles, Cal., Friday P. M., October 28th, 1921

Usual curtain, chair, writing pad and pencil, umbrella, newspaper and pair of scissors. The "guide" amused himself mostly by cutting out faces, animals and figures from the newspaper with scissors and handing them over the curtain. Raised umbrella and held it over the heads of the "sitters" in front.

I asked the guide if my sister Clara was behind the curtain and received the reply (by three raps on the floor with umbrella). "Yes." I asked if she would speak with me tonight on the trumpet and got the reply, "Yes."

After the curtain work was over, father took up the trumpet, but the phonograph made too much racket and he dropped it, saying he would have to try another time.

Another voice came through the trumpet; someone asked who it was for and the reply came:

"For George." I asked, "Is it sister Clara?" and the answer came, "Yes." After the usual greetings the following conversation took place between us:

Clara: "I came to your room night before last to see you."

George: "Yes, I know you did; but you didn't stay very long and I couldn't make out just who it was."

Clara: "I am getting stronger all the time and can do better when I come again."

George: "There was some one with you, Clara; who was it?"

Answer: "It was your mother; she came with me. We heard your voice when you spoke; but couldn't get the answer through."

George: "Sister Amelia wrote me and confirmed all you had told me about the manner of your death."

Answer: "I know she did; I stood beside you when you were reading her letter. But you must listen now to what I am going to ask you."

George: "All right; go aheal, sister; I'm listening."

Answer: "The folks on this side all got your messages and they all pitched in to help me out. But there are such wonderful opportunities here that I want you to keep on working for me; I want to get the full benefit of this side. Do you hear me?"

George: "Yes, I caught it, sister, and I'll keep up the messages until you tell me that it is no longer necessary."

Answer: "That will be a big help to me, brother, and it will help you, too. I must go now; they all wanted to talk with you tonight; but they have been so good to me, they gave me the first chance at the trumpet. Good night, George."

The ex-railroad engineer came in the usual manner, whistled and rang the engine bell; stopped his train; tooted the whistle again after talking for about two minutes and started his train. He called a "Mrs. W." by name, and asked:

"Did you know that I am a brother-in-law to your husband on this side?" The lady replied, "No, I didn't; how is that?"

"My brother married Mrs. S., and Mrs. S. was your sister by marriage."

Ans: "Why, sure, Mr. Blinn, that's right. I never thought about that before. How is my hubby tonight?

Blinn: "He's all right, just waiting to take the trumpet from me." Blinn apparently handed over the trumpet.

Timothy OBoyle spoke next; said he just dropped in to say "how do you do" and "Good-bye", because he had to go to Ashtabula to be with his medium, Mr. Herrick. Some one asked:

"Where is Mr. Herrick?"

Tim: "He has been attending a convention in Detroit and reached Ashtabula tonight. He will speak there and I want to be with him when he makes that speech." (Correct as to Herrick).

Goerner asked: "How long will it take you to reach Ashtabula?"

Tim: "I will be there as soon as I finish talking with you."

Goerner: "Then the railroad strike wouldn't bother you any?"

Tim: "Oh, no; your railroads are too slow for me."

Goerner: "Tim, the other night you said the longer we are on the other side the less frequently we come to talk with our friends on earth. Does that mean that our friends who come to us after long years are earthbound or have failed to progress?"

Ans: "Not a bit of it; talking with their friends on earth is not a punishment; its a privilege. But the longer you are on this side the less interest you take in earthly affairs. People communicate with the earth sometimes who have been here since time began. There is a great deal of misunderstanding on your side about time as we understand it here. But I'll have to go for tonight, friend. Mrs. Jonson is going to gve you all a good treat; I can smell the coffee boiling, and there's pumpkin pie and stacks of fried cakes (he meant doughnuts) out in the kitchen. Its 10 o'clock."

This was correct, as Mr. and Mrs. J. after the meeting, served doughnuts, pumpkin pie and coffee. The clock struck ten just as Tim finished his message.

Viola sang two songs independently (that is, without the trumpet) and two of the male visitors sang through the trumpet.

"Spirit lights" were numerous and hovered about the heads of most of the members at the table.

Krocho spoke through Mrs. J. her usual mixture of jokes, poor English and exalted lectures. She tried hard to give us some advice on the organization of the new Psychical Research Society, but had an awful struggle to pronounce it correctly, as might be expected of an Indian. She called it "Searchical Desuch Something" and various other names and said when she came again she would be able to call it by its right name.

Mr. Bell she persisted in calling "Mr. Ding-dong," and announced that "Elvira Speaks" would now speak through the trumpet. Mrs. Speaks is Mr. Bell's grandmother on the other side, and she too regards her name as a good combination for jokes.

"Spirit hands" passed around the table and greeted each of us by clasping our hand and passing on to the next chair.

Note:—Timothy's statement that he had to go to Ashtabula to be with his medium, Mr. Herrick, turned out to be a very good piece of evidential matter. No one at the Jonson's knew anything about Mr. Herrick being in Ashtabula and no one had any reason to suspect that he would or should go there. This seance took place Oct. 28th. On Sunday evening, Dec. 4th, Mr. Herrick was in Los Angeles and delivered an address under trance before the Peoples Spiritualist Church. Previous to the service I procured an introduction to Mr. Herrick and took pains to ask if he could recall where he was on the evening of Oct. 28th. He replied, "I was in Ashtabula, Ohio." I then told him of the incident at the trumpet seance, and he confirmed the statement, saying, "I was certainly in Ashtabula on Oct. 28th, and so was Timothy."

NOTES ON TRUMPET SEANCE
At Mr. and Mrs. Jonson's Residence, Los Angeles, Monday, 7.30 P. M., October 31, 1921.

The curtain was hung in the usual manner; three sitters took positions in front of curtain—Mr. J., Mrs. Jacobs and myself. The "guide" within amused us by jingling the tambourine, playing a small music box, rattler, dropping flowers over the curtain, jingling the silver bells and writing messages.

At the trumpet meeting our railroad friend came in, tooting his engine whistle, ringing the bell and "blowing off steam." Some one asked what business he was engaged in on the other side and got the reply:

"I am still in the railroad business, but not in the sense you might think; we simply think railroads and they are before us. An engineer on this side soon finds out how little he knew about it on your side. Our work is to project thoughts into the minds of engineers and mechanics on the earth and in this way help develop engineers and engines. That's the way inventions on your side begin. We send out thoughts from this side and help your side to develop them."

My father took up the trumpet and after the usual greetings, I asked if he could tell me who it was that came to my room Sunday night. He replied:

"It was Clara." I asked if Clara had recognized my voice when I sat up in bed and spoke to her.

"Yes, she heard your voice and saw every move you made." I asked who the gentleman was that came to the room and sat in the chair beside my bed.

Ans: "He wants to demonstrate that to you himself."

A few moments later a voice in the trumpet announced, "It's Clara." I asked the same question of her, as to who the gentleman was that came to the room and sat in the chair, and got the same reply: "He wants to demonstrate that to you himself." I asked, does he mean that he will explain it through the trumpet:

Ans: "Yes, he will talk to you later."

Mrs. Jonson went into trance under the control of the Indian guide "Krocho," who with her usual breezy bluster said she had come "to blab" to us for a while. I asked Krocho if she remembered what she had promised to do before we met at the trumpet again and she replied:

"Yes, I told you that I was going to learn how to pronounce the name of that new society and I did. It is called the Psychical Research Society and the other word that I couldn't get is refreshments." (She formerly pronounced the word as "refreshems.")

I congratulated her on her success and she immediately went into the following lecture:

"Now, friend, it's just that way in your life. When there's anything you haven't done right, make up your mind that you are going to overcome it. That's the only way you can succeed in your world or in the spiritual world either. Get in right whenever you are in wrong and help your fellows to do the same thing. Live by the law of love. That's the only law you need know anything about. That's the only way you can come into full consciousness on this side."

I asked, "Krocho how long does it take most people to come to consciousness after the spirit leaves the body and reaches the other side?"

Answer: "That depends upon you. If you make the spiritual life your life and learn to live it, you needn't know any darkness, It's like going to sleep on your side and waking up on this side. Some are so bound to the earth body that they don't want to let go. There are people lying in their graves whose spirits are still in the body. You know there are many people who go through life without being willng to accept any proof of hereafter. They will turn a deaf ear to the truth all their lives. Live in the truth and your eyes will open to the truth. Your creed don't count and any moral law is good; but don't go through the world denying the spirit its right to eternal life."

I asked Krocho if she could see all the members around the table.

Ans: "Just as plain as daylight. There is no night in the spiritual world. When you come into consciousness here you have left darkness forever behind you. But some are a long time waking up. That's because they closed their eyes and refused to see the truth. Do you know, friend, there is only one religion in all the world and in all the worlds of time and space, and one word tells it all—just love. That's all there is to it. Get that through you and you've found it all. You can't go wrong with that."

I asked if the messages I was sending out for sister Clara were a real help and got the reply:

"You know it; if they hadn't been she couldn't have materialized at your room for you. But the help don't stop there; the messages are caught up all along the trail and help many that you don't know about. They came through, all quiet and peaceful enough, but they got through just the same."

Not less than 25 voices came through the trumpet. "Viola" sang "Whispering Hopes" and promised to sing for us under materialization later on. I asked if the time would ever come when spirits would materialize before public audiences and lecture and sing for them and got the answer:

"Yes, when the world is ready for that. But, friend, there are savage tribes who understand the psychic law better than many civilized people and are better able to interpret it."

Before Krocho left, some one in the class asked her what about cremation and the reply came:

"It's better that way. Some day you will do away with the grave and the headstone. Cremate the body and scatter the ashes to the grass and plants. The body means nothing after the spirit is out."

My sister Clara brought a good piece of identification. On Sunday (Oct. 30th), I had written a letter to my sister Amelia in Chicago, in which I expressed some " new thought" ideas on sister Clara's death. Speaking through the trumpet Clara said:

"I read the letter you wrote to sister Amelia yesterday, brother, and it was all right. She will show it to the children and it will help them. They grieve too much for me and it would be so much better if they just wouldn't do it. If they would just believe as you do and know that I still live, and that I am happy and have many friends on this side."

NOTES ON TRUMPET SEANCE

At Home of Mr. and Mrs. Jonson, Los Angeles, Calif., Friday P. M., Nov. 4th, 1921.

On this occasion the chief interest in the cabinet work centered around the messages written on the writing pad placed behind the curtain. The following message came from my sister Clara, characteristic of her writing as she wrote previous to her long illness, when her hand was steady and her eyes good.

"George, this is a pleasure—to come in this way and prove to you that death does not end all; that we still exist and love you still, Clara."

Kitty, the "cabinet worker," always writes in a vein of humor. As stated, she is presumed to have been a New York street waif who was frozen to death in a dry goods box in an alleyway. Her messages are usually written in a child's hand and arranged on the paper in circles. Her message read:

"Oh, Gee! but this is fun. Awful glad, folks to come; hope we can in the other way soon. Kitty."

The reference to coming in "the other way soon," doubtless means that she is waiting for Mr. and Mrs. J. to begin their materialization classes, as Kitty frequently appeared materialized and spoke and joked with the sitters.

Mr. and Mrs. Lambert had a cousin who passed out in the Catholic faith about three weeks ago, whose name was Martha. A message came to the Lamberts, containing simply a Catholic cross drawn on the paper, within which was printed, "Love from Martha."

Mr. J., whose control is "Gray Feather," received a picture of a feather above which was printed the word "Gray," giving the name of the control.

Mr. L., who is part Osage Indian, has a control who appears under the name of "Big Heart." He sent out a message containing the picture of a heart and in the center was printed the word "BIG" in capital letters. (Big Heart was an Osage Chief in life).

As a rule the messages are brief and there come from four to half a dozen of them. They are generally written by the guides behind the curtain placing the writing pad against the back of one of the sitters in front of the curtain, writing the message and handing it over the curtain. Sometimes it will come right through the curtain.

There were only 10 in the circle this night, everybody seemed to be in a cheerful frame of mind and in harmony and the results through the trumpet were exceptionally good. Some friend or relative from "the other side" appeared to every one in the circle, in most cases with good identification or "test messages." For instances, from my sister came this:

"George, did you have a good time last night?" (This had reference to a reception tendered by Mrs. Jacobs on behalf of the Psychical Research Society, which I had attended). I replied:

"Yes, we all had a fine time. Were you there?"

Ans: "Of course, I was there and heard you make a speech. You are going to get good results from the Society. It is going to grow and be heard of everywhere. **Your suggestion to publish the records was a good one,** so all the other Societies everywhere will know what you are doing. You are going to get some wonderful manifestations. Keep in harmony and pick your members for their intelligence and love of the work."

My father spoke through the trumpet, and when I said, "It's really wonderful, father, to be able to chat with you folks after you have all passed over to the other side and we supposed you were all dead."

Ans: "It's only the law as Christ laid it down two thousand years ago, my son. Many people read his book as they would an almanac. Christ said, 'Greater things than these shall ye do,' and, son, you are going to do them through the new Society you are interested in."

Then came this: Mr. and Mrs. Jonson, and Mr. and Mrs. Lombard all took a trip to Santa Barbara and visited the old mission. A close friend of the Lombards, who passed to the other side a few months ago by being murdered, spoke through the trumpet with:

"Lombard, did you know that I went all through the mission with you. I rode in the back of the car all the way to Santa Barbara. Do you remember the Indian woman who gazed so hard at you, the one with the papoose in her arms?"

"Yes, I remember it and was wondering why she looked at me so hard."

"Well," answered the voice from the other side, "she saw the Indian in you; she saw his spirit, and with Big Heart came the spirit of her own chief and she wanted so much to talk with you, and get in your vibration so she could talk with her chief. That's why she followed you up the bell tower, and when you looked down and sent out a message to Big Heart she got in the vibration of her own chief, and when she patted your wife on the face and shoulder she was trying to let you know how grateful she was for giving her chief back to her."

Mr. and Mrs. L., as well as the Jonsons, confirm the details of this message—the visit to the tower, the Indian woman following Lombard to the tower, caressing his wife, etc. Must be some intelligence back of these messages beyond question.

The company went into some restaurant in Santa Barbara and ordered pork and beans. Mr. J. evidently had joked a good deal about the absence of the pork. All through the evening friends of the L's and the J.'s from the spirit side sprung jokes about the pork and beans and toward the end of the seance Timothy broke in with:

"Great goodness! friends, have I got to sit up here all evening swallowing porkless beans? All I've heard tonight is beans—beans beans—nothing but beans. If the Irish had all those beans for shot they would have licked the English long ago."

Question: "Tim, what's going to be the outcome of the Irish fight?"

Tim: "More fight. When they haven't got the English to fight any more they'll be fighting among themselves."

A voice came through the trumpet saying: "George, George! I want to talk with George. It's Wallace." I asked:

"It isn't Dr. Wallace whom I knew in Denver, is it?"

Answer: "Yes it is."

Goerner: "Well, Doc, when did you pass out? I thought you were still on this side."

Answer: "No George, I just passed out. Not very strong tonight. Will come again."

Note:—I knew of three Dr. Wallaces who occasionally came to Denver, though none of them lived there. One of them I knew very well, but I happen to know that he is still alive. Have not yet been able to verify the death of either of the other two.

Krocho gave the usual mixture of jokes, slang, muddled-up big words and wound up with a lecture on "Keeping Cheerful" and "Working for the Other Fellow." These moral talks from Krocho are always good and indicate a control back of her that has a very superior intellect and an original way of presenting the doctrine of the fellowship of man. If Krocho just wouldn't indulge in so much by-play her lectures would be an inspiration in any church pulpit. She does not, however, often mix the two, but generally finishes her clown work before becoming serious.

Viola sang "Whispering Hope" without the trumpet and a male voice sang "Annie Laurie" through the trumpet.

Sister Clara gave this as a parting reminder: "Don't give up the messages, George,—just a word of love every day; that's what helps on this side. You will know the good it does when I tell you that I couldn't come before you this way if it were not for your messages. None of them go astray. They help us all and help you too. Goodnight, brother."

NOTES ON TRUMPET SEANCE
Held at Mr. and Mrs. Jonson's Residence, Los Angeles, Cal., 8 O'Clock Monday P. M., Nov. 7, 1921.

The cabinet work on this occasion was not much of a success. Things behind the curtain went slowly and quietly and the medium, Mr. J. expressed himself as feeling like the results would not be forthcoming. Mrs. J. asked him why it was and he replied, "there's a reason for it, but I don't understand just yet what it is." At this point one of the guides handed a slip of paper over the curtain with the following message, which seemed to explain the situation satisfactorily. The message was from Mr. J's. chemist guide and read:

"In using our medium in this manner we do it more to keep up the vibrations necessary for the grander work to come later on, and are guarding him all in our power, and thank all those who on your side have co-operated with us in promoting means for his protection. Yours gratefully, Silas Webster, Chemist Guide."

The reference to preserving the medium for "the grander work to come later on" we presume relates to the materialization work to come under the Psychical Research Society just organized. The expression of thanks for "those who have co-operated in promoting means for his protection" we presume refers to the method taken to guard him against outside interferences.

The same condition existed at the trumpet meeting; viz: the communicators were not so many as on most occasions; they did not speak quite so long and only the stronger ones appeared. "Timothy" held the trumpet long enough for us to ask a good many questions, and Tim is always ready with a response. I put the following question to start something:

"Tim, I have noticed this on several occasions: Our friends writing to us from the cabinet do not always preserve their own characteristic hand, although it may be signed by them. Is it our own people who write these messages, or do they have an amanuensis on the other side to do it for them?"

Answer. "Both. Sometimes they write it themselves, when the vibration is strong enough for them. Sometimes they call some one else in who can come with a stronger vibration. But the message is from your own people just the same, the spirit who claims it the thought comes through the amanuensis just as it leaves your friend or relative, and you will notice that while the writing might vary, it still resembles your friend. The reason is the same. When the vibration is right the communication is perfect."

Question: "Here's another one that bothers me, Tim: I have noticed that our friends will sometimes tell us that So-and-So (some other friend of ours from spirit life) will speak to us in the trumpet tonight. But my experience has been that the friend mentioned very seldom speaks that night. Why is it?

Note:—Tim evidently read what was in my mind, as my sister had stated that my mother would talk last night, and Tim answered:

"Your mother is with you right now and she is talking to you; but you are not clair-audient enough to hear it. Your friends are trying to help you develop this, and you must not get impatient about it. They know how persistently you have gone into this work and they want you to get all there is in it. And don't forget that there are so many trying to use the trumpet, and one friend on this side will help another by giving him a chance to get in. There are many hindrances between this side and your side; but we are all working for better results."

Question: "Is it true, Tim, that your side is organizing to give us perfect communication?"

Answer: "Yes but its a big job. When societies such as you people are organizing become common all over the world the results will come quicker. But a great deal of the difficulty comes from trying to explain to your side in material language things that are altogether spiritual. That's more trying than you think it is."

Some one asked: "Do people get old on your side? If they reach the spirit world at, say 50 years of age, do they continue to get older?"

Ans: "There is no such thing as old age here. Whatever your age when you reach here, after you get your bearings and get out of your earth environment you are just like a strong young man or woman, feeling good and contented.

Question: "How about religion, Tim; do they preserve the same creeds as they follow here?

Answer: "Not very long. They arrive believing just what they believed on earth. They come as Catholics, Methodists, Presbyterians and Baptists; but in a few days they are all spiritualists. The orthodox churches preach the spiritual life 52 Sundays in a year, but they object to being called spiritualists—until they get over here. Then they find but one religion. The old, old story brought home to them—love for your fellowmen whether they are on the earth side or the spirit side; it makes no difference."

Question: "Tim, I asked once about the work of those on the other side; what is the most important work there?"

Ans: "Work along the border helping the helpless ones when they first come over. Many thousands are active at this work. That's where we get our development. The only development worth while is what comes from helping some one else."

Question: "Do those from the higher planes come to the lower planes often?"

Answer: "Not so very often, but they have the privilege of doing so. As they go higher they visit the palnes toward the earth less. They get busy in the same way then helping others who are moving to higher planes."

Question: "Tim, is there really any such thing as a plane, or is that just an imaginary distinction?"

Answer: "It's distinct enough, but as for any actual separating lines it's like the boundary line between states, or the line you call the Equator—that line is only imaginary, but the distinction is there just the same. You talk of spheres beyond the earth; the term plane is nearer correct than sphere. But this is another case of trying to draw a spiritual picture for an earthly eye to see; it's hard to do."

"Question: "Do you have much beautiful music over there?"

Answer: "Certainly, why not? All music which you have on earth originates here. You heard a song tonight from a spirit who has been over here for forty years, and yet that song has only been known to the earth folks for a few months. The law of harmony is strong here. We have all the great masters placing thoughts in the minds of your musicians. They are still musicians here and they never let loose of the vibrations that make for harmony. Harmony is the key-note. It is one and the same with the law of love. But I've held this trumpet a long time friends and the medium has worked hard." The trumpet dropped to the table.

I broke in saying I wanted to ask just one question of Krocho and then we'd let her go. She answered that she was ready for the question. I put it this way:

"Krocho. when you come to us you come in control of your medium, Mrs. Jonson. Now, what I want to know is this: Does some one control you on the other side? Sometimes you talk with us and ramble on just like a wild little Indian girl; then again you will break out with great fine, beautiful language and give us such a wonderful lecture on morality, on spirit life and good thoughts;— does another spirit control you then?"

Answer: "You got it, friend. I'm just a harum-scarum little Indian girl and never was educated and I like to play with you folks and joke with you: but then when the time comes to say something and be real serious and help you all to understant the law, I go to one of the teachers and she tells me what to say and helps me to get the message through. It's just as it would be with you, when you don't understand a thing you go to some one who does and it you are modest about it, and really want to learn, you can. I control medium Jonson on your side and my teacher on this side controls me, and we all work together like a unit. That's all there is to it—just everybody pull together for good and there's no end to the good you can do. Now, good night, everybody, my medium's very tired."

A palm leaf fan which had been placed on the table, was repeatedly taken up by an unseen hand when the room would become "stuffy" and the entire company fanned vigorously for a few moments until the air was cleared.

NOTES ON TRUMPET SEANCE

Held at Mr. and Mrs. Jonson's Home, Los Angeles, Friday P. M., November 11th, 1921

The cabinet work was tame again last night, and probably for the same reason given at the previous meeting. "Apports" in the way of carnations were the principal manifestation, there being one carnation for every member of the circle, and they were handed out pink and white carnations alternately.

The trumpet seance, however, moved along with more life. There were ten at the table and the seance lasted a little longer than usual. Messages were numerous and every one received from one to three of them.

"Viola" sang through the trumpet. A male voice sang a few notes of "Annie Laurie," in accompaniment with the Victrola, then whistled through the trumpet.

On one occasion there were three separate voices speaking at the same time, one through the trumpet and the other "independent" voices.

Some old-fashioned dance music was started on the Victrola, and a friend of the L.'s, known as "Henry," called off the movements in the Virginia Reel with a strong, clear voice and seemed to be getting a good deal of fun out of it. Then he became serious and assured us of the happiness he found in being able to "converse with the spirits of the earth" and emphasized the fact that we are spirits here the same as we will be on the other side, except that here we are hampered by the physical body and all the ills that harrass the physical being. He stated that we will never know how free we are until the physical body is cast aside and that if we could only realize it death would cease to be an occasion for tears and mourning.

My father spoke through the trumpet for two or three minutes and volunteered the statement that he was glad to get a chance to explain to me at the developing class last Wednesday night the meaning of the voices that had been speaking within me. Said he heard me ask the question of the medium and did not want me to be disturbed but to encourage it in every way as they would come more frequently after they are once started; that after a time I would hear the voice and be able to interpret the message intelligently.

Sister Clara spoke and asked if I didn't think she was gaining strength right along. I assured her that we had all commented upon the progress she had made and every one seemed to think it remarkable. She replied:

"It is the encouragement you have all given me that has helped. I knew how you felt about it. But I want to say this, brother: The next time you go to Chicago don't forget to get the children together and tell them all about the talks you and I have had since I passed over; tell them so they will understand how to talk with me." I replied:

"Yes, I intend to talk it over with them, but do you think they will belive it and understand it?"

Answer: "They will believe you, but they won't understand it at first; but you can make them see through it by giving them the record."

Question: "How did you know I had a record, sister?"

Answer: "I am sometimes with you when you are writing it out. But you always did keep records, George?"

Question: "Haven't you been able to get in communication with any of the children?"

Answer: "No, brother, they don't understand these things. I see them every day, but they can't see me and I can't make them hear my voice. Good night, brother, we have a surprise for you."

A little later another voice called, "George, George!" I asked, "Is it for me?"

Answer: "Yes, my son; this is mother."

I replied, "Well, this is a grand surprise. Bless your dear heart, mother; this is the first time you have talked with me, and its the most wonderful thing in the world to think of hearing your voice again after all these years."

Answer: "They told me I could do this; so I thought I would try."

G.: "Well, mother, it's worth millions to have this chat with you, and I want you to speak every time I come here; because the oftener you come the stronger your voice will get and we can soon work up a good vibration, and every time you come I can hear you that much clearer."

Answer: "Yes, my son, I am going to try to come every time you hold a meeting. Clara spoke to you tonight; she came with me. Now, listen, son to what I am going to say: Sunday night I want you to go to that church where you were last Sunday, and I will meet you there."

G.: "That will be fine, mother; but will I know you are there?"

Answer: "Yes, I will make myself known to you. You will know that I am with you. Good night, son, and good night to the rest of your friends."

Mr. Blinn, the railroad engineer, came with the usual signals, and to hold the vibration some one started the conversation with:

"Mr. Blinn you are a good guesser; we didn't have any railroad strike after all?"

Answer: "Sure you didn't; conditions were not right for it. It was not best that you should have."

Question: "Were you a union man?"

Answer: "Sure, in unon there is strength; but use your strength in the wrong way and something has got to break. That's what happened to the strike."

Goerner asked: "Mr. Blinn, do you believe in the government ownership of railroads?"

Answer: "Yes, and all other public utilities."

Goerner: "I don't believe this country is ready for public ownership yet."

Blinn: "Why not?"

Goerner: "Well, we tried it during the war, and the government got the railroads so horribly muddled up in debt that it will take many years of careful management to get them out. Then, too, I believe new railroad construction would be almost a thing of the past for years to come; it takes too much red-tape before the officials begin to get ready to start to commence anything."

Blinn laughed and asked: "Why is it?"

Answer: "Too much politics in our government."

Blinn: "Do away with it—you will in time."

Goerner: "Yes, we probably will in time but under our present system we have political rings built up in every state and city in the union, and those in power have no wish to change this condition. I expect to see things continue about as they are now for at least 25 years yet. By that time perhaps all the people will be tired of it and demand a change."

Blinn: "That's the way it will be done; but methods for peace and team work with a few level heads at the front will bring the right conditions. All great movements take time." He tooted the horn, "let off steam" and dropped the trumpet.

Then a moment of absolute silence held the company, and Krocho asked:

"What are you all so quiet for; somebody say something and hold the vibration."

I put in with the following question: "Krocho, nearly all the mediums seem to see an Indian guide around me and I'm wondering if you know who the Indian is?"

Answer: "No, chief, I don't; but if you can get his name I can send some one out to look him up. You know it's horrid hard to find some one if you don't know his name. But you will find your Injun in time—when the vibration is right. It ain't right just now. Sometimes you are keyed way up highfaluting; then you are keyed so low down that there's just an awful horrid big space between. You have to keep on a more harmonious plane."

Question: "Is it my fault, Krocho?"

Krocho: "No, that is not what I meant. You are developing along the right lines, but you ain't got there yet. You will in time and when you do your guides will make themselves known to you and they will be with you all the time and help you more than you ever guessed at it. Don't worry about the guide ; you are going to get better acquainted with each other soon." She continued:

"Sister Clara's going to talk tonight." I answered:

"Yes, she has already talked tonight."

Krocho: "But she's going to talk again later. Now, friends, my medium's horrid tired and I am going to say good night."

The reference to my sister Clara "talking again later" was not understood at the time. But, I retired about 11.30 at night. About 2 in the morning I was awakened by a voice on my pillow. I turned over, wide awake, and asked who it was and got the answer: "It's Clara." I answered, "Well, Clara, it's mighty sweet of you to come and talk with me this way, just direct to me, without any trumpet." She replied:

"I am developing this way and you are helping me wonderfully. It was your help that brought mother to you tonight." I asked:

"Clara, are you going to materialize for me when the Jonsons get started, and she answered: "Yes, I am looking forward to that." I spoke again, but the voice had gone.

NOTES FROM "FLOWER MESSAGES"

Given at Peoples Spiritualist Church, Los Angeles, Cal., Sunday Evening, November 13th, 1921.

At the Jonson trumpet seance on Friday, Nov. 11th, my mother requested that I go to the Peoples Church the following Sunday night and said she would meet me there. For record of this trumpet conversation see note of seance for that date.

I accordingly attended the church services on Sunday evening. During the afternoon it occurred to me to take a few roses along hoping that my mother would speak through the flower service.

Mrs. Mary Miller delivered the flower messages. The table was piled with flowers—bouquets, bunches and single flowers, many of them. Picking up the bouquet which I brought she gave out the following:

"This cluster of roses brings me the influence of a mother and she says, 'Tell my son George that I am here and send him love and greetings. When you bought these flowers you said to yourself, 'I wonder if mother will really come.' (Correct). Yes, my son, I am here and have been with you all day. I was with you when you bought these flowers. You first thought you would get one nice large rose for mother; then after you left the store you made up your mind to go back and get a rose for sister Clara, one for sister Annie and one for Minnie. And we are all here to claim our roses. God bless you, my son. I am with you some part of every day and when you go to your room alone at night I am always at your side. Don't be downhearted over material affairs. A change for the better is taking place and you will soon feel more contented. I will be with you to the end."

Note:—The message is correct in detail and the flowers were purchased exactly as described.

Mrs. Miller gave perhaps 20 messages of this character during the evening, most of them with the same attention to detail, and some of them even more so.

During the afternoon I attended the "daylight trumpet seance" at the same church. This was not as successful as the dark room seances at Jonson's. The medium held one end of the trumpet, though there was absolutely no chance for her to talk through it. One party after another would go up and listen at the other end. No one could hear the voices except those who held the trumpet, and the conversations are too brief and indistinct to offer any opportunity for procuring identification. One spirit guide, however, encouraged a continuance of the work and stated that with development the voices would, after a while, become strong enough to be heard throughout the entire hall. I was informed that a few such messages had come at other times.

Here is a piece of evidential matter: Mrs. Miller picked up a flower and pointed out the woman in the hall who had placed it on the table; then said:

"This flower comes from a lady who has been in tears today over the death of a small pet dog. Is that correct?"

The woman answered, "Yes, that's right.'

Mrs. Miller continued: "A little child from the spirit side of life comes as your daughter; she holds this dog up in her arms and says: 'It's all right, mamma; don't cry any more; we've got Bobbie over here with us and he's all right.'

Ignoring the humorous phase of the tears over the dog, the facts are so well connected up as to make very good evidence; for instance, the woman admitted the death of the dog on that day and the tears; also the fact (unknown to the psychic) that she had a little daughter in spirit land, and the child from spirit land had given the name of the dog and it was properly repeated by the psychic.

NOTES ON TRUMPET SEANCE

At Residence of Mr. and Mrs. Jonson, Los Angeles, Cal., Monday, November 14th, 1921.

There were ten members in the circle, all friends and all apparently in harmony with the work . The results were, however, almost negative so far as the cabinet work was concerned. After a while the guide behind the curtain handed out the following message:

"Let Ed and Will change seats." Ed and Will referred to two maiden sisters, the Misses W.'s, who were regular attendants at these circles. Later, at the trumpet meeting, we asked Tim, who signed the message, why he wished the ladies to change seats and he replied: "To get a better vibration; you were not seated just right; the contact was not strong."

We asked, "Did the change improve it?"

Answer: "Yes, quite a little; we could give better results."

Next came one of the characteristic messages from Silas Webster, the chemist guide, whose chief concern seems to be to take care of the health of the medium, Mr. J. This message read:

"Dear Friends of Earth:—If you only knew how we appreciate the kindness shown our medium. We are doing all in our power to conserve his forces to be used later in a greater work."

My mother was the first to talk through the trumpet, and appeared merely anxious to verify her visit to me at the church and then let some one else speak. After the usual greetings she said:

"Didn't I keep my word to meet you at the church, son?"

Answer: "Yes, mother, you did and I felt wonderfully pleased to have you there. But you always did keep your word with the children, and I felt sure you would come. What was it I brought to the church for you?"

Answer: "Some beautiful roses. Good bye, George."

Mrs. J. went into trance and Krocho spoke out: "What makes it so horrid still? Why don't somebody talk?"

I answered, "I'll give you a question, Krocho, that will keep you talking for a whle: What becomes of colored folks after they pass this life? Do they remain black, or are they white?"

Krocho answered: "Here's the idea, chief: It don't make any difference what your color is when you leave the earth; there are no discords here and all are white. If they look black when they materialize to their earth friends, that's just to identify them; and if they are black over here we don't know it, because we only think harmony. It don't make any difference whether its people or pictures or music,—its all going to blend right on this side so there will be no dis-c-cord-ant (she stumbled on this word) impressions. Have you got it, chief?"

"Timothy" appeared at the trumpet, gave us a hearty greeting, as he usually does, and I offered the following question?

"Tim, is it true that the forces on your side are organizing to get a message through that will spiritualize the whole world?"

Answer: "My dear friend, we have been organizing since the beginning of time. The earth plane is just waking up to its opportunity. We are beginning to get your ear now and the work is growing by leaps and bounds. The war had much to do with that. They came over here in such great numbers that many vibrations of the right kind got started in the right direction."

Question: "When the civilized world understands and embraces this doctrine will it mean complete harmony on this side?"

Answer: "No friend; complete harmony in a material world is not possible; but it will mean 75 percent efficiency. When all the nations understand the law then the brotherhood of man will be established over the earth."

Question: "Then that will mean the true millenium?"

Answer: "Very near it friend; the true millenium will be on this side, because its here you get entirely away from material things. But you've very nearly said it: the true millenium will come when brotherly love rules the world. There will be no need for disarmament conferences then."

Question: "Will the disarmament conference in Washington accomplish anything worth while?"

Ans.: "It's a wonderful beginning, and it will have a wonderful ending. But it will take time. There will be a great deal of talk—talk—talk and a mass of what you call red tape. But it will open the way for big things in the future. We are sending out the vibrations and we are building up a machine—not for politics —but for peace and goodwill toward men. It will take time, but it's as much as you can expect when you look at the condition of the world today."

Question: "Will there be any more wars?"

Answer: "It would be out of the question to tell you no when the echoes of war are still sounding in the air."

Mr. L. asked: "Don't you think we ought to do something toward developing mediums here?"

Answer: "Don't worry about that. There will be plenty of mediums when the demand comes. We'll attend to that. But friends I'll have to stop talking; this room is full of spirit folks who want to get at this trumpet." The trumpet fell to the table with a noise as if it had been thrown down violently.

"Chief Big Heart" took it up and addressed Mr. L. (a former friend of Big Heart and member of the same tribe—the Osage), saying that L. was becoming more mediumistic all the time and that he (Big Heart) was going to put him under control soon. Mr. L. complained about having a cold with trouble in his ears and was a little deaf. Big Heart answered:

"Get some fish worms; put him in bottle and cork him up; then hang in sun till worm turn to oil; then put oil in ear; he help him heap quick."

The same instructions were later confirmed by two others at the trumpet, and it seems that this is a favorite treatment for ear ache among the Indians of certain tribes where the secret has been known for many years.

Another incident worth mentioning is this: Timothy was speaking through the trumpet when the telephone bell rang. Tim gave us the name of the caller on the phone and his business in phoning. Mr. M., one of the members of the circle, answered the phone and found the name and business to be correct as Tim had given it to us. No one in the room on the earth side could have given us that information without first answering the phone.

NOTES ON TRUMPET SEANCE

Held at the Jonson Residence, Los Angeles, Friday 8 O'Clock P. M. Nov. 18, 1921.

There were nine in the circle besides the Jonsons. Mr. Jonson was not feeling at his best and we all agreed to dispense with the cabinet work for the evening.

Those who think our departed friends know nothing of the affairs of those on the earth in whom they are interested, might ponder over this:

Krocho commented on the fact that I had come to the "sit-em-down" with the "blues" and I replied:

"What's the remedy for a fellow when he's down in the mouth and hasn't sense enough to smile?" The answer came:

"Just go to yourself, sit down, put yourself in a quiet, calm frame of mind and hold down your nerves. Things haven't gone just right in business today and you are worried. You have gotten out of your own vibration and let this thing work on you until you are keyed way down. Tomorrow you will have better news. Cheer up, think only good thoughts, wear a smile even for those you don't like and you'll soon get back into your right vibration. You don't usually worry. That isn't your style; but you let it get the best of you today. Don't walk the floor. Sit down. But this little circle will help you and you'll go out of here smiling and feeling a whole lot better." (Correct).

My father took hold of the trumpet and he too commented upon the state of my mind and said "you'll be out of it before the meeting is over. I am still with you, my boy, and helping you every day. Things must go cross-wise sometimes; otherwise where would you get your development? Troubles in the material world are part of the law. Goodnight son."

My sister Clara spoke and said: "I see you smiling already, brother. You got your face all red from that ride yesterday."

Question: "Were you with me on that trip?"

Answer: "No, none of us were along."

Question: "Well, I certainly felt some one in the car and tried to talk, but couldn't get any response. Who was that?"

Answer: "It was Emma."

Question: "Who is Emma, sister?"

Answer: "She will make herself known in time. She is with you a good deal lately and you are going to get well acquainted with Emma in the future."

This presumably has reference to a "Guide" from the spirit side. I asked;

"Who is it that goes down the hall with me at night as I go to my room?"

Answer: "Most of the time it's mother. Sometimes I am along and sometimes its Emma and myself. Your mother is often with you. But we are all with you, brother, at least some part of the day. It was very thoughtful of you George to bring those pretty roses for us last Sunday?"

I replied, "It was a great pleasure for me to do it, and the sweetest part of it is to know that you were all there and knew about the roses."

I followed this up with, "Clara, I want you to tell that sweet sister Annie of mine that if she doesn't talk to me through this trumpet soon she and I are going to have a quarrel." The answer came, "She is right with you George." Clara dropped the trumpet and Annie took it up with the following explanation:

"Hello, brother. This is Annie. I haven't been talking to you lately, because you know I have been helping sister Clara, and with the help you have given us she has made wonderful progress. It makes a big difference, George, when we can work together, the earth friends with our side. That gives us the right vibration. But you know I'm always with you George, and we all wanted to talk tonight because you came here with the blues. But you are feeling better now and I can see you smiling."

I asked, "Can you really see me sister?"

"Why, of course, I can. You are sitting between two ladies, with the young lady on your right, and you are leaning forward with your shoulders bent and your face is all red." (This was exactly the attitude I held at that moment).

I put this question as a test: "Sister, who was Minnie De Kover's brother?"

Answer: "It was Seth, but he's on this side, though I don't see him very often." (Name correct. He passed away many years before Annie did). I continued:

"Who was with Minnie and myself on the night Minnie and I tried to talk in the hallway, but were afraid of being heard by the teachers?" (This took place at school in Washington, D. C.)

Answer: "I was there myself, brother,—just you and Minnie and myself." (Correct).

She continued, "Minnie was always very fond of you and we all know that you have thought of her many times during all these years. Minnie stands right back of your chair now and is going to put her hand on your shoulder, so you can feel it."

A hand went on my left shoulder and I greeted Minnie and thanked her for her remembrance of me. Annie replied:

"You know what a sweet girl Minnie was on your plane; well, she's just as sweet a spirit. Before I go, George, I want to thank you for the roses you sent us, and I want you to know how it helps us on this side to get your messages at night. We get them invariably, —not one of them goes astray.. Now, brother, we've kept the trumpet a long while, and it's really hard to do this the first time we try.

Goodnight. You are going to have good company after you get better acquainted with Emma."

Every one in the circle received just such messages with similar "test questions" and identification. The fact is, these efforts to convince us who the spirits are that talk form a very definite part of the conversations, and the "other side" seems especially anxious to prove their identity to us. Little jokes, puns and family reminiscences of an evidential character enter very largely into these conversations. There is also an evident desire to help us all by bits of good advice as to the health of some one in the circle; messages of good cheer for those who come with a burden on the shoulder; sane suggestions for overcoming some temporary physical defect, etc.

Viola spoke through the trumpet and apologized for not singing to us; said she didn't want to deprive others of the trumpet. She too commented upon the state of my mind and offered a message of encouragement and cheer to overcome it.

"Timothy" took up the trumpet with his breezy, good-natured salutation and followed this, as he usually does, with an Irish joke or pun of some kind. Some one asked his name and received the reply:

"A fellow in St. Louis once called me, "Say, Timothy—Hay!" I asked:

"Tim, it there anything to the doctrine of re-incarnation?"

Answer: "No my friend, there is not. Life from your side through eternity is one of progression—not retrogression. When you leave the earth you have graduated from it. From that time on your life is one of progress. There could be no progression in going back to the earth. It is the school for infants. There is no graduating on this side except from one plane to another and higher school in the next. What advantage would it be to me to leave the earth as an enlightened human being and then have to return either in the same form or some lower form? That isn't progression, friend. That would be going backwards."

MEMORANDUM FROM FLOWER MESSAGE

At Peoples Spiritualist Church, Los Angeles, Cal., Sunday Evening, November 20th, 1921.

On the above date I again purchased four roses to take to the church, hoping to have another flower message from mother. I wrapped a piece of writing paper around the stems, on which I had written: "A rose for mother; one for sister Clara; one for sister Annie and one for Minnie, from George."

I stated to Mr. Shank, a business associate in the office, that I had done this as an experiment to see whether or not any of the folks from "the other side" could tell me at the Jonson trumpet seance tomorrow (Monday) who they were intended for and what I had written on the paper.

Mrs. Miller delivered the flower messages, as usual. She took up my cluster of roses and read the message as follows:

"These beautiful roses bring me the influence of a dear sweet mother. She comes so happy and pleased to know that you thought to bring them. There are four who come and you brought a rose for mother, one for sister Clara and one for each of the other two— I do not catch the names clearly but your mother says, we are all here to greet you; we saw you wrap them up and we know who they are for. You don't have to wait until tomorrow, my son. We can tell you now. We are all here."

Mrs. Miller continued: "Your mother says, don't worry about anything, George. I am always with you and things are not going to remain so uncertain much longer. Be patient a little while and you will have much to be thankful for. We are all here tonight."

There were probably as many as 30 messages given out by the two mediums—Mrs. Miller and Mrs. Inez Wagner. While a few incidents of unconscious mind-reading seen apparent here and there, the greater part of the messages is so intimately related to events known only to one or two persons on earth and family members on the spirit side, that it would be out of the question to attempt to account for more than one-fourth of the results by telepathy.

Mrs. Wagner delivered an exalted lecture, under trance, on "What is a Christian?" I believe most of these lectures come from her spirit control. But if there appear to be intrusions of the subliminal self entering into the message toward its close, by reason of a partial return to her normal self, it could hardly be wondered at in view of the confusion with which she has to contend,—automobiles outside the building, members in the hall coughing, sneezing, whispering, dropping hymn books, scuffling their feet, etc. The wonder is that she overcomes these difficulties as well as she does.

NOTES FROM TRUMPET SEANCE

At the Jonson Residence, Los Angeles, Monday, 8 O'Clock P. M.,
November 21, 1921.

Father was one of the first to speak in the trumpet. I put the following question:

"Who is it, father, that has been speaking to me on my pillow at night lately? This happened two or three times, but I am not just sure who it was."

Answer: "Your sister Clara and I have both spoken to you in this way, and we will do so again."

I thanked him and told him to keep these visits up and come as often as he could. Then he put this question to me:

"What happened to your pillow last night son?"

Answer: "Well, I know now what happened. Some one got under my pillow, doubled it up and raised it so high that I woke up with my head propped up in the air." He laughed heartily at this and seemed to think it was a good joke on me.

I asked if he would meet me at Mrs. Miller's tomorrow (Tuesday) afternoon for a private chat through the trumpet.

Answer: "I will if it is possible, George,—if I am not too busy."

Following this sister Clara spoke. At first I did not catch the message very clearly and she jokingly suggested that I had better get some of that worm oil and put in my ears. She referred to the roses which I took to the church Sunday, saying "all these attentions help us so much on this side; everything in the way of a good thought comes through to strengthen us in our work. We never fail to receive them. We knew you were planning the private trumpet meeting and we'll all be there."

I asked after sister Annie and got the reply: "She stands right beside you and can hear you and see you smile."

Question: "Clara, can you really see me?"

Answer: "Yes, why not? And in a little while you will be able to see us."

Then followed a period of silence and Krocho broke in with, "What makes it so horrid still? Don't hold the silence too long; it weakens the vibration."

I answered, "All right, Krocho, I'll ask a question that will keep you going for a few minutes. Here's what I want to know:

"In order to pass from the earth plane to the higher plane, on the spirit side, we have to die, as we call it. Now, then, after we get on your side when we progress from one plane to a higher one is there anything like death, or any other very decided change to go through in order to get higher up?"

Answer: "No Goerner chief, there is only one death. After that its life eternal. Passing from one plane to a higher one on the spirit side is just quiet, peaceful progression. Life is everlasting. Some progress faster than others. Those who have lived a spiritual life on the earth, who have learned the law and followed it, are better prepared. Very few go right through to the highest realms. Christ did it because he was prepared and he ascended into perfection. If you know the law and obey it, it is possible to do the same thing. But all have the same chance on this side. The law laid down by Christ says, 'love ye one another.' Live that and you don't have to ask what's going to become of you after death. He is the great spirit over all. Do you know, friend, that no man can afford to lose his respect for the memory of Christ?"

I thanked Krocho for the message which she gave me last Friday that good news would come on the following day and I would have occasion to cheer up, and remarked that she was a "good guesser." But she snapped back with this:

"Wrong chief. I didn't do any guessing at all. I knew what was going to happen. When some person on the earth plane wants to do something that just causes a lot of trouble, makes people unhappy and does no good, we can often plant a thought in the right place, so he can see his duty differently, and that's what happened."

Minnie spoke through the trumpet and we had a good long chat, discussed old school days and joked and laughed over earth affairs. Finally, she said: "I want to talk with you alone, George; I have something to say to you."

I asked her to be present at the private trumpet meeting tomorrow and suggested that this would give us a good chance to chat. She answered, "Yes, I'll be there. I wanted to get a little message through to you at church Sunday night, just to thank you for the roses; but didn't get chance."

In a few minutes mother placed her hand on my head, then moved the trumpet very close to me, saying:

"George, isn't it wonderful that we can come to you in this way and prove that we still live, and can communicate and let you know that life is not ended with death; that death is only the beginning, and that we are still with you. Thank you so much, son, for the pretty flowers you brought to the church; it was so beautiful because they came from my son. Goodnight my boy. I will talk with you again tomorrow."

Here's an amusing little incident: Krocho likes to play with a little metal snapper which she calls "the bug" and sometimes when she thinks a spirit has talked too long she finds great sport in "popping them out with the bug", as she puts it. Generally some of us hide the bug to see if she can find it in the dark; but she never fails. Last night some one hid it way up on the moulding on the wall, back of an oil painting. She moved the trumpet up in the air and back of the painting, fished the bug out with the trumpet, put it in the trumpet and dropped the bug on the table. This she did independently and while her medium (Mrs J.) was seated in her chair.

During the cabinet work Mrs. Jacob, who was formerly acquainted with Prof. Hyslop of New York, stated that she could see W. T. Stead and Prof. Hyslop both standing in the floor. Later, at the trumpet seance, Timothy confirmed this, saying Mr. Stead and Dr. Hyslop had both been in the room during the entire manifestation. He emphasized that "this is Prof. Hyslop, the psychologist and the great skeptic; some day he's going to talk to you in the trumpet—just like the rest of us; he's had his eyes opened since he came over here." (Mrs. Jacobs is both clairvoyant and clair-audient).

FULL RECORD OF TRUMPET SEANCE

Held at Residence of Mrs. Mary Miller, No. 844 W. 9th Street, Los Angeles, Cal., Tuesday Afternoon, November 22nd, 1921, One P. M.

Reached Mrs. Miller's by appointment. The seance takes place in a small room with one door between this room and the hall. The door is closed tightly and it would be impossible for any one to come in or go out without being heard. The curtain is drawn in front of the glass portion of the door. An aluminum trumpet is placed on the table and the light turned out. The room is entirely dark.

At any trumpet seance, speaking through the tube gives a certain similarity in tone. But the main cause of this similarity is that the communicating spirits draw upon the vocal cords of the medium —whether she be entranced or not. The medium is not conscious of this use of her vocal cords and she may be even using them herself, speaking in a loud tone, while this is being done.

But those who know the communicating spirit well will have no trouble recognizing the characteristic mannerisms of speech. But the thing to tie to is the evidential matter of a personal nature recornizable among old friends. To me there is no doubt that the speakers on this occasion were the spirits they claimed to be. I have attended seances enough with them to recognize them immediately as they appear. A stranger must look for the style of speech, the integrity of the medium and the links of personal matter that go to make up the chain of evidence. If necessary ask such questions as will bring out the desired identity.

These voices are all strong and as clear as one would use in an ordinary conversational tone. There is nothing that cannot be definitely heard. Mrs. M. knew nothing of me except that I had occasionally attended her church and had two flower messages there. She knew nothing of my folks on "the other side"; did not even know my last name and I am prepared to credit the work as genuine.

The success of these trumpet seances may be said to depend, first upon the state of development of the medium for trumpet work; secondly, the psychic development of the sitter and his frame of mind. A doubter or skeptic is very likely to create an inharmonious vibration.

The first voice was a strong, husky man who introduced himself as Dr. Worthington, saying: "I generally procede and end the seance. You are George Goerner. I have seen you at the church once or twice and know you by sight. I am glad to meet you and we are going to get better acquainted. The forces coming to you this afternoon are gathering around you. You are strongly psychic yourself and your friends are already drawn to you. Good day brother."

Following this came mother with a sweet spiritual message: "My son, this is such a happy meeting; and, oh, to think that we can still meet and talk. My boy, through all the years since I left your plane I have walked at your side. I have guided your feet through life. The way has often been hard; but I have many times called on the Master Spirit to give you courage and sustain you, and when I saw the ground slipping from under you there was always help from on high to carry you through. And now sister Clara and Annie and their little ones are all here and we are all so happy. There is no death. There is no death. Keep a cheerful heart, don't worry; you have gone through the worst you will know and we are all helping you. And when you brought the flowers to the church you didn't know that you brought mother's favorite rose; but you did. My old body lies many miles from you and you couldn't put them there. But the grave doesn't matter, son. It means nothing. The spirit lives. The roses were sent to the hospital; so they did more good than you knew. Goodbye, and God bless you."

Father spoke jokingly of raising my pillow last Sunday night and was still laughing over it. He said, "my boy, I just wanted to have a little fun with you. That's what makes us all happy. We all know what an uphill time you had in the past. But that's over with. You are going to have plenty of success and you are going to do a great deal of good. I am always with you and helping you in this work and in business."

I replied, "Well, father, you know I have never tried to use any one on the other side for business purposes. My greatest happiness is meeting with you all and chatting with you and knowing that you still live and care for me."

Answer: "Yes, we know how you feel about it and we are helping you just the same. Better put some weights on your pillow, son." (He laughed heartily and put down the trumpet).

Sister Clara followed with: "Father must have his joke and he thinks its good fun to play a little trick on you. You know he always did like that. Well, after all, brother, we are here to make you happy and bring all the smiles we can. George, I am so glad you are going to send the record to my children and grandchildren. There are so many of them and if you will just show them how to reach me it will make us all very happy. I see them and talk to them every day; but they can't see me and can't hear me. But you can show them how. Just think, brother, we used to hear the old preacher tell us that we would sleep in our graves and way off in the years to come the trumpet would sound and we would all arise. He didn't know that we could stand at his side in spirit and listen to his sermon, and he didn't know that we could take the trumpet and talk to our friends without waiting for the judgment day. Oh, George, if I had only known what you know about these things. You must teach them to my children. Its too wonderful for them to miss it. I'm going to say goodbye, because you are going to get a surprise now."

The next voice was just the dearest kind of a little child's voice calling, "Hello, Uncle George! You don't know me, but I am little Mary."

I asked, "Who is little Mary?" The answer came: "I'm mamma's little girl."

"Yes, but who was your mamma? I don't know of any little Mary that belongs to any of our folks."

Answer: "No, you didn't know me, Uncle George. I was just so awful tiny. I only lived in spirit. You think it over. Papa told you about it once. "I'm sister Clara's little girl."

Note:—I now recall that sister Clara's husband mentioned this incident to me in Chicago many years ago. But little Mary and I got well acquainted through the trumpet and had a nice long chat together. She wound up by saying,

"Did you know that we had little George over here too? You don't know little George either. But he's here and he's Aunt Annie's little boy. We call him George after you and he wants to talk with his Uncle George." Throwing kisses she put down the trumpet.

"Little George" spoke and we had pretty much the same sort of a chat which I had with little Mary. George was a baby who also passed out in spirit. This incident confirms the statement once made to me by sister Annie through the psychic, Mrs. Pettit, at which Annie informed me that, "I have my little boy here with me." See also Mrs. Wallace's reading of Aug. 31, 1921. Later it was confirmed by my sister Amelia in Chicago, who happened to be living with Annie at the time of George's birth.

Next came a strong cheerful voice, calling: "Hello, George Goerner!" I asked, "Who is talking."

"Think I'll keep you guessing, George. You know. Try it again. I told the folks I'd have some fun with you today."

I replied, "I think I know who it is, because the medium made the same mistake they all make and said you stood beside me like a brother. But I want you to make yourself known."

The answer came: "You call the name and I'll promise to give you identification."

Answer: "All right, its Harold Cook."

Harold: "Why, sure it is. You and I used to dig holes in the ground for the same company. How's that for identification? And father raised the money."

Goerner: "That's fine, Harold, and I'm still digging holes."

Harold: "But you are going to win out, George. Your friends are all with you and there's another miner going to talk today."

Goerner: "How are you getting along now, Harold?"

Harold: "Fine, George; everything is lovely, and I am happy."

Goerner: "How is your dear old father and grandmother?"

Harold: "Father advances very rapidly. You know what a wonderful character he was. That's why he's so strong over here. And grandmother is just the dearest soul you ever heard about,— just the sweetest old lady in the world."

Goerner: "Harold, I want to get straight on one point: At

Mrs. Pettit's you told me one time that your mother was still on the earth plane. I always thought your mother had passed away and was with you in spirit land."

Harold: "No, George, that was wrong. Mother is still on your plane; but she is very feeble and will be with us about Christmas time. She doesn't know it; but we are all preparing to meet her over here and are going to take good care of her. She is very old now and her health has broken so much lately."

He continued: "Speaking of the mine, George: You are going to make good. Where you went last you stumbled on to something that most engineers would overlook. Work along that line. Goodbye, old fellow, and if I don't talk very often remember its because I'm trying to give some of the other folks a chance at you. We get most out of the world by helping others most. Goodbye—goodbye—goodbye."

Mrs. Miller then said, "There's a mining man going to talk with you and he dresses like a miner and says he came that way to your room and you thought he was Harold." I guessed it to be John Thomas, but waited for identification. The voice called:

"Hello, Goerner!" I answered, "Who is it?"

Answer: "Its John Thomas, and I'm awfully glad to talk with you. You know I'm helping you in your mining work and we are going to pull that thing through. Stay with us; keep in close touch with this side and don't let go of the work. Things are shaping themselves right. Don't hesitate to ask for advice. We know you don't want to commercialize us; but that's all right. We are going to help you see it through."

Goerner: "Well, that's fine John. Its fine of you, because you and I never met on earth, and I know that any boy that belongs to Jim Thomas is going to be the right sort of a boy."

John: "Well, dad was a dear old fellow, and he is yet. He always thought a great deal of you and he still does. He just follows you around. But you and I are going to get better acquainted. So I'm going to let dad talk."

Came this: "Hello George Goerner, old scout! Do you know who I am?"

Goerner: "Yes, you are my old friend, Mr. Thomas."

Thomas: "No, no mister about it; just plain old Jim Thomas."

Goerner: "Well, Jim, this is surely a great meeting. I was in hopes that you would come, because I want to thank you again for the wonderful work you did on those drawings up north. I saw your fine hand in it and in the contract you drew up back East. I want to thank you again for it."

Thomas: "Well, I want you to put the machine on your properties; because we are going to improve it even more but it isn't best to do it until you work it out in a more practical way. It needs strength and I'm going to show you how to get it. But it is going to be all you expect of it. Don't worry about that. As for the contract back east; just go right ahead. Don't try to rush it. You can have all the time you want. Take it easy and work it out along the lines John suggested. He knows what he's talking about."

Goerner: "Thank you very much, Jim. I want to tell you that I finally got in touch with your son, Gordon."

Thomas: "Yes, Gordon is correct. You got it wrong the other time. But I'm glad you located him. I knew you would. Send him the record. We want to get in touch with him, because we can help him so much, and he will understand things better if he gets the record and the better he understands it the better we can help. You wont lose anything by it. It will all come back to you, old pal. Ever since I passed away I have been on your trail and I'm going to stay with you and we are all working for you. John thinks a great deal of you."

I thanked him and asked, "How is Mrs. Thomas?"

Answer: "She's fine now George. It was better for her to come over here. Life was hard for her on earth and we are all so happy here together. But we want Gordon to know about the things you understand so well. Tell him we've got old Rover here with us."

Goerner: "All right; Jim, I'll see that he does know. But you found things very different over there from what you expected, didn't you?"

Thomas: "Yes, I did. If I had only known what you know. But, you're a lucky lad, George, and you'll find it out when you get on this side. Oh, but it does help so much to get in the right path before you pass over. Well, goodbye, old pal—goodbye—goodbye."

"Sunbeam," the flower guide at the church, spoke through the trumpet; told me who she was; said she was so happy to deliver the messages to me from mother, and she knew we would get better acquainted and that was why she wanted to talk a little today. Her greeting was full of good cheer and she put down the trumpet with: "We will meet again often."

Dr. Worthington again spoke, bade me good day and dropped the trumpet to the floor as an indication that the seance was over. Following this Mrs. Miller said:

"A very sweet spirit just came through the door and walked right back of you, placed one hand on your shoulder and says:

"Tell George I am so sorry I was late. But it couldn't be helped. I had some work to do looking after some little children that just came over and they needed help so badly. But tell him I'll make it up to him and we'll have that confidential chat before long. Tell him its Minnie; he knows and he knows that I am always with him. I didn't forget and I just stepped in at the last minute so he would know."

Note:—Mother's reference to the roses going to the hospital is correct. I learned on inquiry that the flowers placed on the table at the church for the "flower messages" are sent to the hospital after the church service.

The appearance of little Mary at this seance will probably account for the name "Mary" written on the slip of paper which came from behind the cabinet at the Jonsons on Monday, Oct. 24th. (See record for that date). Mary would be an appropriate name for this little tot, as this was the name of both of her grandmothers. It is also probable that the "John" on the same slip of paper was intended for John Thomas, who appeared at today's seance.

Mr. Thomas' request to tell his son Gordon that "We've got old Rover here with us," evidently has reference to a family dog, although this was the first I had ever heard of him.

The reader should note this: The Thomas family and the Cook family were not acquainted with each other on the earth plane. Neither was either of these families acquainted with my relatives or Minnie on the earth. Yet they all seem to be very close to one another on "the other side" and most invariably come all together to commune with me when the door is open through the medium. Their identity is complete and to me there is no question as to who they are. Also observe that at the Jonson trumpet seance of Nov. 21, I made a definite appointment with my folks in spirit land to meet me the next day at the Miller seance, and they were all there to keep the appointment. Can you still question the intelligence of spirit folks and the perpetuation of memory after death?

NOTES ON TRUMPET SEANCE

At Residence of Mr. and Mrs. Jonson, Los Angeles, Friday P. M., November 25th, 1921.

The cabinet work was slow again and this will probably be the case until this work is abandoned for the materialization meetings. The object of the guides on the other side seems to be to give Mr. and Mrs. J. an opportunity to rest up and conserve their strength. The manifestations consisted mostly of handing out small roses—one for each member in the circle, and writing notes.

Silas Webster, chemist guide gave this: "To the Circle: We on our side are waiting very patiently for the day when we can go ahead with our regular work and hope you will be able soon to gratify our desire."

A note from sister Annie, written in a very good imitation of her own hand when on earth, read: "Dear George: We were with you when you bought the roses and you are seldom alone. Be of good cheer; we are helping you in every way possible. With love, Sister Annie."

Mrs. Lambert had a message from her cousin Martha, who just passed out a few weeks ago, containing the Catholic cross, in which was written "I. H. S." Before the trumpet work began there was a discussion between Mr. and Mrs. L. as to the meaning of the initials. Later Martha's mother (from the other side) spoke through the trumpet and corrected Mrs. L's. interpretation, saying the letters stand for, "I have suffered."

"Little Mary" took up the trumpet and announced that it was "Mary Ellen" for Uncle George. I asked,

"Is this the same little Mary as my sister Clara's baby?"

"Sure, it is Uncle George. Didn't we have a grand talk last Tuesday?"

Answer: "We surely did, sweetheart, and we are going to have another one soon."

Mary: "I'm glad of that; I can hardly wait. You send us such good thoughts that it makes it easy for us to talk with you."

I asked: "How is little George?"

Answer: "Oh, he's fine and waiting for another meeting."

Then came a moment of silence and I asked, "Have you gone, Mary?"

Answer: "No, I came here to stick; but somebody else wants the trumpet." Throwing out kisses she laid the trumpet down with "Goodnight, Uncle George."

Father spoke very briefly, saying "How do you do, son; just wanted to greet you."

I replied, "You haven't been planning any more tricks on my pillow, have you father?"

Answer: "No, I'll come in a different way next time. Goodbye, son; I am always with you."

Sister Clara placed the trumpet very close to my ear, standing back of my chair, as there was another voice using the other trumpet. She said:

"I was there George?"

George: "Where, sister?"

Clara: "At the trumpet meeting Tuesday?"

George: "Well, bless your heart, sister I know you were. Didn't we have a good meeting?"

Clara: "Oh, that was grand it was so easy to talk."

I asked, "Did you speak to me on my pillow last night?"

Clara: "I tried to make myself heard, but didn't get along very well."

George: "What else did you try to do in the room, sister?"

Clara: "I tried to materialize, but didn't have much success. But I did it for development; your vibrations are good, George, and it helps us to come to you. Now, listen, brother: You get one of those trumpets that you were talking about, and put it in your room and when you go to bed at night let it set on the table close to the bed and we'll come and talk with you direct."

George: "How did you know I thought of getting a trumpet?"

Clara: "I heard you talking about it at Jonsons. (Correct). But you were afraid you might not be able to get any results, (Correct). You will, brother; its getting easier all the time to get close to you."

George: "I'm glad to hear that sister and I will surely get the trumpet."

Later we were all expressing the wish that Viola would sing for us and some one suggested starting "Whispering Hopes" on the Victrola. The moment the Victrola began Viola started to sing and sang the song all the way through, going clear around the circle and singing first at one chair, then the next, etc.

Timothy first went all around the circle, tapped each and every one of us on the head with the trumpet; then gave us a greeting and Goerner asked:

"Tim, are there any differences in language on your side of life?"

Tim: "No, friend, we all speak the same tongue."

Goerner: "Is it true that you speak through thought vibration instead of the voice as we use it on this side?"

Tim: " That's right; the language here is the language of thought; its the universal tongue. But this isn't so easy to make clear in the language of the earth; there is a difficulty to overcome in giving you the right understanding of this phase of our life here."

Goerner: "Well, Tim, the Hindoo guide who came to Mrs. Lombard tonight spoke in Hindoo. She can't understand Hindoo; why didn't he speak in English?"

Tim: "He only used his native tongue for the purpose of identification. When he talks to her clair-audiently he'll use the thought language and communicate by vibrant force."

Some one asked: "Tim, where do the spirit guides get these flowers which they hand over the curtain to us?"

Tim: (Laughing) "I wont tell you, friend; because I don't want you to think you can go right out and get a whole lot of roses for nothing. But the explanation given by most of the scientific writers on the subject is sufficient for now."

Goerner: "Tim, a few nights ago, you told us that you had met Dr. Hyslop, from New York?"

Tim: "Yes, I met him once."

Goerner: "Well, when the professor was on earth during all his psychical research work his great exacting principle was, evidence. He was always demanding evidence. Now, when you see him again you tell him that we want him to come here and talk with us through the trumpet; but be sure to tell him that he had better come well prepared with credentials, because we are going to be just as exacting about evidence as he was."

Tim: "That's right, friend hand it right back to them. Some of those fellows spend all their time making investigations instead of living the life and when they get on this side they find out that it isn't the research that gives them their standing."

Goerner: "But he left a good monument behind with the books he wrote; they are being widely read now."

Tim: "That's right, friend; he did his greatest good after he was gone. The same way with Isaac Funk. He's here too."

Goerner: "Yes, I have read his 'Widow's Mite.'"

Tim: "That's a wonderful book and has helped all over the world."

Some one asked: "Were you a Catholic, Tim?"

Answer: "No, I was an Orangeman. They are Protestants. But its your character that counts; not what you profess."

Question: "Is there any such thing as a day of judgment?"

Tim: "Yes. its every day that you live. But there is no judgment day in the sense you mean. Every man and woman is brought to trial every day they live. If you don't live down your weaknesses on your side, you've got to do it on this side."

Question: "Is there any such place as hell?"

Answer: "Not in your orthodox sense. There is punishment enough on this side; but it is mental rather than physical and is in just proportion to the deeds done in the body. A man is responsible for his wilfull wrongs only. To punish a man through eternity when he has only lived a few years of wrong doing under full responsibility is not fulfilling the doctrine of Christ. The mistakes you make and for which you cannot be held responsible are not the things that bring darkness after death. There is no such thing as eternal punishment unless a man wants to be punished eternally. In other words, the door of reformation is never closed either on your side or ours. Purgatory comes nearer expressing it, but the priests have no strangle-hold on purgatory. It has been a law since the beginning of time that no man shall be denied his chance to go forward. The Catholic is oppenly opposed to spiritualism; but at heart he's a spiritualist just the same. Take spiritualism out of catholicism and you havn't much left. But don't think any man can escape his responsibility. He pays at one end or the other."

At this Krocho snapped the "bug" and Timothy laughed, saying: "There's Krocho popping me out; I've talked too much," and threw the trumpet on the table.

Note:—The name "Mary Ellen" applied to sister Clara's child brings out another good piece of identity. This name would be appropriate for her, as her grandmother on her father's side was named "Mary Ellen." (See Trumpet Seance of Nov. 22nd).

Regarding flowers brought in as "apports", at a later seance one of the spirit guides explained to us that these were taken from gardens in the neighborhood of the Jonson home; and qualified this with the statement that the forces from the "other side" gave the soil, roots and stems treatment by which the plant lost nothing by the plucking of the flowers.

Notes on Psychic Experiences taking place Sunday November 27, 1921.

I attended the Peoples Spiritualist Church, New Hampshire Avenue and 12th Street, Los Angeles, taking with me a cluster of roses, naming one rose for mother, one for sister Clara, one for Sister Annie, one for Minnie and one for little Mary Ellen.

Mrs. Mary Miller read the "flower messages." Taking up the roses I had brought she said:

"When you wrapped up these roses you gave them all names. There is one for mother, one for Clara, one for Minnie;—the others I do not catch, as the forces that are for you are beginning to come thick. There is your father; then comes a man named John, and with him comes Jim. They are all here and all want to greet you. Mother says, "tell George if he only knew how his work helps us here, and how we love the flowers." Minnie walks right in front of you, as a sweet spiritual woman and thanks you for the roses."

The "John" mentioned is doubtless John Thomas and "Jim" is his father.

Those who wonder what becomes of a limb or other part of the body lost on the earth may find the answer in this:

Mrs. Inez Wagner was delivering messages to the members in the hall, and asked: "Who in the audience would recognize a man who calls himself Pegleg Smith and says he wants to talk with his old partner?" She pointed the man out (although she was blindfolded) and he identified Pegleg. She then continued,

"Tell him I've got both my legs now and can walk as well as anybody."

In my room at night, after I had retired, sister Clara spoke to me on my pillow. I asked,

"Is it sister talking?"

Answer: "Yes, its Clara. I told you I would came often."

I replied: "Well, it's very sweet of you sister and the oftener you come the better I understand things on the other side. Do you think we can talk any plainer after I get the trumpet?"

Answer: "Yes, I know we can. I want to thank you for the roses."

With this the voice left. It was followed by some one tapping on the pillow. Father does this sometimes on the trumpet at the Jonson seances and I asked, "Is it father?" He answered with three taps, meaning "Yes" and said he had just come to let me know that they are all with me.

The heavy male voice which I have heard several times before, and to which my father referred at the trumpet seance of Nov. 11th, and also at the Wednesday evening developing class Nov. 9th, speaking within me, spoke several times last night. The sound was clear enough, but the only intelligible words I could catch were, "Keep on with the work; keep on with the work."

I placed my right hand up on the pillow, down toward the edge, and a small hand like that of a child's crept into my hand. I held it for not less than five minutes, felt the fingers, the thumb and the palm. I asked whose hand it was, but received no reply. I was not asleep, my eyes were wide open and the hand was certainly there. It was neither warm nor cold, but what might be called "medium." I suspect it was little Mary Ellen's and will make further inquiry at the Jonson trumpet meeting tonight.

Note:—Unfortunately, these manifestations coming to my room are matters which I cannot prove to any one else, as can be done with seances held in the presence of others. I am always alone in my room, and it is doubtful if they would occur in the presence of a stranger who had had no previous training in psychic work. To me, however, they furnish exceptional proof, for the reason that I know to an absolute certainty that there is no one else in the room and the messages can come from no human voice. The conversations could not be carried on unless I was wide awake and my mind clear so I can respond to the questions and answers given. It is no dream and no hallucination. Furthermore, they most invariably connect up with some previous bit of evidential matter taking place at other seances or psychic readings and in most instances form a definite connecting link.

NOTES OF TRUMPET SEANCE

At the Jonson Residence, Los Angeles, Cal., Monday Evening, November 28th, 1921.

There were only ten present at the meeting, including Mr. and Mrs. J. The cabinet results were almost negative for three-fourths of the time. This was doubtless due to a weak vibration resulting from a generally depressed feeling on the part of both Mr. and Mrs. J. on account of their daughter having left that day for the hospital for a serious operation.

Finally "Gray Feather" took control of Mr. J. just long enough to say that he wanted to "lift him up" and told the circle that he was going "to tell on his medium; my medium he go today to sit down to table to eat when squaw went out, and he cry just like little baby. He still feel that way; that's why can get no big noise."

Some one asked Gray Feather if Lottie would be safe at the hospital and received the reply: "Me don't know. Sometimes no look good; but heap good work being done; maybe she be all right."

Then Timothy got into the cabinet and cut up a few antics making comic figures out of paper with the scissors and soon had the circle in a lighter frame of mind.

When the trumpet circle opened the vibration was very strong—the strongest we have yet had—and the results for every one were unusually good. All the communicators "from the other side" commented upon the even, harmonious conditions; said the vibration was almost perfect and would bring better results than we had ever had."

This proved to be the case. The voices were strong and followed close on one another without the usual music to start them.

Father took the trumpet and I asked if he had been to my room the night before.

Answer: "Yes; do you know what else I did?"

Goerner: "No, father, what was it?'

Answer: "I went to that church and saw all of you there and I got into the vibration of every one of you and that helps us all. We have a better contact now."

Goerner: "Father, do you know anything about the hand that crept into mine on the pillow last night?"

Answer: "No, it didn't happen while I was there. I am going to talk with you at Mrs. Miller's tomorrow afternoon."

Goerner: "Did you know I had an appointment with her?"

Answer: "Sure, I heard you make it at the church just as you went into the door."

Note:—This is correct; Mrs. Miller was at the entrance of the church as I passed in and I made the appointment at that time.

Little Mary Ellen called, "Hello, Uncle George!" I answered:

"Well, bless your heart, dearie, I'm glad to hear you speak again."

"Well, I was at the church last night. You looked so happy and full of smiles."

Goerner: "Why shouldn't I; when I knew you were all there; I couldn't help feeling happy. But what else did you do last night, dearie?"

The reply came, "Why, I stole into your room after grandpa left and you took my hand."

Goerner: "Well, bless your heart, that's just what I wanted to know and I was waiting to see if you would tell me about it. Well, sweet soul, you can just put your hand in mine any time and I'd just love to have you."

Answer: "Well, it wasn't anybody but me, Uncle George, and I'm coming soon again."

Goerner: "Will you come to the trumpet meeting tomorrow?"

Answer: "Sure, we are all going to be there. Goodbye."

I said to sister Annie: "Sister, you know father was considered a good physician and surgeon when he was here on earth, and we all want him to look out for Lottie while she's at the hospital and take good care of her."

Annie: "That's just what I was going to speak about. All of our forces are working for her. They know its serious and we are doing good work here. Rest easy all of you and send out your best thoughts for her while she's away and that helps so much."

I asked if she would be at the trumpet meeting tomorrow and she answered, "Yes, we will all be there; Clara stands right back of you now with her hand on your chair. Goodnight, brother."

Timothy came in, saying that if he didn't get in and say a word the ladies would have it all their own way. He asked, "What's the question tonight?"

I put this one: "We have spoken before about animals living on your side: Does the animal actually exist in the same sense that you and your other spirit friends do; or isn't the animal there really as a mental reflection of the dog or horse that we loved and cared for on this side?"

Answer: "Not a bit of it, friend. That dog and horse are alive just as much as I am, or any other friends you may have here, and in exactly the same sense. There is no mental reflection business about it; its the real thing."

Krocho broke in with, "The shams are all on the earth side, chief; its on our side that you get only what's real."

Timothy: "That's true, friend; Krocho put it to you just right."

Previous to this Mrs. M.'s father had spoken and referred to his lameness. Afterwards Mrs. M. said to Timothy: "I am puzzled as to why my father should have said he was no longer lame. He never was lame on earth. Why did he say it?"

Tim: "I don't know either why he should have said it if he was never lame; what did he die of?"

Mrs. M: "He had a stroke of paralysis."

Tim: "Oh, well, that accounts for it, lady. That was just his way of expressing himself. If you had a stroke of paralysis you'd feel pretty lame after it too."

"Catherine", a relative of the M. family, appears to have overheard this conversation and she spoke to Mrs. M. independent of the trumpet and confirmed Tim's explanation, saying father wished her to explain that he didn't mean that he was lame and couldn't walk naturally; "but he just felt lame all over."

Some one asked Krocho what sort of homes they had on the other side.

Answer: "The kind of a home you have built for yourself on the earth plane. Your mansion will suit your character. If its a poor one when you reach here its your privilege to keep building it up as you move higher until you reach the home not made with hands, eternal in the heavens. As many beautiful thoughts as you think just so many beautiful flowers will you find in your home here, and you can sprinkle them with the waters of love and kindness and they just keep on multiplying and growing brighter and prettier all the time."

W. T. Stead announced himself through the trumpet and said he had come to encourage us in the organization of the Psychical Society; said he was greatly interested in it; said he saw a chance to build up to the Bureau which Julia wanted him to found before he went down on the Titanic. He assured us of success and said Julia (who wrote the "Letters from Julia" through Stead's hand after Julia had passed to the other side and while Stead was still on earth) had taken such an interest in it that she came along to say a word of good cheer and to encourage us.

"Julia" followed Stead, saying she couldn't resist the desire to assure us of her cooperation in the society and said, "You must not stop there; but encourage the growth of other societies until it becomes world-wide."

Krocho concluded the seance with: "Well, friends, my medium's had the blues all day; and she's tired and I'm going to pop myself out. All keep a good thought for little squaw until she comes back to you and we are all going to work for her from our side. But you know friends, there comes a time when we must all come over and when that time comes nothing can stop you and you just have to be popped out. We can't tell today just how its going to come out, but I feel like its going to be all right and the little squaw is coming back to you all real soon. But when your work is done, and when you can do more good on our side than you can remaining in that old tight body on earth, it aint a death; its a birth. Goodnight everybody."

Note:—Those who have read the "Letters from Julia", written automatically by W. T. Stead previous to his passing away and dictated under the signature of "Julia" will understand the reference to establishing "the bureau" for bringing general proof of spiritualism, or spiritism, to the world. W. T. Stead was for many years the president of the British Society for Psychical Research. Julia had been a friend and co-worker with him and this will account for their appearance together on this occasion and their interest in the local society being formed here.

FULL RECORD OF TRUMPET SEANCE

At Residence of Mrs. Mary Miller, Los Angeles, Cal., Tuesday, 1 O' Clock P. M., Nov. 29, 1921.

There was no one present in the seance room except Mrs. Miller and myself, as on previous meeting. The trumpet she uses is aluminum and this is first emersed in water—the water acting as a conductor. The trumpet is placed on the floor and taken up by the different communicators, who sometimes come very close to the sitter, and even manifest their presence by tapping him on the head, face or shoulders in an affectionate way.

Dr. Worthington, trumpet control, came first again and greeted me about as follows:

"Good afternoon, Mr. Goerner. I am glad to see you back again. I thought we would get better acquainted. There are good forces here for you and they are already assembled in the room. You are mediumistic and becoming more so right along and it makes it easy for your friends on the other side to reach you. Keep up a smiling face and a cheerful heart and the results will come."

Next came Minnie and we had a very good little chat, much of it being of a personal nature relating to past associations before she left the earth plane, schoolday topics, friends of bygone days, etc. Finally, I asked if her brother Seth was with her and received the reply.

"Yes, he is here now and I see him often. He hasn't forgotten you and still thinks a great deal of you. You know he passed out before I did and was here first." (Correct).

I remarked, "Minnie are we going to have that confidential little chat soon that you spoke of?"

Answer: "Yes, but I am going to wait until you get your trumpet; then I'm going to magnetize it for you and when we can talk all alone, with no one but you and me to listen, I am going to tell you what I wanted to say. Goodbye. We'll have many talks together soon."

Little Mary Ellen spoke and said she came just to let me know how happy it made her to talk with Uncle George, and again confirmed the incident of Sunday night by saying, "I put my hand in yours on the pillow Sunday night and I'm going to do it again soon, and when you get your trumpet I'm coming often. They are all here to talk and little George is holding up his hand for the trumpet." She threw several kisses through the trumpet and handed it over to George.

Little George and I chatted pretty much as an Uncle on the earth would chat with a nephew on earth that he cared for, and he seemed to be remarkably pleased at a chance to chat with Uncle, and said he came to the church too with the rest of the folks.

Then came Mr. Thomas with: "Hello, George, I'm John and I was with you this morning at that conference in the office. I went all through it with you. I looked after the mining side for you and there were others with me to look after the business end. You can go right ahead on this line. They look like a good pair and we are going to help you pull it through."

I asked: "How is your mother, John?"

Answer: "Oh, mother is getting along fine. We are all together now and everybody is feeling fine and happy. Rover is still here he stays right along with us. We couldn't do without him." He put down the trumpet and was followed by his father with the same greeting:

Hello, Goerner: "This is your old friend, Jim."

Goerner: "This is surely fine, Jim. I'm expecting lots of good chats with all of you after I get my own trumpet and have it in my room.

Thomas: "I'll be there, old boy. Do you know who is going to be your trumpet guide?"

Goerner: "No, I don't Jim." He did not go farther with this point just then; but continued:

"I just dropped in to tell you that I was with you this morning at the conference. John was with me and we both took a good look at that pair. You know the old lawyer we used to have in Denver?"

Goerner: "Yes, I know who you mean."

Thomas: "I took him along with me just for safety, to see that your feet didn't slip. Now, let me tell you, George: You needn't be afraid of Tom————; he will pull this thing through and look out for you too. You can trust him to handle the other fellow. They mean business and I am going to stay right with you to the finish."

Goerner: "Can I trust them, Jim, to play fair and give us a square deal?"

Thomas: "Yes, George, you can go right through with it. Mr. ————isn't as hard a man as you think; —his word is good. But here's what I want to do: We are planning some fine work for you later on; but we must first get you on your feet so you can move about. After we get the mine going you can work without these hindrances that make it hard for you to do anything now. We have got to get you out of the squeeze. That's why I appointed myself your trumpet guide. I am going to help with that, so we can keep close together."

Goerner: "That's fine, Jim, and I know that we are going to get great results."

Thomas asked: "George can you see old Rover sitting near you?"

Goerner: "No, I am not clairvoyant enough for that and am wondering if I will ever be able to get that far."

Thomas: "Yes, you will; you are right on the verge of it now. You are too psychic not to get it. A year ago it would have been impossible. But you have made good headway and you know the results have been coming right along. Just keep it up. Do you know, old boy, that when you once get well into this work you can never turn back because you will never want to. But Mrs. Miller can see Rover; ask her to describe him."

Mrs. Miller then said, "he sits right beside you, down on his haunches with his forelegs up and his head turned looking toward you. He is a black-tan with just a little white spot on his nose; big intelligent eyes and his big tongue hanging out of his mouth."

Thomas: "That's right; he wont keep his tongue in his mouth. He always did let it hang outside. That's Rover exactly."

Goerner: "You know, Jim I located Gordon and I am going to keep in close touch with him until he reaches you. I'll get the record to him just as soon as I can find a way to get it out."

Thomas: "Yes, that will be fine. His mother will be so glad. Gordon had a setback to his health and we can be of help to him, and can help him so much better when he understands these things."

Mrs. Thomas followed Jim and we renewed our acquaintance of earth. I asked if she knew how close together she and my sister Clara passed out and she answered:

"Yes, Mr. Goerner, we both passed out at the same time, I in August and she in September, and we meet over here and have been great friends ever since. You know Denver was so cold, and so much snow in the winter. I don't blame you for living in Los Angeles."

Another voice: "My boy, this is mother. I didn't just come this minute; I have been with you all day. We all love the beautiful flowers you brought to the church Sunday. They brought such a sweet message to us all. Then they went to Prof. Bronson and when he took them to his home he sent out such a wonderful vibration and it made it so easy for us to reach you last night and today. He is so spiritual and his influence goes far. So you see just a little kindness, just a word of love, just a cheerful message, and it keeps growing as it goes. Be of good cheer; we are helping you and remember always that mother is with you to the end."

"Sunbeam", the guide who controls Mrs. Miller in delivering the flower messages at the church, came in as bright as her name with:

"Do you know, brother, that you get your greatest wisdom at night?"

Goerner: "No, Sunbeam, I didn't; but I am glad to hear that."

Sunbeam: "This is true. It is why your friends come to you at night. They are helping you in this way. After you lie down long enough to get your nerves quiet and become receptive, they steal into your mind so peacefully and put good thoughts there. So when you bring your flowers to the church the word goes out long before you think it does and the dear ones are all there to meet you. You know they are there and that's why you keep your mind open to receive them. You know they are here today and your face is just full of smiles. Goodbye for today, brother."

Dr. Worthington took up the trumpet, delivered a farewell address and was about to drop it when Mrs. Miller said:

"Just this moment a dear old gentleman came through the door. He comes with the influence of a father and walks very rapidly to your chair and throws up his hand as a signal to Dr. Worthington and says, 'Doctor, don't drop that trumpet till I keep my word with my son. I promised him last night that I would be here today and I must keep my promise. Hold the vibration just a moment."

Father then spoke, said he had been almost too busy to get to the meeting and said "Doctor Worthington was good enough to keep the door open." After a moment's chat he dropped the trumpet with Goodbye, and God bless you my boy I am always with you."

Notes:—The conference at the office, to which Mr. Thomas and his son referred, took place on the morning of this seance. I held a business meeting with two associates who came for the purpose of arranging to raise capital for some mining interests. I went directly from the office to Mrs. Miller's, without conversing with any one at all about this conference, and Mrs. Miller could have had no possible way of getting any advance information on it. The name "Tom———" was correctly called, and neither any of my friends on the spirit side nor any one at the Miller home could ever have known this party on earth.

The statement made by Mrs. Thomas that she and my sister Clara had both passed out the same time—"I in August and she in September" is approximately correct, although I have not been able to get the exact date of Mrs. Thomas' death. Sister Clara passed over Sept. 28th, 1921, and Mrs Thomas sometime late in the summer of the same year.

The statement made by my mother, that the roses afterwards went to Prof. Bronson, is also correct. Usually they go from the church to the hospital, but on this occasion after the flower messages were given my particular cluster of roses was handed to Prof. Bronson as a reward for his lecture on "The Master's Cup."

I have omitted sister Clara's message from this record, as it was most entirely of a personal nature relative to her children in Chicago; but wish to mention the fact that she too spoke of my having ordered the trumpet and from the tone of her message she seemed to know all about it,—when I had placed the order—the fact that I had to send east for it, and seemed to know just about when it ought to reach me.

Father's statement that he had promised me last night that he would be at the trumpet meeting today was correct. The appointment was agreed upon between him and myself at the Jonson seance the night before. This seems a good piece of evidence of intelligence on the spirit side, as Mrs. Miller knew nothing of my having attended the Jonson seance and knew nothing of the appointment with my father.

RECORD OF TRUMPET SEANCE

At Residence of Mr. and Mrs. Jonson, Los Angeles, Friday, 8 O'Clock P. M., December 2nd, 1921.

There was the usual crowd of ten members present. The cabinet work was limited mostly to messages written on the pad left in the chair behind the curtain. Most of those present had a message from some one on "the other side." Silas Webster, chemist guide to Mr. Jonson, handed out the following:

"To the Circle: It is always a pleasure to come to you in this way, or in helping in the animation of the physical objects used for our physical work here back of the curtain. But you all being in perfect harmony assists us greatly, as nothing without that can be accomplished satisfactorily. Remember, friends, the saying a house divided against itself cannot stand. Do not allow any unkind thoughts to prevail, either within or outside of your seance room, as such are most detrimental to your spiritual development and a hindrance to the manifestations. Think only good and aspire to the highest and you will build up around you such a storage of physical force that we will be able to accomplish most anything we attempt. Yours, Silas Webster."

"Kitty" sent out one of her childish scrawls, written in circles: "Well, I did not get a chance last time so I am going to write this time. We want our medium to stop worrying. We will all help aunt Lottie all we can. Be cheerful and we can all work together."

After the curtain seance was over I read the messages to the circle and placed the ones from Kitty and Silas Webster in my pocket. At the trumpet circle my sister Annie mentioned this, saying:

"Brother, I had to grab this trumpet on the run before somebody else got it. Just wanted to tell you that I am going to write you another letter soon."

I answered: "I think it's about time, sister, that I was getting another one," and received the answer:

"How many do you want at one time, brother, you've got two in your pocket now."

Mother spoke of the meeting held the evening before for the reorganization of the Psychical Research Society; said we were attended by a good band of helpers and that was why everything went on in harmony. Said she was glad that that I had taken the presidency of it, and added:

"That was arranged from this side, my son, and you have such a strong helper in this work."

I asked: "Who is my helper, mother?"

Answer: "She will make herself known to you in her own way. She is getting very close to you lately. That was such a lovely meeting we had Tuesday, son. It is so wonderful that we can meet and commune together this way. I will be with you at the church Sunday night —we will all be there. Goodbye—goodbye."

Sister Clara also spoke of being present at the meeting of the society; said there were good forces on the other side working for us; said she would be at the Church Sunday and try to get a message through, but "If I don't, brother, you will feel our presence and know that we are there. Little Mary sends her love and says she is coming to see you soon."

"Catherine," who comes to Mr. and Mrs. M. as a guide was asked by Mr. M.:

"Catharine, what do you think of the selection we made for president of the society?"

Answer: "It's all right. Things will move along now. He isn't afraid to speak out. We are back of him and back of the society, because we want to see you lead up to big work."

All through the trumpet seance references were made by one communicator after another to the reorganization meeting of the society. Evidently we had a substantial group of visitors from the spirit side; they seemed familiar with every detail of the meeting and spoke of the subjects discussed by us in a knowing way. There seemed to be nothing that escaped them.

A male voice spoke through the trumpet, announcing his name as "Frank Shaw."

Question: "Who are you for?"

Answer: "I'm for everybody."

Krocho then broke in with: "Oh, he's the man that used to make such good stink-up stuff."

Shaw: "I am Frank Shaw from Toledo, Ohio. I used to manufacture perfumery. If you will all lay your handkerchiefs on the table I'll perfume them for you."

Krocho: "Oh, we are all going to get stunk up."

Each and every member placed a handkerchief on the table. Every handkerchief was removed, saturated with perfume and put back on the table where it belonged. The room was then sprinkled with perfumery until the place was scented with it.

We tried a little experiment with the trumpets. Most of us prefer only one trumpet on the table at a time. When there are two both of them are often being used at once and the two voices create confusion, especially for those whose hearing is not very acute. The decision we reached was to put both trumpets on the table, but to "send out a thought to the other side not to use but one at a time," and see what would be the result. "The other side" carried out the program to the letter; used only one trumpet at a time, although frequently one communicator would eagerly hold the loose trumpet in hand waiting for the present speaker to finish.

When things got quiet and Krocho thought it necessary to say something to hold the vibration, I asked:

"Krocho, do the folks on your side of life have to sleep?"

Answer: "No, chief, we don't sleep. We just rest in a quiet, easy way and we don't get tired enough to need what you call sleep; but we get the rest, the quiet and the strength we need. It's just like when you go in an eating place; you don't know it but some of us are with you very often, and while we don't eat your food we can get the essence of it and that's our way of eating."

Timothy announced that he was ready for questions and I asked:

"Tim, we can all understand the beginning of things with us on this side; but I don't think any one has a very definite idea about the end of things: After we reach your side do we actually keep right on living, progressing, going ever onward and upward, everlastingly and without end?"

Answer: "Well, friend, it would be hard for me to say because I haven't lived that long yet. Life is eternal if you can comprehend what eternity means."

Goerner: "Have you actually met any people who have been on the other side for hundreds or thousands of years?"

Tim: "I certainly have, sir."

Goerner: "Then if they have been living for several thousand years it would be reasonable to assume that life is everlasting?"

Tim: "That would be a reasonable conclusion and I see no objection to it. Christ has been here for 2000 years."

Some one asked if he had seen Christ.

Answer: "No, I have not. Others may have seen Him, but I haven't; but we all feel His influence and His power constantly."

Goerner: "Does Christ exist as a spirit in the same sense that you do?"

Answer: "It would be reasonable to suppose that he does, because He was a scriptual and historical character and lived in the flesh the same as the rest of us did."

Goerner: "Does God exist as a personality, or does he stand for the universe?"

Answer: "None of us have ever seen God. You may call him the great universe—not a personality."

Goerner: "How would it be to define Him as the consummate of all the spirit forces, or of all the physical forces?"

Answer: "That would be very good, friend. None of us here know anything about a personal God in the sense that we know the personal Christ. God is perfection, but that does not mean personality."

Krocho started to "pop him out with the bug," but I asked for one more question:

"Tim, in the past few days a little niece and a little nephew of mine who never lived to learn to speak on this side, now talk to me in very good English. Where did they get it?'

Answer: "Just as you got yours, partly from your parents and partly in school. We have many schools here—much better ones than you have."

Some one asked: "Tim is prohibition the best thing for the human race?"

Answer: "Temperance would be better. A man prohibited from following his inclinations has no choice, no selection. It's a normal right to follow or resist temptation that builds character, and not resistance under a barrier which prevents you from doing anything but resist."

He put down the trumpet and Krocho said she was going to "pop the whole circle out, because my medium's horrid tired. But don't forget friends that I love every one of you, and I wouldn't say one thing to hurt anybody's feelings. Sometime some of you come here with a sad heart. I know all about what's the matter, and I could help you so much if we could just sit down alone and let me tell you how to get away from it. But I don't do it—why? Because it's a little personal matter of your own and I know it would embarrass you to have me talk about it in the circle. Good night, everybody and God love you all."

Note:—The "Frank Shaw" incident is good; inquiry developed the fact that there was a man by that name in Toledo, Ohio, several years ago engaged in the maufacture of perfumery.

Here's another one: The little "bug" which Krocho seems to regard as her property, was placed in the tambourine on the chair behind the curtain when arranging the cabinet. When we were ready for the trumpet seance no one could find the bug. Mr. L. accidently put his hand in his coat pocket and found it there. No one knew how it got there. Later Krocho admitted that she put it there herself. We believe this, because no one else present had handled it after it had been dropped into the tambourine and we have the assurance of all the members that they had nothing to do with placing it in Mr. L's. pocket.

Mr. and Mrs. L. had arranged to start for San Francisco by auto the following morning and had mentioned this at the Jonson home before the seance began. At the circle "Big Heart" and "Gray Horse" (spirit guides) both spoke of the trip through the trumpet, as did also Mr. L's. sister Minnie (deceased); they said they were with the L's. in their preparations and would be with them on the trip. The folks on "the other side" knew as much about the proposed car ride to San Francisco as the L's. themselves did.

Do not overlook the fact that the members of this circle are personal friends. We know one another by close association and repeated meetings and we have had a long intimate acquaintance with the mediums, Mr. and Mrs. Jonson. None of us are trying to fool ourselves or the other fellow. We are not playing any tricks on one another at these seances, but are all earnestly trying to **get the evidence and arrive at the truth.**

NOTES ON TRUMPET SEANCE

Held at Residence of Mr. and Mrs. Jonson, Los Angeles, Monday 8 O'Clock P. M., Dec. 5th, 1921

The work behind the curtain was lively from the beginning. The sitters were Mr. Jonson, Mrs. Jacobs and Dr. Wetherby. These clasped hands tightly, so that both hands of each sitter were firmly held throughout the seance. Two red electric lights were on and the room was light enough to see every move made and even to read clearly the messages that came over the curtain.

Finally Mr. J. remarked that "something was happening"; said he felt chilly all over and his coat was being taken off. Mrs. J. then went to the curtain and Mr. J's. coat was handed out over the top. It had been removed from Mr. Jonson while both hands were clasped and held by Mrs. Jacobs.

At the trumpet seance some one asked Gray Feather if he had taken it off and he replied. "Yes, me want to show you how good vibration you all had." I asked Gray Feather if he would tell us how he took the coat off without ripping the sleeves.

Answer: "Me no tell; cause you go take somebody's blanket off."

Note:—The assumption is that a part of the coat was dematerialized in order to get it from Jonson and then materialized again. This took place in the presence of ten witnesses and there was no chance for any sort of trickery.

Sister Clara wrote the following note: "Dear George: I am so pleased to be here tonight; but we miss the influence of our dear friends who are gone. But they are all right. With love, Clara."

At the trumpet table sister Annie was the first to speak and gave me this:

"You know brother, I promised last week that I would write you a letter tonight. (Correct). But I didn't do it, because I wanted to give sister Clara a chance. I'll write next time."

Goerner: "All right, sister that's very good of you and I'll be glad to get the letter. But, listen, sister; a week ago last Wednesday you said you were going to whisper something in my ear soon. Did you forget about it?"

Annie: "No, indeed, I didn't brother; I am just waiting to get the right chance—when you are all alone and no one else can hear. We've got a surprise for you. You do this: Bring your trumpet down to the Jonson meeting and use it at the table that evening, so it can come well under the vibration from our side. That will help to give you a good result. Goodbye, goodbye."

Mother gave this through the trumpet: "We were glad to give sister Clara the chance to write to you tonight. You know Clara seems to do these things better than the rest of us. She came so recently, and has built up so strong, that she gets within the earth condition so much easier. You know, son, when your father and I passed over no one used to speak of spiritualism at all during those days. The wonder of it all was never known by us. But your sister Clara remained long enough to see great strides in the work and she came better able to understand it on this side. Goodbye, my boy; I am with you always."

Father gave this: "What happened to your hair son?"

Goerner: "You've been pulling my top-knot have you? I felt your hand just a moment ago and was sure you were around. But mother had her hand on my shoulder all the time she was talking and I just thought she put it on my head; but when some one pulled my hair I knew it was you."

He laughed at this and went on: "Say, son, I was at the hospital today to see Lottie. She's getting along nicely and I feel that all danger is passed. But, oh my, they did do some cutting-up on that girl!"

I asked if he was going to materialize for me when we get started on the work and received the reply: "You just watch me trot out from behind that curtain."

A voice came announcing that it was "Admiral Moore of the British Navy." Said he heard us discussing his books and felt at liberty to come into the circle. Some one asked if his last book "Glimpses of the Next State" could be bought in the United States.

Answer: "The American edition is exhausted. It is still in print in England."

Mrs. Jacobs asked: "Admiral, you used to know Dr. Hyslop of New York; can't you tell him to come and talk with us some time?"

Goerner: "And tell him to bring plenty of evidence with him, because we expect him to be able to satisfy the American society of his identity."

Moore: "I can tell him, friends, but it won't do much good for sometime."

Question: "Why?"

Moore: "I'll tell you why: That man is no farther advanced today than he was when he first came over here. He is still in a daze. He hasn't come too yet."

Question: "We are sorry to hear that. Why is it?"

Moore: "There's a reason for it. Hyslop was always an egotist. He held himself above his fellowmen. But he hasn't yet been able to square accounts with this side. You know he was very exacting and very inconsiderate of the mediums whom he employed for his work. He condemned them all and accused them all of being dishonest and tricksters. Now you know, the medium is the instrument through which the spirit must give the results which the investigator is after. But you can't get them by abusing the medium, and the spirit forces resent this attitude toward their instrument."

Some one asked: "Can't you help him out, Admiral?"

Answer: "Not to any great extent. The law of compensation comes in here to a considerable degree. We can all help one another, but that doesn't mean that a man may merely ask for help and shift the responsibility for his earth life."

Later Mrs. Jacobs' son, from "the other side," confirmed what Admiral Moore had said regarding Hyslop and he (Jacobs) said: "That's all true, mother. Hyslop wasn't big enough to do any different on this side than any one else with the same weakness."

"Esther," a very strong spirit guide for Dr. Wetherby, commented at length upon the new Psychical Society and said it would develop into something bigger than we anticipated and that there were some big surprises to come to us; that the phenomenon of removing the medium's coat while both of his hands were tightly clasped in front of him, was a small item to the things that were awaiting us after we got well into the work.—"We did this only to demonstrate the strength of the vibration you are building up."

Note:—Sister Clara's statement that "we miss the influence of the dear friends who are gone," doubtless refers to Lottie at the Hospital and to Mr. and Mrs. Lombard, who always attended the seances, but happened to be away in San Francisco on this evening.

NOTES ON TRUMPET SEANCE

At Residence of Mr. and Mrs. Jonson, Los Angeles, 8 O'Clock Monday P. M., December 12, 1921.

There were 12 in the circle, including Mr. and Mrs. J. The "battery" was arranged as usual—black curtain hung across one corner in the room; chair behind curtain with small music box, a child's "rattler," pair of "minstrel bones," writing pad and pencil. Two red electric lights were left on and furnished light enough to read the messages and see clearly.

Silas Webster, chemist guide, handed out: "There are many things I should like to write about, but do not wish to use up the energy or force that we desire to use later on; but we wish you to realize that we are all doing what we can to attain our objects."

Sister Clara wrote: "Dear George: We are all so sorry that each one cannot write an individual note, but that is impossible. But we are all with you and interested in your welfare. With love, Clara."

The "sitters" in front of the curtain consisted of Miss Worrall and myself, besides the medium, Mr. J. All three clasped hands so that both hands of each sitter were firmly held, and none could release hands without the others knowing it.

After a while Mr. J. complained of being "very cold" and said "something was happening." Miss Worrall said she felt the chill very noticeably and I felt it slightly. Finally one of the guides handed Mr. J's. vest over the curtain.

Bear in mind that previous to sitting before the curtain all of us in the room had commented upon the fact that something of this kind might occur, and we had all noticed the fact that Mr. J. had his vest on, completely buttoned up, and his coat over this. The vest was removed without removing the coat and while both of Mr. J's hands were tightly held. When the vest was handed over the curtain every button was still fastened.

Later, at the trumpet table, we asked "Gray Feather" how he did it and received the reply, in his Indian style of talking, "Me just take back out of back, then put back back again." We presume he tried to explain that he dematerialized the back part of the coat and vest in order to get the vest off without unbuttoning it, while J's. hands were held, then materialized the back again.

Mr. Blinn, the ex-railroad engineer, came in with his signal of whistle, steam and rumbling of the train. Some one asked if he left this world through a railroad accident and he replied:

"No. Mr. Jonson saved me from that. I attended one of their seances and was told not to go out on my engine the next morning because it was dangerous. I told the master mechanic that I wanted him to examine the engine first. He found the crown sheet worn as thin as paper and the engine was scrapped. You all don't know it, but I loved that old engine that I just cried when I saw it on the scrap pile. Mr. Brown used to run on the Clover Leaf with me, and Jonson told him in Toledo not to go out on his engine; but he went, got caught in a collision and was killed. He's over here with me now."

Mr. and Mrs. J. both confirm Blinn's story and vouch for it. When Blinn announced that he was going out, we asked him to give us a good imitation of his train in action. He called for a little phonograph music to strengthen the vibration; then went through the usual noises of tooting the whistle, blowing off steam, starting the engine and moving off with the rumbling of the train gradually dying in the distance.

Some one more clairvoyant than the rest of us stated they could see great white clouds rolling over the table; following this an Indian guide took up the trumpet and announced himself as Chief White Cloud and said it was his signal.

Mother spoke briefly, thanking me for the roses which I took to the church Sunday. I asked if the folks would all be present at the trumpet meeting at Mrs. Miller's Thursday. She answered: "Yes, son, you don't have to invite us; we will all be there when the door is opened."

Krocho gave us a brief moral lecture and wound up by saying: "Forget the body when death comes and keep only the soul and the spirit." I asked:

"Krocho, is there any difference between the soul and the spirit?"

Answer: "Yes, chief; the soul is the life; the spirit is the form through which the soul is expressed after what you call death. Its like the tree: The tree is the form through which the life, or soul, of the tree is expressed."

Timothy announced: "You had better close the seance, friends. Mrs. Jonson's got a fine treat for you. She's got two big plates full of fried cakes (as Tim calls the doughnuts) and a big pot of coffee. You are getting fine results and you are going to get bigger ones in the new society's meetings."

Some one asked Tim if he knew what time it was; he answered: "Yes, its nine-thirty and time to quit." The light was turned on, we looked at the time and it was exactly 9.30. Mr. L. remarked that he wished he could do what Gray Feather did with Mr. J's. vest, and Tim shot back with: "Oh, that wouldn't do, friend; you'd soon have all the pocketbooks in the country."

NOTES ON SEANCE OF DEVELOPING CLASS

Held at Residence of Mr. and Mrs. Victor Severy, 4304 S. Western Ave., Los Angeles, 8 O'Clock Wednesday P. M., December 14th, 1921.

This is known as the "Wednesday Evening Developing Class" and at present consists of nine members, four ladies and five gentlemen. These meet at the same hour every Wednesday. The class has been organized for nearly two years, although during that time there have been several changes in the personnel and the results have doubtless been slower than if they had been able to keep the same membership right through from the beginning.

The meetings are conducted by Miss Mary McLain, a well developed clairvoyant and clair-audient medium from one of the Los Angeles spiritualist churches. Mrs. Severy is also very mediumistic and is usually in a trance for the greater part of the seance, and it is during this trance period that we get the best results.

The events of this night will be better understood by going back one week to Wednesday, Dec. 7th. At that seance my father, sister Clara and sister Annie appeared to be "very much present" and although I could not see them myself they were described by both Miss McLain and Mrs. Severy, and I could feel their hands upon my head and shoulder very plainly and sense their presence.

At the same meeting I remarked that I saw clairvoyantly my little niece, Mary Ellen, and nephew, "little Georgie"; but was not sure of this until the following Friday (Dec. 9th) when this was confirmed at the Jonson trumpet seance by Mary Ellen, speaking through the trumpet, said she was with me Wednesday evening and, "you looked right at me, and little Georgie was there too." At the same (Jonson) meeting she referred to Mrs. Severy's three little children as being "darlings" and said: "I just love little Marian."

Note:—This much is a certainty: Mary Ellen never knew any of the Severys on this earth; still she called the number of the children correctly and the name of little Marian and the evening of the seance was also correctly called.

At this Jonson trumpet seance she (Mary Ellen) also promised that she was going to "surprise me the next time." No more was thought of this remark until the meeting on this particular evening—Wednesday Dec. 14th at the Developing Class.

The meeting convened at the usual time—eight o'clock—and we all took our accustomed places. On the previous Wednesday we had discussed among ourselves the advantages or disadvantages of working in total darkness or providing a little light; but none of us were very clear as to which was the better course to pursue. So I suggested that Miss McLain ask her guide "Alice" for instructions. We received the reply:

"It depends upon what you wish to develop first. If trumpet, total darkness is better; if materializations, then a little light is better. Choose which you prefer first; then govern yourselves accordingly."

So at this seance we had a mild red light, sufficient to see all persons in the room. The meeting opened with the Lord's prayer, as usual, one or two hymns; then perfect silence for about 45 minutes. The trumpet was discarded.

During this silence my father stood back of me and my sister Clara at my right, leaning against my shoulder and my arm with pressure enough to be readily felt. I could not see them but the clairvoyant members could and described them accurately. During this entire time I kept up a call within my mind to my friend Minnie and asked her to appear so that I could see her.

Finally a form stood up in the center of the circle; it was to me about the height of Minnie and within me I seemed to "sense her presense," although the form was (to me) in the shape of a human figure (head, shoulders, arms and body clearly defined) it was still too hazy for me to outline the features of the face. Finally, Miss McLain described her as a slender, medium height lady, with dark hair, eyes light, face narrow, very pretty and very spiritual-looking. I replied: "That's certainly Minnie" and Miss McLain answered: "Yes, she smiles and nods her head, 'yes'."

Note:—This was also confirmed by Minnie at the Miller trumpet seance of Thursday, Dec. 15th.

Just at this point I saw the form of a child come very close to me and remarked that "little Mary Ellen must be in the room, because I see another figure; but it is too small to be Minnie." This figure was also clearly outlined, but not clear enough for me to distinguish the facial features. But as I spoke the figure climbed into my lap and sat upon my right knee. It was tenuous, or cloud-like, seemed to have no weight and no solidity but was nevertheless visible to me and brought with it a distinct feeling of the child in my lap. Miss McLain also saw this and described it.

Note:—This was also confirmed by Mary Ellen at the Miller trumpet meeting of Dec. 15th, and this confirmation came without any effort on my part to bring it out. This was probably the "surprise" which Mary Ellen said she was going to give me.

Mrs. Severy was in trance during most of this time and the form of her son Victor, who passed away about 7 years ago, was seen standing in front of her; but seemed to have difficulty in "building up," athough he has appeared to the Severys a number of times.

During the seance I suggested that Miss McLain ask her guide, Alice, if the conditions were more satisfactory.

Answer: Yes, and the improvement in the results was because of it. I would suggest that you arrange a cord from the light into the cabinet, so the guides may adjust the light themselves. You will get better results still and you are all going to be surprised very soon now."

Alice is presumed to have been on the spirit side for more than a thousand years. Her advice usually comes with a clear logic and a definite purpose. Will try the string on the light next time we meet.

RECORD OF PRIVATE TRUMPET SEANCE

At Residence of Mrs. Mary Miller, 1512 Magnolia Ave., Los Angeles, Thursday 1 O'Clock P. M., December 15th, 1921.

Mrs. Miller had changed her residence since the previous seance I had with her. Dr. Worthington, her trumpet guide, opened the seance, as usual. He commented upon the new surroundings; said we would derive better results than Mrs. M. had expected, as the new home she was occupying had been used by one family almost the entire period of its existence; that they were good people and the walls were well magnetized. He continued:

"I am glad to meet you again, Mr. Goerner. We are becoming well acquainted. Your friends are already in the room and you are going to have a very nice chat with all of them. I notice you brought your own trumpet along to have it magnetized; that's a good idea and your friends are now passing it among themselves and are all helping it. (I felt on the table and the trumpet was gone). Your trumpet guide, Jim, now has it in the air and he will use it when he speaks to you. Mr. Thomas is going to make a strong guide for you and you are going to have good success with the trumpet voices. Well, I wont take any more of your time; the folks are anxious to talk."

Mother then held the trumpet and with her came the blue light, which I have noticed before. I commented:

"Mother, I see that pretty blue light that comes with you so often. Is that your light?"

Answer: "Yes, son, that is my light."

"What does the light mean, mother?" Mother usually delivers a very pretty spiritual message and this question gave her the opening. She answered:

"It is a signal, my boy. We all have our spirit lights, some of one shade, some of another; some one form, some another form. It is a spiritual candle that burns as a symbol of life, hope and happiness. To you it is a message. I want you to keep it before you. Be of good cheer, be hopeful and keep a high principle. There is much good that you can do. The Master Spirit has his light. We follow that. It is his message of love, of hope and help. He has answered many a prayer I have offered for you, my boy. I have watched you in the darkness when the storms seemed to overcome you. All the world seemed wrong. But never did the Master's light fail me; faintly sometimes it glowed, but always there was enough light to lead you into a better way. Through all the years when the cup was bitter, when you went without a religion, and even when you denied the Master, he gave you his hand at my call and helped you over the rough places. But we are not forgetful of the battle you fought and we are helping you to put it behind you. Be of good cheer, my son. You have seen the worst you will pass through. The Master's light is always burning. Keep it before you and all will be well."

Note:—These lights sometimes come as flashes of irregular shape,—sometimes in blocks, sometimes in globes, sometime in streaks like lightening, sometimes long, narrow, wavy curtains rolling and furling like a soft, silky flag in the breeze. They are blue and red and green and purple and violet and sometimes variegated. Sometimes they last just long enough to get a glimpse of them and are gone; sometimes they flash and die and return; sometimes they will hover in the air continuously for a few seconds to a few moments.

After mother came Mr. Thomas. He held my trumpet well up in the air; said he was giving it a magnetizing and said he liked it better than the metal trumpet which we formely used. Said he was glad to be constituted my "trumpet guide" and that he would be able to keep close to me during the years to come, "for, I am with you through life, and when you come to this side you will find me at the door to meet you. You have helped us all so much, and we will not forget it. We can help you in your world, and when your work is through there we will help you across. Keep to your mother's sermon and carry a high principle; let your word stand for truth and everlasting honesty, so that when you come to this side your friends of earth will say: 'Well, Goerner's word was always good.'"

I asked: "Jim, what sphere or plane are you on?"

Answer: "I am not very high, George; I knew nothing at all of the things that you understand so well. Spiritualism was merely a by-play with me. But when I got over here I found that it was the real thing. But I had my good points and we get full credit for them over here. We are all happy and all united—except Gordon. I appreciate so much what you are doing for him, and we are going to pay. You are helping us every night with your messages and every day with your good thoughts and we are all working our way through."

Goerner: "Jim, do you still follow masonry?"

Answer: "No, George we have no need for it over here. If a man lives up to the moral ritual of masonry he will be a good man. But if he lives the doctrine of Christ and loves all mankind, that's masonry enough."

Goerner: "Jim, some one just put his hand on my shoulder; who was it?"

Answer: "That's John. He stands right back of you and will talk in a few minutes. He is looking out for the mine and you are going to have a good new year. Goodbye and God bless you. A Merry, Merry Christmas and a Happy New Year."

He then placed my trumpet on the table and took up Mrs. Miller's aluminum trumpet, spoke through it and called attention to the difference in tone and seemed to prefer the fiber trumpet to the metal. He commented upon the correspondence between myself and his son, Gordon, in Chicago; knew just how many letters we had passed between us and the contents, and added: "His mother is so happy over this."

His son, John, spoke briefly, just a Christmas and New Year's greeting, and his mother followed, thanking me for my efforts to get her son, Gordon, in communication with her. She seemed glad for a chance to chat with me and looked forward with great pleasure to being able to talk with Gordon before long.

Minnie spoke next and voluntarily mentioned that she was with me at the developing class on the previous evening. "I heard you call, George, and came to you as soon as I caught the vibration. It made me so happy to know that I could hear you and let you know that I was there. Your voice will always bring me to you. Through all the years that kept us apart I walked beside you and many times listened when you spoke to others, waiting for the time when I could get within your vibration and make myself known to you. But we had such a grand visit last night and I will soon be able to materialize for you. I will keep close to you now until you come over here; then there will be no more parting. I could talk for hours, George; but the rest of the folks are waiting for the trumpet. I worked with your trumpet at the Jonsons the other evening and am helping to magnetize it today. We will soon be able to use it with you. Goodbye, goodbye."

Sister Clara took me by surprise by saying: "I am so glad, George, about the plans you are making to get the children in Chicago in communication with me. I will be so happy then, and it will help you and them, too."

I asked if she was able to tell me what the plan is.

"Answer: "Yes, you are fixing up the record so you can have it printed and send them all a copy, and then tell them how to get up a developing class once a week with a medium, so they can all talk with us through the medium. That will be grand."

Note:—The above was exactly the plan I had mapped out, although I had mentioned the developing class part to no one. I simply had thought it over in my own mind and decided on that course.

Little Mary Ellen followed Clara and said that she (Mary Ellen) was going to pick the medium for sisters and brothers in Chicago and said: "And I am going to pick a good one." Then came this:

"Listen, Uncle George, you know last night I climbed up on your knee and I sat there such a long time, and mamma said I was staying too long; but I told her, I love Uncle George and I want to sit here; so she didn't make me get down. Didn't we have a lovely time last night?" She referred to the roses and I asked her if she got hers at the church.

"Why, yes," she answered: "Don't you remember the medium called out one for me?" (Correct).

"Little Georgie" (sister Annie's child) followed Mary Ellen, saying he was so glad that his mamma had "teached" him to use the trumpet "so I can talk to my Uncle George." He said that when Mary Ellen came to me at Jonson's he was coming too. (Presumably he referred to the materialization meetings).

Sister Annie also made reference to the prospect of materializing for me at the Jonsons or at the Wednesday evening developing class. They all have the date of the first materialization seance on their calendar; all seemed to know when the first meeting would take place and all seem to be waiting for the chance to appear.

Father informed me that he was going to give me "identification enough to last for sometime." He then began talking to me in German and when I answered that I understood so little of German, he spoke in French and followed this with a rather lengthy quotation in Latin.

Note:—During his earth life father was very strong on languages and evidently has not forgotten them.

I asked him if he was still a physician and surgeon on the other side:

Answer: "Yes, my son, and the trouble that carried me off need not worry you. You seem to think you have a tendency to appendicitis; but that is not true. Get rid of that thought. I told you at Mrs. Petitt's that your only weakness was an occasional attack of gastritis and I am taking care of that. You have noticed less of it lately and it is yielding to my work. I have been your only physician all through your life; you have had very little need for medicines, and when I passed out I still held the job."

Note:—In this he had read my mental attitude correctly. Father passed out from appendicitis and sometimes I have suspected that I had a tendency to the trouble. He did, as stated, advise me to the contrary through Mrs. Petitt and lately it seems to have gone most entirely. No man has had less use for medicines than I have had and all through life I have been singularly free from accidents and sickness.

I asked what joke he had been playing on sister Annie at church last Sunday night. He laughed and said: "Well, you know the medium called off a flower for all the ladies except sister Annie. I told her that I would see that she didn't get any flower. But she got ahead of me. When the medium didn't call off a flower for her she went over to you and sat right down beside you. I know you felt her presence, son. Now, remember this, keep a happy disposition because you are going to have a good New Year. Friend Thomas is a fine business guide for you. You can trust to his judgment. Dont get tangled up in too many interests for a time yet. Get the old mines opened first before you scatter your effects. Goodbye and a Merry Christmas and a Happy New Year. We are going to be with you all through the New Year and the years to come."

"Sunbeam" (Mrs. Miller's flower guide at the church) spoke, just to give me a Christmas greeting, and said there would be a "good little Indian" added to my helpers soon and that we were going to be great friends. She too predicted a very successful year in 1922.

Following this Dr. Worthington took hold of the aluminum trumpet to close the seance, when I broke in with:

"Doctor, will you please tell my friend Harold Cook that I want him to talk with me the next time I come here."

Answer: "Harold stands right back of you and has been here all the afternoon. He has his hand on your shoulder. He is helping you with the mine and keeps looking over your maps. He and John Thomas have that well in hand. The reason he didn't talk today was that he wanted to give the other folks a chance. He is such a fine generous chap; but he will talk with you through your own trumpet before long. Goodbye, friend; we have all had a wonderful evening and I am going to wish you a Merry Christmas and a Happy New Year."

Note:—Knowing all the communicators above as well as I do, and being personally acquainted with them here on this earth—except in the case of the two children and John Thomas—and being familiar with their own peculiar style of speech, the characteristic phrases, the intonation of the voice and the personal traits, I am prepared to accept these messages as genuine and coming from the spirits claimed. If the telepathic hypothesis is advanced to account for them, then the telepathy would in most of these cases have to come entirely from the spirit and not from the medium, as might be the case if the medium were in a trance and the spirits were communicating through her. Furthermore, they have all appeared to me so many times now—over and over again—and their identity is too well established by too many bits of evidential matter to give room for any argument to the contrary.

MEMORANDA FROM TRUMPET SEANCE

At Residence of Mr. and Mrs. Jonson, Los Angeles, Friday P. M., December 16th, 1921.

The following incidents may serve to give an idea as to the condition in which some people reach "the other side" after passing out of the body.

The circle was small on this occasion, there being only 10 present, including the Jonsons. The vibration was good, however, and the trumpet results perhaps a little better than usual. The cabinet work was "tame" and we concluded that it was getting so close to the beginning of the materialization classes that the forces were trying to conserve the strength of the mediums for that occasion.

We all had the usual visits and chats with our own friends and relatives.

Then a strange voice, speaking broken English—with a German accent—came in crying, "Hello, Hello,—vere am I?"

We asked: "Who are you for?"

"Vass is dat?" We repeated the question and he replied: "I don't know. Vere am I? Vas iss dis place?" We told him it was a trumpet circle.

"Vell, vas is a trumpet circle? I vant to get back to Philadelphia. Vill somebody show me my house?"

We replied that he was a long ways from Philadelphia and that he was in California.

"Oh, iss dis California? How did I get here? I am going back to Philadelphia."

We began to understand that it was some spirit that had just passed over and had not yet come to consciousness. In other words, he didn't know that he was dead. But by keeping up the conversation and encouraging him he finally began to talk more rationally. We asked how he got into our circle and he replied:

"A big Irish fellow named Tim took me by the arm and said he was going to help me. I said I didn't vant no help and vas going back to Philadelphia then he said I can't go back to Philadelphia because I am dead. I aint dead and I'm going back to Philadelphia."

We finally got the name of Johanes out of him and that he had evidently been a track walker on the railroad at the Philadelphia yards; but he didn't seem to be able to tell how recently he had left the body. He seemed to realize that he was coming too. We realized also that Tim had brought him to us to "give him a lift" and help him come to consciousness.

Johanes held on to the trumpet for a long while, talking more coherently toward the end. We all promised to send out our good thoughts in his behalf and help him on his way. Toward the last he seemed to understand what this meant; but still didn't appear to quite catch the idea that he was dead and held to the thought that he must get back to his job in Philadelphia.

A little later a character picked up the trumpet, whistling some jovial, care-free air and brought with him the distinct impression that it was some shiftless indifferent fellow that wanted nothing in this world better than to "hobo it."

We asked who he was and the answer came: "Santa Fe John."

Question: "Well, who is Santa Fe John?"

Answer: "Hanged if I know—and nobody else."

Question: "How did you get that name?"

Answer: "Riding the bumpers up and down the Santa Fe."

Question: "Where was your home?"

Answer: "Most of the time in the blind baggage. The cops kept me moving. They wouldn't let me stay anywhere very long."

Question: "Well, say, Santa Fe John, tell us this: when did you pass out—when did you die?"

Answer: "I passed out every day there was a train going; but I aint died yet."

Question: "What did you do for a living here?"

Answer: "What yer all trying to do, get something on me?"

We answered: "No Santa Fe, we're just trying to keep up this vibration so as to help you come to yourself."

"Oh, I guess this old Irishman here will get me in right. He's a good old guy; he aint hard on a baggager."

He whistled some more and dropped the trumpet.

Later Tim spoke to us and said: "Now friends, I brought those two fellows to you just to let you see how much good you can do both on your side and ours. These fellows need your good thoughts and a helping hand. That Dutchman was the limit,—just an innocent ignorant old fellow that never did anybody any harm and nobody any good. He lived all to himself and for himself and his vision was just that limited that he never thought that he couldn't take his savings with him. He came over here dazed and terribly out of mind. He has been wandering around trying to find his way back to Philadelphia and keeps talking about getting docked if he don't report to his job. He came over here with some fellow that soon woke up and told the Dutchman: "You durn fool you, you don't know you're dead"—and he didn't. So I took him by the arm and brought him to you people and he's already getting his eyes open. That visit did him a lot of good. And I want you all to remember this: When a stranger butts into your circle, just open your arms, throw the doors wide open, because he is more than likely struggling to get into the light. Don't confine your good messages to your own loved ones. There is much else you can do, and from now on I want you to make a charity circle out of this and go in for helping the newcomers over here."

He continued: "But you ought to have seen Santa Fe John when he first came here,—all shot to pieces with liquor—believe me, friends, he was a sight. All he could see was a railroad track and he stood right alongside of it looking for a blind baggage; nothing but a chance to ride had any hold on him. He was one of the knights of the road, just a shiftless, lazy, indifferent cuss that had to keep moving; his reputation wouldn't stand a landing place. But I got hold of him and he's beginning to see where he is. The little talk you all gave him made a big difference and he's all smiles now and began to pick right up.

"Now, let the good work go on. Treat these fellows with kindness,—just a little encouraging word, just a good thought here and there. It will do wonders for them and when you come over you will find the pretty lights all around you to remind you of the good you have done. If you could see what I can see right now,—just so many beautiful lights for the good deeds done in the body—you would know what a wonderful thing it is. Don't be afraid of death; its a great change to look forward to."

Note:—This is a good answer to those who persist in the belief that death is going to make us perfect—those who do not realize that a spirit is not perfect until it has progressed to perfection any more than a human being is. What you are at the time of your death here, that you will be when you reach "the other side" until you have advanced to something higher and better.

During the cabinet work I called Mrs. Jonson's attention to a figure standing in front of me. I could not make out who it was and asked of she could describe it for me. She answered, "Yes, he's a clean-cut young fellow, with dark hair, dark clothes and very dressy." I remarked, "It must be either Harold Cook or John Thomas." She answered, "Its John Thomas, because he turns his head towards you and smiles and nods 'Yes.'"

At the trumpet sister Clara asked if I knew she was in my room the night before. I replied that I woke up about one o'clock and seemed to sense the presence of some one, but decided that I was either mistaken or else they had gone. She answered:

"I tried to materialize enough for you to recognize me, but didn't quite make it. I'll try it again tonight."

Note:—I retired at eleven o'clock and about one awoke with a clear vision of a form in the alcove of my room. The head, arm and shoulders were easily distinguishable. I asked if she would speak to me and the voice came in whispers on my pillow, "Its sister— its sister."

I asked: "Which sister dearie?" The answer came, "Its Clara; I told you I would come." I spoke again, but the voice had gone.

I put this question to Krocho: "I have on the spirit side a nephew and niece who passed over before they had any life on the earth side at all. If they had lived here they would both be about twenty years of age. But, when they come to me now they are still little children."

Krocho answered: "That's for the purpose of indentification. Children here grow to where they are no longer at the helpless or feeble state as they might be on your earth. They grow to what you call maturity; then live the lives of healthy, contented, happy beings. There is no what you call 'process of decay' here; we have no sickness, no pains and no infirmities. So there is no such thing as old age here."

REPORT ON MATERIALIZATION SEANCE

Held at Residence of Mr. and Mrs. J. B. Jonson, Los Angeles, 8 O'Clock P. M., Friday Dec. 23rd, 1921.

This seance was the beginning of a series to be held at the Jonson home under the auspices of the Society for advanced Psychical Research. The Society is incorporated under the California laws and has for its object the investigation of any psychic phenomena brought to its attention. The first work undertaken is a study of the materialization work of Mr. and Mrs Jonson and these meetings will be held weekly or by-weekly for such length of time as the society may deem necessary for a full investigation of this phase of manifestations.

The cabinet arrangement and method of conducting the meeting was the same as described in previous records. We had just the number present advised by "Gray Feather" (Mr. Jonson's control.) At one of our trumpet seances he requested that we have no more than "four times five fingers"—twenty members. About a dozen members examined the cabinet and the premises for the purposes of the minutes of the meeting. The chairs were arranged in a horse shoe around the walls, so as to give as much room as possible for the spirit controls, or other visitors from the other side and give all sitters a clear view. Mr. J. took his arm chair in the cabinet; but after becoming entranced returned to the main room and sat in full view of the society throughout the evening. Mrs. J. also remained outside, in her normal state and called the various members to the curtain as they were wanted by visitors. The light was enough to take notes and read them.

There seemed to be the best possible conditions for good results. The vibration was good, everyone seemed in harmony, expectant of a satisfactory evening and there was a distinct feeling of good will all around—a very essential requirement. All the spirits appearing were strong, came with good voices and remained in full view longer than at most previous seances.

The first visitor was "grandmother Truax," grandmother to the two Worrall sisters. She has appeared to them a number of time before and they accept the identification as complete.

Next came my old sweetheart of school days, Minnie DeKover. She was dressed in beautiful white robes with a long veil of some filmy material, such as we are told is worn by those of a high spiritual station. It has been about 30 years since Minnie passed over, and although I was satisfied that it was she, I asked for a little identification and received the reply:

"Yes, I was in your room last night with sister Annie and gave you my name three times." (Correct)

I was glad to see this old school day friend and had the conviction that she was just as glad to see me and that death had not taken all of the human element out of her. Several times she repeated her happiness at being able to come in this way; passed her hands over my head repeatedly and followed the outlines of my face with the fingers of both of her hands, saying: "I am so happy to be with you again, to speak with you face to face and to hear your voice and know that it is George. I have waited all these years to get your attention, and it seems so wonderful now that we can meet in this way."

We chatted for about five minutes; then the figure gradually grew closer to the floor and finally disappeared altogether.

Mrs. Jacobs' son "Bobbie," who was drowned in 1905, came third,—a strong, active-looking young character full of good cheer and smiles. He seemed delighted to be with his mother and after exchanging family greetings he disappeared behind the curtain.

Fourth came a young lady unknown to any one in the circle. When asked who she was for she waived her hands out to the circle and said: "For all." We asked her name and she replied: "I am the Star of Hope and have been sent as a guide to the circle." Dr. Wetherby handed her his trumpet and asked if she would magnetize it. She took it in her hands, made a good many passes over the trumpet and handed it back.

Following this came a spirit giving the name of Margaret Sinclair. She was a friend of the Severys when on earth and was sufficiently recognized. We asked that when she leave she disappear in full view without going behind the curtain and she did so.

Our little "cabinet worker," Kitty, greeted us through the curtain. Mrs. Jonson asked what she thought of the new circle and she replied: 'Its salubrious." I asked if she was coming out to see me and got the answer: "You didn't bring that box of candy you promised me." I replied that I would do so the next time if she would tell me what she wanted. The answer came: "I only like chocolates."

One of the society told her that he had some candy in his pocket which she could have, but she answered: "I don't like gum drops because they stick up my teeth." (Gum drops was what he had in his pocket).

The statement that I had failed to bring the box of candy promised has reference to a seance held on Wednesday, May 25th, 1921, at which time I told her that if she would come down to chat with me I would bring her a box of chocolates. (See record for that date).

Next came my sister Annie. I did not need any identification, for it was certainly sister Annie—there could never be any mistake about that in my own mind. She was dressed the same as Minnie was. We had a very delightful little chat. She too confirmed the visit to my room with Minnie on the previous night. I remarked that it seemed like old times to be able to meet her again and she answered:

"I am happy to be able to come in this way and to bring you proof that I still live and that all is well. I am coming to your room every night and talk with you until I can come to you stronger."

I asked why she spoke on my pillow instead of through the trumpet in my room. She answered: "We are developing you for clair-audience."

Then came a very pretty little tyke of a girl with dark curls around her shoulders. She was in bare feet; called for Mrs. Majors and said she had been sent as a helper to assist her in her development work. She gave her name as Crystal Dahlborn; said she had lived in Spearfish, So. Dakota, and passed out of this life at the age of twelve years. She came with a good deal of light and seemed glad to stay. We asked if she could come down farther into the room, but she replied that she may not be able to get back to the cabinet. We told her that we would all give her a strong vibration and help her back; she then grew less timid and came well down into the center of the room.

Note:—In saying that she was afraid she might not be able to get back to the curtain, she doubtless meant that the vibration might not be strong enough for her to hold up the materialization that long. This sometimes occurs and they will then disappear wherever they happen to be when the vibration gives out.

An interesting visitor was a stranger who gave the name of Zara and said she was, when on earth, a Spanish gypsy dancer. Several of us chatted with her in Spanish and she seemed very glad to be able to talk with some one in her earth tongue. When the circle all sang "La Paloma" she danced a Spanish dance, snapped her fingers in imitation of the castanets and joined us in singing La Paloma in Spanish.

Mrs. Lombard's mother came, a dear old lady, with her glasses on her nose, and when Mr. Lombard remarked that that was not the way mother used to carry her spectacles when on earth, she promptly shifted them to her forehead after a well-known habit with her before she passed away.

The last figure to appear was a stranger giving the name of Florence Mayne; she said she had been appointed a guide to assist Miss Blakely in her work as recording secretary for the society; told Miss B. that she formerly lived in Philadelphia, but passed over many years ago; said she would aid Miss B. in getting evidence for her record; instructed her to record every item, no matter how small, and said the importance of it would be appreciated later on.

The meeting closed at 9.45 to convene again on Friday, the 30th.

Note:—It should be borne in mind that the chocolates, to which Kitty referred, would not be taken by her to the other side; but would dematerialize on this side at the same time that she disappears. The same thing happens to flowers, etc., passed to spirit forms in the seance room. These tests we make often and they are always interesting. It is one thing to account for "apports" brought into the seance room by visiting spirits; but what becomes of the dematerialized objects is a harder question to answer.

EXTRACT FROM TRUMPET SEANCE

Held at Residence of Mrs. Mary Miller, 1512 Magnolia Avenue, Los Angeles, Cal., Tuesday 2 O'Clock P. M., December 27th, 1921.

Meeting was in accordance with appointment made with Mrs. Miller the day before. No appointments of any kind had been made with the folks on the "other side." They were all there just the same—thirteen of them—and I felt their presence plainly as soon as I entered the Miller home.

Dr. Worthington, trumpet guide to Mrs. M., opened the seance as usual with greetings; wished me the compliments of the season; stated the folks had already assembled in the room and were anxious to talk. Said Mr. Thomas, my trumpet guide, had taken up my trumpet and the folks would use that instead of the medium's.

Mr. Thomas then spoke and for a moment I had a very good view of him clairvoyantly. He seemed to know that I could see him and remarked that it was proof of clairvoyant development and the folks were all doing their part to help me along with this.

He commented upon the Christmas dinner which I had attended. Said all the folks were there and that he realized that I felt their presence; but remarked: "Your friends at the tables didn't know you brought a houseful of spirits." Spoke of the jolly evening we all had; complimented the "gentility" of my friends and said he was glad I attended the dinner. He seemed to know that I had been trying to form my own opinion, looking over the crowd, as to which ones were most psychic in temperament and said that I had not missed it.

Mother spoke for three or four moments; said she was also at the Christmas dinner and was glad I had changed my mind about accepting the invitation; told me she knew how I felt about wanting to meet her at the church, but said she had induced me to phone back and accept the invitation, because they "didn't want me to spend Christmas day alone." She concluded with: "We were all at the dinner with you and were glad that you knew it."

There is a good evidence of spirit intelligence here. I had an invitation to dine with some friends; at first I declined it, but a few minutes later I felt a strong impression to phone back and accept it. I felt at the time that the other side had suggested it, but was not sure until the Miller seance.

While at the dinner table I had also tried to figure out in my mind who were the possible psychic temperaments, and the folks on the other side seem to have known what my opinions were.

Then came a chat of perhaps ten minutes with sister Annie followed by Minnie. We first discussed the materializations at the Jonsons; then followed a few private instructions from Annie which she wished me to get to her daughter in the east. Then a confidential little chat with Minnie.

Little Mary Ellen seemed peeved because Kitty, the cabinet worker at the materialization meetings, did not give her a chance to materialize; but said Kitty had so much work to do and "she promised me a chance real soon."

John Thomas spoke mostly in a business vein with regard to developments on our mining interests and predicts a good year for us. He said: "We are all planning some fine work for the future for you; but we must first get business matters in shape for you so you can do the things we want you to do, and when you get far enough for that you will just begin to realize what a wonderful work can be done when you co-operate with us on this side."

Mrs. Thomas also spoke and she, too, seemed well posted on the events at the Christmas dinner party; seemed to know just about how many were there and evidently caught the atmosphere of the crowd on that occasion.

Then came this: "Hello, Mr. Goerner; this is Kitty; I just butted in here for a minute. Say, tell my medium I was here; will you?"

I answered: "Of course I will. Are you coming down to see me next Friday and get those chocolates?"

Answer: "You bet I am. Sunbeam says she's coming too and get some."

Sunbeam followed and substantiated Kitty's statement and said she would help her get rid of the chocolates. Then followed a well-worded New Year's greeting, after which she said:

"Little Georgie is just having the time of his life running around the room, and he's waiting now to get the trumpet."

Georgie spoke for a moment and passed the trumpet over to Harold. We had a few minutes greeting about times in Denver, business affairs, and his own folks on the other side. He closed by extending the New Year greetings, and predicted good success with my psychic work by the end of the year.

Father, mother, sister Clara, Annie, Minnie and Mary Ellen have been in the habit of coming to us at the Wednesday evening class. They all took pains to tell me that they were cooperating with us in every way and predicted a big success for the class; said we need not feel discouraged, that we would certainly get even better results than we expected, and advised by all means to keep at it. They complimented Mrs. Severy for her patience and perseverance; said they wanted to thank the entire class for our loyalty to the cause, and finished by urging: "Don't give it up, because it is helping all of you more than you think."

Little Mary Ellen said: "Uncle George, I just love those Wednesday evening classes so I can hardly wait for Wednesday to come. Ain't the Severy's wonderful. One of the communicators said there were "big things in store for Mrs. Severy in this work."

Here is a remarkable piece of pictographic work: Before the trumpet voices actually came Mrs. Miller described a visitor in the room as follows:

"There stands beside you a dear sweet old lady who comes with the influence of a very close relative, but not a blood tie, as if she might belong to a sister or brother by marriage. She is medium in height, has gray hair, with a little curl right down the middle of her forehead. She has no upper teeth in front, but all of her lower teeth seem to be there. She has a way of holding her head downward and a little forward; has a most wonderful smile; wears a striped dress of calico and has a little checkered white and brown apron. She says she is grandmother and yet I am sure she is not a blood relation."

I replied: "I couldn't fail to recognize that. Its grandmother Fowler—my sister Clara's mother-in-law."

Mrs. Miller answered: "Yes, she nods her head and seems so pleased that you recognize her."

This description is letter-perfect—even to the loss of the upper teeth—the little curl in the front of the forehead—the habit of holding her head downward and forward—and the striped dress with the checkered white and brown apron. I do not recollect ever having seen grandmother Fowler with any other kind of an apron, although I lived in her home in Washington for more than a year.

RECORD OF TRUMPET SEANCE

At Residence of Mr. and Mrs. Jonson, Los Angeles, Cal., 8 O'Clock P. M., Tuesday, December 27, 1921.

There were ten members present on this occasion, including Mr. and Mrs. J. By consent of all we dispensed with the cabinet work and opened the trumpet seance at eight o'clock promptly.

We occupied a smaller room for this purpose and received the favorable comments of some of the communicating spirits for doing so. They stated that within the smaller space the magnetism was more confined and that the little room worked pretty much as a cabinet would in holding the vibration and giving good results.

Sister Clara spoke briefly, saying she just came in to greet me, because she had already spoken with me at Mrs. Miller's seance in the afternoon; expressed delight at the chat we had at Miller's and said she always enjoyed these meetings.

Johannes, the German from Philadelphia, who appeared at the seance of Friday, Dec. 16th, took up the trumpet; said he had come to thank us all for the help we had given him; said we could not realize what awful darkness he was in, and how he was grabbing at the air to get about. But said the good thoughts we had sent out to him brought the light and since then he has been moving on very rapidly; said he would always remember us but could never thank us enough.

Santa Fe John, the fellow who came on the same evening with Johannes and advised that he got his name riding the bumpers up and down the Santa Fe railroad, also passed through the room,— and just passed through. He did not attempt to speak, but simply came whistling in that careless, indifferent way that he used before, and whistled himself out. It was enough to identify him as the same as the previous "Santa Fe John" and was doubtless merely to let us know that he remembered us and wished us to know that he was progressing, or had at least come into the light.

Then came a bit of pathos that must have moved us all to tears. Just a dear little child's voice begging in the most plaintive way: "Folkses, wont you p'ease help me find my muvver."

We asked: "Well who is your mother, dearie?"

The answer came mixed with sobs: "I don't know, folkses· p'ease take me to muvver."

We asked: 'Can you tell us your name, little girl?"

Back came the answer: "No, I don't know what my name is. I dess want to find my muvver; p'ease take me to muvver. I tant find my way home."

The trumpet then dropped to the table and Krocho spoke up, saying one of the guides had to hold the trumpet for the little tot; then continued:

"Now, friends, that's just another case to show you how much charity work you can do in this little circle and how much good you can do. That's a little baby girl, about four years old, that came over today and of course she can't understand her surroundings yet. She is in good hands and will have a mother just suited to her and lots of little playmates; but you can all help her a great deal if you will go into silence for a moment and send her out a bright thought and help her to come to an understanding of her new life; the happiness it will bring to her will well repay you."

Father spoke a little longer than usual and said he could do this because he didn't take up much time at the Miller seance. He complimented us on the selection of our members for the new psychical society; said we would get even more wonderful results than at the last materialization meeting. He then addressed Mr. Majors, who had been complaining of some trouble with his back; told Majors to lie flat on the floor and exercise his arms and legs systematically, just as if he was swimming, and do this every day until the muscles of his back relaxed naturally and this would relieve the unnatural strain on the muscles causing the trouble, if he would lie on his back while exercising.

Mr. L. had been speaking of reducing his stomach; father offered him the same advice and told him to keep this up for a few weeks and if he followed it persistently he would get rid of the excess flesh; but for him to lie on his stomach instead of his back.

Krocho complained of some one having hidden her "bug" and said she wanted Goerner Chief to give it up. I replied that she ought to be able to find it, but she said she didn't want to have to fish into my vest pocket to get it. I told her I had taken it out of my vest pocket and she should locate it.

I at first put it into my pocket; then passed it to Miss Worrall. Miss Worrall passed it back to me and I handed it to Krocho, and asked why couldn't she locate it in Miss W's. lap. She answered: "Because she got depressed about joining you in hiding it from me, and when one's mind is in the dumps it isn't so easy for a psychic to reach them. Remember that, chief, and never go to a medium when you're down in the mouth. Always go with your head high; your mind cleaned of all the cobwebs and keep cheerful. Then you'll get good results if you go to the right kind of a medium."

An incident that seems to explain certain apparent inconsistencies is the following:

Several weeks ago Minnie made the statement to me at a trumpet seance that she had something to tell me when she could talk confidentially. A couple of times afterwards I reminded her of this and asked if she had forgotten that confidential chat we were going to have. The answer came both times: "No, I am waiting for the right opportunity."

At the materialization seance on Friday, Dec. 23rd, when she materialized and I talked with her face to face, she made clear to me what it was she wanted to tell me confidentially. Then at the Miller trumpet seance on Tuesday, Dec. 27th, she confirmed this.

Finally at the Jonson trumpet seance of the same evening, (Tuesday the 27th), we both spoke of it—merely intimating it— and she impressed upon me the fact that it was to be a little secret between the two of us; said the more I thought of it the more wonderful it would become, and that after I passed over and reached the other side, the beauty and wonder of it all would be even greater.

At this point Krocho broke in, saying: "You'll tell me about it, wont you chief?"

I answered: "No, I don't believe this is for any one except Minnie and myself;" then speaking through the trumpet to Minnie, I said: "But she can read my mind, Minnie."

Minnie replied: "No, not in this case George. Krocho is so good at finding things, let her find out what this is. But this is not for Krocho and Krocho will never know what it is."

After Minnie dropped the trumpet, Krocho gave me this:

"Chief, your sweetheart was right. That is a blessed secret between you and Minnie; it is being reserved for you until you reach here. It isn't for me to know and I was only having a little joke with you and Minnie. It is not for me to interfere with the happiness of any one and you will enjoy this secret more by keeping it always between you and Minnie until you reach this side. I don't know what it is, and there is no way I can find out, because it is not in the psychic law for me to know."

Note:—This incident seems to explain another side of the telepathic theory. So much comes to me at seances to show too plainly that my friends on the other side read my mind constantly. But here is a case of a matter strictly between myself and a friend on the spirit side of life, and something that will be the more cherished by being kept absolutely between us, and it seems that even on the other side it is not within their powers to know it by reading either my mind or Minnie's.

Note:—In an effort to get proper identification of "grandmother Fowler" right at the start (as she will probably appear often from now on), I asked father who was the first visitor to come into the room at the Miller seance and got the answer:

"It was grandmother Fowler." This verifies grandmother's claim and makes future identifications easier so far as she is concerned.

REPORT ON MATERIALIZATION SEANCE

At Residence of Mr. and Mrs. J. B. Jonson, Los Angeles, Cal., 8 O'Clock P. M., Friday, Dec. 30th, 1921. Under Auspices of L. A. Society for Advanced Psychical Research.

Conditions were not so favorable on this evening as at the previous week's seance. This was the result of a depressed feeling throughout the circle—especially the Jonsons—because of severe sickness in the Lombard family. As they are very close friends of the Jonsons the two mediums were not in the frame of mind calculated to bring the best results.

The meeting, however, proceeded. Mr. J. first asked that we all go into silence for a moment and throw out our best thoughts to the Lombards and ask the assistance of the forces on the "other side."

After Mr. J. became entranced Mrs. Lombard's grandmother appeared; said she had come in response to the thoughts we had sent out; that they had been received on the "other side"; instructed us to keep up the good work, and said she had come to tell us that while the situation was grave their spirit forces would cooperate with us and do all that was possible; cautioned us not to worry, but keep a happy thought and all would be well. She then dematerialized.

Minnie appeared just for a moment; did not seem quite so strong as on the previous visit—due quite likely to a lower vibration arising from the depression in the circle; said she could not stay long, but would return at another time, and disappeared.

Mrs. Jacobs' brother Henry came through the curtain, talked with her in whispers; did not appear very strong. As soon as he left, her son Bobbie stepped manfully through the curtains, walked well down into the room after his mother, pointing his finger at her and beckoning her to come to him, saying: "I am here too; I brought him along."

Then came a little girl, perhaps ten or twelve years of age, in appearance, gave her name as Dorothy; stated she was a spirit child to Mrs. Jacobs, and that "Bobbie brought me along." Mrs. J. seemed satisfied with the identification, but was willing to accept her own psychic intuition for the facts.

The "Star of Hope" again appeared, a strong spirit with a good light, beautifully dressed in white robes and drapery, and gave us the following greeting, extending her arms to the circle, and speaking in slow, well chosen language:

"I bring you love, peace and happiness for the New Year. The angels send their greetings with light and love and truth."

Another good visitor was the sister of Mr. Drake, the vice-president of the Society. She remained for perhaps ten minutes, bringing a good light; stepped well down into the room and joined the circle in singing a hymn. She had a bunch of violets fastened at her waist,— an apport which she must have procured from some nearby garden. When she left the circle she entered the curtain, her face to the curtain and her back to the circle. This is the first exit of this kind I have seen. All the others have invariably disappeared facing the sitters.

Then stealing out from under the curtain, creeping on hands and knees on the floor, stealthily as an Indian might creep upon an enemy, came "Fleetfoot,"—a guide to Mr. and Mrs. Majors. When well out of the curtains he suddenly jumped to his feet, raised himself to his full height, folded his arms, threw his head back haughtily and surveyed the crowd, then pointed to his head and called our attention to his feathers. We asked what tribe he belonged to and he replied, "I am Sioux." The circle sang "Redwing" and he danced to the tune with a very lively action, clapping his hands at the same time. He was dressed in Indian attire, feathers on his head and mocassins on his feet. This character often talks with us through the trumpet and is always a strong spirit.

We had another visit from Mrs. Major's guide, "Crystal." She was less timid this time and seemed quite at home in the circle. She spoke mostly in whispers, but appeared to be trying all the time to raise her voice. Finally, she concluded very audibly with: "Happy New Year to everybody —I'm going all to pieces," and vanished.

In telling us that she was "going all to pieces," she doubtless meant that the vibration was giving out and she could not hold the materialization longer.

Came also Mr. W. T. Stead, whose figure could be seen in the room most all the evening by the clairvoyant members. He spoke in whispers at some length with Mrs. Jacobs, who has been in correspondence with Stead's daughter and requested Mrs. J to send his love to his dear daughter.

Occasionally strange characters will come in for apparently no purpose—unless it be either to gain strength immediately after death, or to give us a chance to study a greater variety of manifestations. One of these was an Italian girl, dressed in the bright colors of the peasantry, who gave the name of Stella de Lucca; spoke in Italian with Mrs. Baker and when the music box was started she placed her hand upon it saying: "All same street music, with de monk" then began to dance to the tune. What she had in her mind was probably the familiar New York street scene of the Italian organ-grinder with the monkey.

During all this work Kitty remained behind the curtain in silence. Finally, I asked if she wasn't coming out to get that box of chocolates. She answered:

"Yep, soon as I get stuck up. I need a little more mustard back here." ("Getting stuck up" is her expression for building up spirit forms).

We waited a while and chatted with her in this way until she came through the curtain and walked toward my chair. I handed her a small box of chocolates, which she took in her hand, saying:

"Oh, gee, ain't that dandy!" I asked:
"Are you going to give little Mary Ellen and Georgie some?"

"Yep, I'll give 'em all some."

I said: "You mustn't let them make you sick." This evidently struck her as amusing, for she laughed heartily as she backed into the curtain.

Note:—After the seance was over several of us examined the cabinet, but there was no trace of the chocolates or the box anywhere. But we have seen articles dematerialized at seances so often that we have come to accept the phenomenon as a fact too well established to admit of further doubt.

The spirit "Florence Mayne," who comes as a guide to our recording secretary, Miss Blakely, came in at the end of the work; gave Miss B. instructions as to keeping the records with attention to minute details, offered encouragement in our work and closed with: "God bless you all; we love every one of you and greet you with peace and happiness for the New Year."

The meeting adjourned to Friday, January 6th, 1922.

NOTES FROM FLOWER MESSAGE

Given by Mrs. Mary Miller, Peoples Spiritualist Church, Los Angeles, Sunday Evening, January First, 1922.

This was a rainy evening and there were not more than thirty present in the auditorium. Those who would come out in the storm would naturally be "believers," and the very fact of their being willing to face a heavy rain for the benefit they feel they may derive from the service would tend to produce a strong vibration and bring good results.

This may account for the fact that what few messages were given were clear and the identifications somewhat better than at most services I have attended with a "full house."

I had taken a cluster of five roses, as usual, naming them after mother, sister Clara, sister Annie, Minnie and little Mary Ellen. Mrs. Miller called the names correctly except as to sister Annie, which she missed. Stated there was also present Jim and John—doubtless Mr. Thomas and his son. They came with greetings for the New Year and the assurance of their hearty cooperation in my behalf in matters both material and spiritual. Mother gave this through the medium:

"We are working for your spiritual enfoldment. We have already touched you and you have felt the influence. During this year you will see much improvement. You will have the gift of clairvoyance, clair-audience and success in trumpet work. You will see us and talk with us before the end of the New Year. You will get much in the way of materializations that you do not now expect. We have a work for you to do and are opening the path that you may walk through. We are with you to the end. We are all here tonight and we greet you with love and peace. Be not disturbed; keep a calm mind; we are working with you and for you. Minnie says, tell George I am here too with the New Years greetings.

Mrs. Wagner gave the "test messages" blindfolded. To explain this: Those in the hall will write messages, which are sometimes sealed in envelopes with an identification, such for instance as: "G-743", "M. K. T.", or other initial or number. During these tests Mrs. Wagner is under the control of a spirit giving the name of "Blossom." Messages not sealed in envelopes are usually folded over, concealing the contents. Mrs. Wagner does not as a rule take the messages into her hand until she has first called the initial or number; not only this, she will often read the message and initial and then pick it out from among the numerous messages piled on the table. She will in many cases, blindfolded, point to the person in the auditorium who wrote any particular message, and give the answer as it comes to her from the control.

One of the spirit controls, speaking through Mrs. Wagner, predicted that spirit voices would sing to large audiences in the church before five years and vouched for a tremendous out-pouring in behalf of spiritualism among all nations during that period. This prophecy came through Mrs. W.'s inspirational message. Spirit singing before congregations, however, does not seem so startling in view of the strength and beauty of the voices that have come from "the other side" at our trumpet circles.

Note:—In Mrs. Miller's message father gave this as a test: "Some people call my son Gorner; but that is not correct. It should be Gerner." The name is spelled Goerner—the "o" being silent, but there are some who persist in pronouncing it as if the "e" following the "o" were not in the name at all.

REPORT ON TRUMPET SEANCE

At Residence of Mr. and Mrs. J. B. Jonson, Los Angeles, 8 O'Clock P. M., Tuesday, January 3rd, 1922.

There were seven members present, including Mr. and Mrs. J. The voices came in lively succession, each member having from two to four communicators. Every one seemed to be in a more or less humorous frame of mind—both on our side and the spirit side—resorted to puns and jokes and made rather a "jollification" meeting of it.

Timothy repeated several verses of comic poetry; most always has a good pun ready and has plenty of characteristic Irish wit.

Father spoke mainly on the wonders of spirit return and spirit communication, saying:

"Friends, do you know that all over the world the orthodox preachers are beginning to wake up to the beauties of spiritualism; but they are slow to admit its truth. You have pastors who have become mediumistic since they entered the ministry and the light has been shown to them many times. Still, they don't dare turn away from orthodoxy and they continue to preach something which they no longer believe. It's the same thing as living a double life and many a one has reached this side to find out that it doesn't pay. It has kept more than one of them in darkness when all it required was to follow the light given them when they had the chance. With a congregation before them with ears to hear their opportunity was great. Preachers still stand at the grave delivering the old sermon of a resurrection way off in the years to come, and do it while the spirit already stands resurrected at their side listening to a false system of teaching."

He concluded with, "Well, my son, I will talk with you again at Miller's Thursday. We will all be there. Goodbye to you and your friends; a happy New Year to everybody and God bless you all." I broke in telling him I had a question to ask before he put down the trumpet and asked if he could tell me how many and who were in my room on the night before. He answered:

"Yes, the whole family was there. I was there for part of the time. Your mother was with me. Then afterwards sister Clara and sister Annie went in to be with you for a little while.'

"Father, who was it that tried to materialize in the alcove?"

Answer: "That was sister Annie."

Later Minnie took the trumpet and I asked if she was in my room the night before and got the reply:

"Why do you ask that, George? I am there every night and there is never an evening that I don't come to you. You hear my voice most of the time and I can always get your answer.'

Minnie then sang "Dollie Gray" through the trumpet. The voice was very strong and could be heard at the end of an auditorium seating 500 to a thousand people. Then something happened. She suddenly stopped singing and Timothy and my friend Jim Thomas both sang the song as a duet—a grotesque imitation mixed with laughter, and we decided they were trying to have some fun with us, when I reminded Mr. Thomas that he used to say that he couldn't "sing for sour apples" and that I believed him. The answer came:

"Well, George, this Irishman said he could beat me singing Dollie Gray, and I just thought I'd take a chance with him. Wasn't it awful?"

Minnie then explained that Jim asked for her trumpet and Tim took the other one and said she would have to finish the song another time. After Minnie put down the trumpet Krocho gave this:

"Say, Goerner chief, I want to tell you something: You don't know it, but that sweetheart of yours is a wonderful spirit. She is beautiful and her spiritual station gives her great influence over here. You can afford to be proud of her because when you get over here you are going to find out how wonderful she is."

Previous to starting the seance some of us were discussing Kitty's age. No one seemed to know very definitely; so when she spoke through the trumpet Krocho whispered to me to ask her how old she was and this is what Kitty gave me for my pains:

"It isn't polite, Mr. Goerner, to ask a lady her age." She laughed and dropped the trumpet with, "Give another guess."

I put this question to Tim:

"Tim, so far as this little circle is concerned we are all satisfied that our friends from the other side are just the spirits we think they are; but would there be any chance for an interloper to step in and give the name of one of our friends and try to create the impression that we were talking with our friend when it might be a stranger?"

Answer: "Not a chance, friend. What do you suppose I'm here for? Don't I know every one of your friends? Do you think a stranger could get in here if he was an undesirable? There is a band of protectors right around this circle, with an outer band around that one, and so long as you desire good, true and uplifting influences that's what you will get. Don't have any misgivings on that point; your visitors here are just who you think they are."

Question: "But how would it be at Mrs. Miller's, Tim?"

Answer: "The same way. Mrs. Miller is a good woman and she has strong protectors. That protects you whenever you go there."

Little Mary Ellen said she just took the trumpet to thank me for the beautiful rose I took to the church for her Sunday and said she was looking forward to the chance to talk with me at Mrs. Miller's, "because we always have such a lovely chat there."

Clara spoke quite at length and said that I must not be disappointed because she has not materialized yet, explaining:

"It isn't as easy as it might seem. If the vibration is exactly right it wouldn't be hard to do. But we must wait for just the opportunity and may be then we can't develop so as to remain long enough to carry on a conversation with you. But we are working all the time and before this year is out you will see us materialized in your room and we will be able to talk with you much stronger because we would get an unmixed vibration. You are helping us and we don't want you to get discouraged, because your development makes it easier for us to work with you. You are now impressed with the wonder of all these things, but you will look at them as perfectly natural when you understand them. I am counting on the next visit with you at Mrs. Miller's and we can talk more about this next Thursday."

Mr. Thomas informed me that he and his son, John, were in my office during an important business conference I had with two associates on Monday morning. Said they both stepped in the moment "the little blackheaded fellow sat down," and remained there during the entire conversation. I asked, "How does it look?"

Answer: "If you once get the big fellow to work with you instead of with the little Hebrew, you can take his word. He may put up a hard bargain; but he's a straight-shooter and his word once given is good. But don't tie to the little fellow except through the big man. You will have to watch the little fellow and take no chances. Get him in black and white . Don't be discouraged. We are with you to the finish. If you don't get the contract you want through them it will come from other directions. It wouldn't be wise to rush things. I am going to talk with you about this again on Thursday when we are alone."

Here is another case where they all seemed to be well posted on my plans. A few moments before I started for the Jonsons I made the appointment with Mrs. Miller for Thursday by phone and by the time the Jonson seance opened they all seemed to know about it on the other side.

In some way the subject in the circle turned upon Col. Robt. G. Ingersoll, when Krocho said:

"Do you know folks my medium used to get writings from Mr. Ingersoll and when they first started she was so orthodox that the shivers used to run up her back like a rat running up a sugar sack. But let me tell you something: That man Ingersoll never had any darkness on this side. He made money like water and gave it all to charity and kept quiet about it, and the dear little children, no matter how poor or homely, never had a better friend than they had in Mr. Ingersoll. He loved them all. He believed what he preached. He had the courage to say there was no personal God—he believed it. He said he wouldn't talk eternal punishment for any man because there was no such thing, and there isn't. My medium had lots of writings from Mr. Ingersoll after he passed out of the body and they didn't any of them come from the realms of darkness. The Valley of the Shadow of Death, friends, is nothing. Learn all you can of the psychic law; live a clean, spiritual life, true to what you believe, and you—every one of you in this circle—will find me and the rest of your friends at the door ready to open your eyes at once and take you by the hand and lead you on to the light and the full enjoyment of the hereafter. Good night everybody and God bless you all. My medium's tired and Gray Feather has gone home and I'm going, too.

During our conversation with Tim I put this question to him and worded it carefully:

"Tim, I have read the writings of many of the scientific investigators of spiritualism. Most of them have spent from 10 to 25 years in the work. They all take a great deal of space talking about fraud mediums, the tricksters and charlatans they have met in their work; talk about lack of dependence to be placed in the communicators from the spirit side, and then wind up by producing a few small driblets of evidence in substantiation of psychic phenomena; but lose no opportunity to comment at length upon the 'objectionable phases' and the 'repellant features' of the seance room. Now I have attended more than 100 seances of all kinds, with one medium after another, and I have never yet encountered these so-called 'objectionable' and 'repellent' features, and I'll guarantee that I can produce forty men and women right in Los Angeles whose experience has been the same as mine. Why is it, Tim?"

The answer came: "My dear friend, your scientific investigator is the most gullible man in the whole work. He starts out expecting to find every medium a fraud and every seance room a mud-house, and he gets exactly what he goes after. The law that like attracts like is strong on both your side and ours. Your scientific investigator knows that straps and ropes to bind the medium, handcuffs around their wrists to hold them in the cabinet, can all be removed and replaced by the spirit control right before the eyes of the investigator; and still he tries to hide his identity under a mask and an apron, gets himself introduced to the medium by a false name and all that sort of flapdoodle. He hasn't yet got it through him that the medium is the instrument of the spirit control and that the spirit resents his attitude toward this instrument. A little courtesy and a little tact and consideration for the medium would get the results much quicker and better. There is a band of guides around this circle to protect it from intrusions of uncongenial forces, and there would be around the investigator too if he took the right method."

NOTES ON TRANCE SEANCE

At Residence of Mr. and Mrs. Victor Severy, 4304 S. Western Avenue, Los Angeles, Wednesday P. M., Jan. 4th, 1922.

This was the regular "Wednesday Evening Developing Class." There were nine members present. The seance began promptly at eight o'clock with prayer, then singing a couple of hymns; then silence until Mrs. Severy went into trance. Some fresh flowers were placed in the room in compliance with suggestion from one of the guides from "the other side." Flowers, we are told, appear to the spirit side as lights and they also tell us that they draw strength from them for producing their manifestations.

The "Big Chief," who has been controlling Mrs. S., and who has not yet given us his name, appeared as a "transfiguration," or "transformation," as it is usually termed in the seance room. This, as near as we can learn, is made up by the spirit forces using the "aura", or "fluidic emanation" from the body of the medium as well as from the rest of the sitters in the room. From this circle they draw their force and the method of drawing is sometimes plainly visible, their hands reaching out to the various members in the circle and turning them over, working backwards away from the circle, carrying on the process repeatedly.

These "transformations" appear as etherealized, or partially materialized, figures and the visitors (spirits) can in most cases be recognized by those in the circle who knew them in life. There will, however, frequently come visitors unknown to any one in the room and introduce themselves by various names, perhaps stating the object of the visit.

For instance, one woman appeared, first over and above the body of the medium; then sat on one arm of the chair; then on the other side. We asked who she was and received answer that she came as a guide to the circle. Further questioning brought out the reply that she was an Egyptian, but would withhold her name until later; said she had dark eyes, but not black hair and stated that "all Egyptians are not dark; some of them are fair." We asked if she had been on the other side many years and she replied: "Yes, I passed over many years ago, but I am not old."

In saying that she was not old we presume she meant that there was no aging after reaching the spirit side, as this same explanation has been pressed upon me at other seance rooms.

My father appeared, and although the figures were all more or less hazy, a close-up view showed sufficient for a recognition. We asked who the visitor was for and the reply was very clear, "for Mr. Goerner." Thinking at first it might be mother or one of my sisters I asked: "Are you going to talk to me, dearie?" and got the answer:

"You don't have to dearie me, because I am not a lady. I am a relative and a close one."

I then put in with: "Oh, then it must be father."

Answer: "Yes, I am father and you can confirm this at the other meeting tomorrow."

This was good identification—or what we call a "test." At the Jonson seance on the night before I made an appointment with father at Mrs. Miller's trumpet seance for Thursday, and his reference to this appointment would make good his claim as to who he was.

There were fourteen of these transformations during the evening, each sitter in the class having a visitor and some of them more than one.

In speaking to us in this way the spirit controls use the vocal cords of the medium, and while the voice is distinctly not that of the medium, and she knows nothing about it when she returns from the trance, the voices all have pretty much the same tone and are seldom raised above a clear audible whisper.

The medium was in a deep state of trance during all these transformations, coming out of it with a slight headache and complaining that her face felt "pulled out of gear"; said it seemed twisted and her jaws for the moment appeared to be "out of joint." In two or three minutes, however, she was entirely normal again and after Miss McLain (who is a spiritual healer) applied her hands to Mrs. S.'s head for a couple of moments she said the headache was gone.

Several of the communicators assured us that these transformations were the next thing to materializations and that from now on the results would become stronger and more convincing; stated the right guides were assisting us and complimented us for our patience in keeping up the work in the face of many discouragements and setbacks in trying to hold the class together.

Note:—At the Miller trumpet seance the next day (Thursday, January 5th) father spoke through the trumpet and confirmed his visit to me at the Severy seance. As soon as he spoke at Miller's I asked: "Where did I talk with you last, father?" and the answer came:

"At Mrs. Severy's last night; I told you you could confirm it." He was very definite in having me understand that he was there and that there was no mistake about it.

FULL REPORT OF TRUMPET SEANCE

At Residence of Mrs. Mary Miller, Los Angeles, Cal., Thursday, One O'Clock P. M., January 5th, 1922.

Contrary to the usual custom at these Miller seances, Dr Worthington was not the first speaker on this occasion. The light had hardly been extinguished when I could see at least half a dozen etherealized forms moving about the room. Mrs. M. could see more than that number and see them more clearly. She described some of them with excellent detail.

Little Mary Ellen began speaking in whispers independently; then gradually raised her voice until she was talking, without the trumpet, in a perfectly natural tone so that every word could be heard. I complimented her on her success in this attempt and she seemed wonderfully proud at the achievement, saying:

"Uncle George, I don't want to use the horn any more. I don't like the horns and I want to talk to you without them. You know I came to you at the Severy's last night all by myself. I didn't need Big Chief to fix me up. I came independent. Did you know that? I am going to keep trying till I can materialize for you."

Mother spoke briefly on the happiness she derives in visiting with me at the seances and coming to my room. I asked if she had anything to do with getting me into spiritualism and she replied:

"Indeed, I did, my boy. Your father and I worked for years to get your attention. But it seemed impossible to get within the vibration. Your frame of mind was against all our efforts. We were with you at mediums several times; but we saw it would take a very strong demonstration to reach you. Then we saw one of your friends at the Jonsons and we sent out the thought that induced him to speak of it in your presence. Next we sent the thought that brought you to inquire into it. Father and I took you to the Jonsons. Since then it has been easy to reach you and we have all been so happy in the talks and the wonderful visits we have had."

Clara spoke somewhat along the same lines, speaking of the work she and the rest of the folks were doing to bring about my clairvoyance and clair-audience, so they could talk with me direct. Said the visits to my room were helping all of us.

"You don't know it, George, but I am in your room every morning, as well as many times in the evening. You can sometimes see us at night, but you can't in the daylight. You will before long. Do you know who it is that wakes you up in the morning?"

I answered: "No, Clara, I don't," and was told:

"It's little Mary Ellen. She loves to come to the room with me in the morning and wake you up. We all enjoy these meetings at Mrs. Miller's, because we can be alone and there are no mixed vibrations. Goodbye, brother, and God bless you.'

Minnie talked quite at length on the wonders of the spirit side of life; spoke of gardens surpassing anything known on the earth plane, and said:

"I am looking forward to the day when I can meet you on the spirit side, that you may know for yourself the great things that are in store for you. You can't realize what our opportunities are. There will be no parting after I meet you at the door. The meeting will be for all eternity. There is so much I can tell you when you develop more."

I asked: "Will I soon be able to see you clairvoyantly and be able to carry on a conversation with you?"

Answer: "Yes, you will, and it will be sooner than you think. You seldom miss my voice on the pillow and I can always hear you when you answer back. You are not far from receiving the things you are asking for. We are all helping you."

I thanked her for singing to the circle at Jonsons the other night and told her to tell my friends Jim and Tim that they couldn't sing for sour apples. This brought a good hearty laugh that was perfectly natural and certainly reproduced the laugh of the Minnie I knew at school years ago.

Sister Annie gave me a piece of new information. I thanked her for her materialization in my room and she informed me that she did so well because Kitty came along to help her. Kitty is the cabinet worker at the Jonsons materialization seances. She is a very strong spirit herself, and her work consists in building up the spirit forms behind the curtains. Kitty confirmed Annie's information, saying:

"I guess you didn't know before that I come to your room sometimes with the folks. Well, I do because I want to help them to materialize for you. I like you because you are good to my medium and I want to help you develop."

Up to this point the communicators—excepting Mary Ellen—had been using Mrs. Miller's trumpet. My own trumpet was lying on the table and I had placed around it an aluminum band covered with 'radium paint." This band is luminant in the dark. My trumpet guide, Jim Thomas, took up my own trumpet, moving it about the room, back and forth and up and down. With the luminous band these movements could be plainly seen. During all these movements we kept up a conversation, mostly of a business character in which he gave this advice:

"I told you at the Jonsons that I would talk about this business again today. I did not want to say much in the presence of the rest of the circle. But I injected the thoughts into your mind that brought out the speeches you made to the little Hebrew. I want you to understand how to handle him. He is more anxious to get hold of your company than you think he is, but is trying to give you the notion that he doesn't care about it. But you go after him right from the shoulder, tell him just what terms you want and you will find that he will give in rather than lose the deal. He can raise the money, but he is not working for your interest. I wanted to keep you from committing yourself in a hurry. You have a good thing there and if you don't make a contract with the Hebrew and his friend you will hear something in a few days that you can use as a club over him. We are working to help you, because we have a grand plan laid out for you and are trying to get you in shape so you can carry on our work. When we once get you into it, it is going to give you a wonderful amount of happiness and be a monument to humanity. Keep close to John, because he is working for you and he's level-headed. When you get in a tight corner and don't know which way to turn, call on us."

After thanking him the subject turned on the Jonson seance and I asked:

"Jim, where did you and Tim learn to sing?" His answer was:

"Say, wasn't that rank? Well, we just wanted to make you laugh a little. We like your circle and we like your frends and we all had a good time."

To my surprise Timothy came in with: "Who said I couldn't sing? You didn't expect to find me here, did you?"

I replied that I was glad he came whether I expected it or not and told him that he was just as welsome at Millers as at Jonsons.

"Yes, I know it, friend and I felt at perfect liberty to come. But you know how I feel about Jonsons—it's home to me. I feel as if I was going back to mother when I go there."

Father spoke just long enough to verify his visit to me at the Severys the night before and said he wanted me to know that there was no mistake about it, he was there.

John Thomas gave pretty much the same advice as his father did with regard to business matters, saying:

"Now, George, I have looked all over the ground at the mines. You've got a good chance there and we want you to make the most of that opportunity. I am going to keep close to you while these negotiations are under way. Call on me at any time and we'll go hand in hand with you to the finish."

Here's another good one from little Georgie, my sister Annie's spirit child:

"Say, Uncle George, you didn't know that I went with you from your office to the street car and came out to Mrs. Miller's with you. But I did. I took your hand and walked at your side. I like to go down the street with you, because I love Uncle George."

Here is a phenomenal narrative. To a stranger in psychic work it might seem incredible; but I have gone far enough with these investigations to know there is nothing unusual nor unnatural about it, nor will it compare with the higher forms of phenomena:

Sunbeam (Mrs. Miller's guide who controls her when delivering the flower messages at the church), took the trumpet and said: "I came in because I heard you and my medium talking about my picture. I painted that for her."

On the wall in Mrs. Miller's seance room is a beautiful picture of a young girl, apparently around 18 years of age. It is certainly the picture of a "Sunbeam," with smiling blue eyes, golden curls around her shoulders, complexion of just the right shade of marble and rose. Around her shoulders a drapery of some soft white goods with delicate blue stripes, and in her dress a pink rose.

Mrs. Miller explained that she has never seen Sunbeam except clairvoyantly and at materializations. She is said to have left this world at the age of four. After she had been on the spirit side about twelve or fourteen years Mrs. Miller asked for one of her pictures. Sunbeam promised her one. Later she instructed Mrs. Miller to lay some pieces of cardboard in her seance room and permit no one to touch them. In about three weeks she found on one of the cardboards a picture labelled "Sunbeam," with all the features of the face and shoulders drawn.

She instructed Mrs. Miller to place the picture within a gilt frame with a glass over it and she would in time color it. Soon the colors in her face were all there; the shade of her hair; the white in the dress and the delicate blue stripes and all the creases and folds in the drapery.

Next, Mrs. Miller stated to Sunbeam that as she was only known to her as a flower messenger, the picture should have a flower in it. A few days later the beautiful pink rose was there.

Mrs. Miller vouches for this narrative, and those who know her character and have listened to her messages of truth and spirituality, and know something of the wonderful phenomena produced under her mediumship will not question her statement.

Note:—Within a few minutes before I started for Mrs. Miller's for this seance, I remarked to one of my associates in the office that I felt strongly the presence of some one from the spirit side, and believed I would have company to Mrs. Miller's. This probably bears out little Georgie's statement that she went with me from the office to the street car and out to Mrs. Miller's

In mother's message at Mrs. Miller's she thanked me for the roses which I took to the church the previous Sunday, and said she was glad they were divided between Mrs. Miller and Mrs. Wagner, and "Mrs. Miller still has some of them in her room." After the seance was over Mrs. Miller confirmed this, stated they were divided between Mrs. Wagner and herself and that she (Mrs. Miller) still had two of them in a vase in her parlor—which she showed me.

MEMORANDUM REPORT OF TRUMPET SEANCE

Held At Residence of Mr. and Mrs. J. B. Jonson, Los Angeles, Cal., Monday P. M., Jan. 9, 1922.

For a little diversion we had about thirty minutes of cabinet work, in which the demonstration from behind the curtain consisted mostly of apports in the way of violets handed out, some of them over the curtain, some of them through the curtain and others left strewn on the floor in the cabinet after the work was over. "Timothy" and "Kitty" gave some vigorous manifestations in the use of the tambourine, the "bones" and the music boxes.

When "Bobbie"—Mrs. Jacob's son—took the trumpet, Mrs. Jonson began gasping for breath, said her heart began to ache and she choked, saying she felt as if she was drowning. Mrs Jacobs recognized in this the symptoms of Bobbie's death and asked if he had produced that effect upon the medium. The reply came:

"Yes, mother, but I didn't do it intentionally. She is so sensitive that as soon as I appeared she felt all the pains and the choking that I did at the time of my death."

I asked Clara who made the attempt at materializing in my room on the night before and she replied: "It was sister Annie." I then asked: "Was any one with her?"

Clara: "Yes, Kitty came to help her."

George: "Did any one speak on my pillow besides you, sister Annie and Minnie?"

Clara: "Kitty, did and you heard her."

This conversation was followed by Kitty who confirmed the visit and the voice on my pillow. But these visits have become so frequent lately, as well as the voices on the pillow, that (like the chats through the trumpets) I have grown to recognize and identify them at the time; but for my own satisfaction like to have them confirmed in the presence of some else.

Minnie spoke of the roses I took to the church Sunday and when I remarked that I would be disappointed if I didn't get a message from her through Mrs. Miller she replied:

"But you must not feel disappointed, George. The difficulties are greater than you think. We are always there, but there will be times when so many other flowers will be on the table that they are more or less piled one upon another and the vibration is interrupted, so that it is hard to get a message through. We are with you just the same and can usually make you feel our presence.

"It is the same way with materializations. I will materialize for you at every opportunity I get; but it takes a great deal of strength to do it, especially at the beginning. Later we can come stronger. But I was happy to know that you saw me clearly the last time and could talk with me. So if we fail to come to you, it isn't that we are not there, but the vibration is not always strong enough for us to manifest so you can see and hear us."

Some of our friends will throw kisses through the trumpet on leaving, and last night one of the circle jokingly remarked: "That sounds like mush." I retorted:

"I think some of you are jealous because you haven't any sweethearts to send you any kisses." Then came this from Krocho:

"That's right, Goerner chief. A little mush spread around here and there does a great deal to brigthen up your old world and bring happiness to the lonely hearts. Its mush that puts the laugh wrinkles around your eyes and makes your peepers sparkle. When you go home tired and things haven't gone right through the day, don't it make a heap of difference to have some one come up quietly and put their arms around you and whisper a little mush in your ear? The trouble with your world is that there isn't enough mush to go around. All the mush you spread this way is stored up to your credit on the big shelf in the hereafter and when you come over on the spirit side you can look up on your shelf and you will find great bowls of mush, and these will be the good deeds you have done, the kind things you have said and the glad smiles you have sent out to make some one else happy. That's all you're living for, friends, and if you don't know it, don't wait another day; but get right into the harness before the New Year gets any older and begin spreading the mush because it's good for the soul."

At this point Gray Feather humorously put in: "Yes, and good for the tummy, too."

Tim followed with: "What's the matter with your Los Angeles this New Year friends? With the murders, burglaries and court scandals every day, you are not making a very good start. Can't you see how your old world works against all our efforts? We talk harmony, kindness and the brotherhood of man, and the material man turns a deaf ear and works right against his own inner self. Why so much selfishness when just a little love, just a little thought for your brothers means so much happiness and so much sweetness and so much rest and peace to you all."

Hester, a spirit guide to Dr. Wetherby, sang "The Isle of Somewhere"; Viola sang, "Whispering Hopes," and John Kennedy, a deceased cousin to the Lombards, gave us "I Walked With You and I Talked With You." This was a treat for us all and it is difficult to get away from the feeling that one is listening to "the music of the angels," for to us who know the conditions, and know each and every one in the circle, and the earth life of the communicators, there is no chance to question where these voices come from.

Catharine, a guide to Mr. and Mrs. Majors, startled us with her intimate knowledge of the recent applicants for membership into the Research Society. Her advice was:

"Be careful about your new members. You have one on the list whom you had better drop for the present."

We asked: "Can you give us the name?"

Catharine: "I would prefer not to mention names; but you may guess."

Question: "Is it one of the ladies or the gentleman applicants?"

Catharine: "The ladies on the new list are absolutely satisfactory and will cause you no trouble."

Question: "Then it must be Mr. F———? What is the objection to him?"

Catharine: "His racial training is against his acceptance of spiritualism. He is by heredity a materialist. His mind is not in tune with your efforts. He will bring that feeling into your circle. It will get into the spirit of the medium and your entire circle will suffer in results. Don't take the chance—not now."

Question by Mrs. Jacobs: "But, Catharine, he seemed so much in earnest about it."

Catharine: "Yes, that is a character of the race and he is using that against your sympathetic nature. Did he not tell you that he had read greatly and visited many mediums and had never yet had one bit of conviction brought home to him? Why? He went with his mind against conviction and he will come into your circle in the same way. If your heart moves you to help him, then advise him to continue his reading; continue his visits to the mediums; enter an elemental class and keep out of the higher phenomena until he has trained his mind to remain open—receptive—ready and willing to receive the truth. When he has done this he will get in harmony with the spirit side; but not before. The Jewish race doesn't take to it."

Crystal, another guide to the Majors, has only recently been coming to our circle. But in conversation with Dr. Wetherby she seemed to have become very well acquainted with most of the members. She spoke of having visited Dr. W. at his office and when he asked as a test:

"What kind of an office did you find me in?" she answered:

"You pull their teeth for them—no,—no, you don't pull them—not any more. You just fix them in—you fix them in."

After the seance I interrogated Dr. Wetherby on this point and he advised me that he stopped pulling teeth about 15 years ago, and since then has confined his practice to what is known as "constructive denistry"; that is, bridge work, crown work and plate work.

At the last materialization seance, Crystal had told Mr. Majors that if he would bring her a box of candy, she would dematerialize it for him. In the meantime it seems that he had purchased the candy and had it at his home. She knew all about this; could tell the kind of candy it was—the kind of a box he had—the size of it—the table on which he had placed it at home, and wound up by cautioning him "not to forget to bring it to the materialization Friday."

The mother of the Misses Worrals spoke through the trumpet and seemed anxious to give her sister back in the East some proof of her continued existence and of spirit return. She spoke of the preparation being made by the two girls for their return to their eastern home; instructed them to give her sister all the details of these conversations through the trumpet, and as a convincing test, ended by saying: "I can tell you how her bedroom is arranged and you can convince her that way." She then described the position of the various pieces of furniture in the room, including some changes in their location which had lately been made.

Bear in mind that these are things that are still unknown to the two Misses W.'s, residing in Los Angeles, as they have not been to their old home in the east for several years, and the descriptions are being looked up.

Timothy gave us a pun on Mrs. Jacobs' name, Dr. Wetherby's and the Worral girls, saying:

"Guess I had better climb Jacobs' ladder to see what the weather be. Don't that beat the worl'?"

At the end of the seance a spirit hand was placed on my head. I asked Krocho if she could see who it was, and she told me, "Why, yes, it's your blessed mother." I then said: "Mother is that you?" For reply she tapped three times on my head, "Yes."

Dr. W. asked Hester why she had not materialized for him since the seances were resumed and received the following instructions:

"You were not seated in the right position. Do not sit beside Mr. Severy. He is off-setting the vibration. Take a seat as distant from him as you can get—go down toward the end of the room in front of the chiffoniere and I will be able to come to you."

Here's good evidence that our spirit friends do not necessarily lose their humor after passing out of the physical body:

Dr. W. is perfectly bald and when talking with his spirit guide, Hester, he complimented her on her beautiful hair and suggested that he might be tempted to bring a pair of scissors and cut a lock for a keepsake when she next materialized. Her reply was:

"Shall I cut one of yours in exchange?"

MEMORANDUM OF MATERIALIZATION SEANCE

Held At Residence of Mr. and Mrs. J. B. Jonson, Los Angeles, Cal., Friday P. M., Jan. 13, 1922.

One of the members of the Society was absent on this occasion and a new member made his first appearance. These changing conditions always seem to have some effect on the result, although it may only be slight. It does nevertheless make a difference in the strength of the vibrations and this is reflected more or less in the strength of the visitors from the "other side," the light they bring, the clearness in voice and the length of time they can remain with us.

The instructions given by Hester (Dr. Wetherby's guide) relative to the position he should occupy in the circle were followed as outlined by her through the trumpet on the evening of the 9th, and the results were as she had predicted. She was the first one to appear from the cabinet; walked well down the center of the room; chatted confidentially with Dr. W.; took his trumpet for magnetizing, passed her hands over it repeatedly, waved it through the air gracefully several times and handed it back.

Previous to Hester's appearance, Mrs. J. asked Gray Feather (Mr. J.'s control) if he could give Mrs. Baker a treatment for some trouble of the spine. He assented and Mrs. Baker stood in the center of the room, while Gray Feather passed his hand up and down her back. I asked if she felt any benefit from it and she replied:

"Yes, I should say I can; I can feel the vibrations going clear through me. She afterwards expressed the effect as being "quiet and refreshing." Gray Feather, however, seemed to take a "different view of it, saying: "Oh, no; can do no good work with harness on."

The second visitor was "Aunt Jane" for the two Worrall sisters. This is a familiar spirit to us all; speaks through the trumpet often; comes with a good deal of strength, but seldom ventures more than a few feet outside of the cabinet. She has come so often that to the Worrall's the identification is complete.

A new figure was the mother of Mr. Oaks' wife. This was her first appearance; none of the rest of us knew her, but Mr. Oaks stated he had no difficulty in recognizing her and that there could be no mistake about it with him.

"Bobbie"—Mrs. Jacobs' son, is always a strong figure, both at the trumpet and at the materializations, although on this visit he announced to his mother that he did not have strength enough to assist her much in magnetizing her trumpet but instructed her to bring it another time. These "varying moods" among the spirit folks can usually be traced to changes in the circle members, or to illness among them or some adverse condition of mind.

Our friend "Viola," one of Mrs. J.'s guides, this night made her first appearance since the seances were resumed. She never fails to create a refreshing feeling among us all, is full of smiles, messages of good cheer and always seems glad to be with us. Some one asked if she would dance if we sang her favorite song, "Rock-a-Bye Baby," and as soon as the song began she started dancing, kept it up until one verse was finished and then disappeared within the curtains.

Henry Marshall, a spirit guide to the Lombards, came with Mr. L.'s Indian guide "Big Heart." When on earth Big Heart always dressed in citizen's clothes and when he appears at the seances he is still dressed this way—never in the Indian attire that most of them wear.

Came next my friend John Thomas, a fine, handsome young fellow, of about thirty years of age, "natty" and well dressed as he always was in life. Although I was very intimate with all the other members of the Thomas family, I had never met John before he passed away and I could only recognize him by his photographs which were plentiful at the Thomas home in Denver. He seemed anxious that I should be sure that there was no mistake about his identity and gave this as evidence:

"You know I called at your room last night. I wanted to tell you that I would appear for you here tonight; but wasn't strong enough to get the message through." I replied:

"I knew you were in the room and caught your name, but could not catch anything else." He answered:

'Well, I was there, George, and I wanted you to know that I would come tonight." He then went back to the curtain and as I started for my seat he stepped out again, walked briskly down the room, tapped me on the shoulder with his hand in a friendly way, waved a goodbye and again disappeared.

Another stranger to us was a lady merely giving the name of "Rose," and called our attention to the beautiful red rose in her hair; said she came "for the entire circle and the rose is to you a message of love, light, beauty and truth."

Crystal fairly jumped out of the cabinet, in bare feet as usual, and immediately let us know that: "I've come for my box of candy; seemed wonderfully pleased; said she would have a time dematerializing so many candies, and guess she'd have to get Kitty to help her undo the strings on the box. She appeared in no hurry to go; chatted for a long time and finally made a very graceful exit, slowly diminishing in size until she reached the very floor, with the box in full view and finally both Crystal and the candy disappeared in full sight of the circle.

Mrs. Lombard's mother, a dear old lady who always dresses as she did on earth and never fails to bring her spectacles, has no trouble identifying herself. Mrs. L. called me up and introduced me to her mother—just as one might be introduced in a parlor of society folks, and the acknowledgement of the introduction was just as natural and one is for the moment divested of the idea that he is conversing with some one who has been called "dead" for many years.

One member suggested that Mr. Carpenter sing "La Paloma" in Spanish and see if we could induce "Zara" to come out and dance for us. "Zara" is the Spanish gypsy dancer who appeared at a previous seance. The song had the desired effect; she joined in singing, danced to the tune and frequently snapped her fingers as though imitating the castanets. She was given a good encore, acknowledged it gracefully, bowing and waving her hands, then with a final "adios" disappeared as suddenly as a flash behind the curtains.

Little "Dorothy", who came at the last seance as a spirit child to Mrs. Jacobs seems to have made good her claim, since she has been vouched for to Mrs. Jacobs by her son "Bobbie", by her brother Henry and by Mrs. Jacobs husband—all on the spirit side of life. Mrs. J. seems happy to accept the relation and she may well feel proud of these visits, for Dorothy brings a delightful influence with her— very beautiful, timid as a girl ten or twelve years might be, and very spiritual. We were all anxious to have her remain a while and Mrs. Jonson, in order to hold the vibration as long as possible, asked the circle to sing a hymn in low tones; Dorothy joined in singing "Jesus Lover of My Soul", and sang it with her head bowed and her hands clasped as if in prayer. The effect was decidedly a reverent one and the entire circle seemed to have caught something sacred in her presence.

MEMORANDUM OF TRUMPET SEANCE

At Residence of Mr. and Mrs. Jonson, Los Angeles, Cal., Monday P. M., 8 O'Clock, January 16th, 1922.

Extra visitors came to the class this evening. There were 18 in the circle including Mr. and Mrs. Jonson. The light had hardly been turned down when the guides behind the curtain began to get active. The usual physical demonstrations took place first with the musical instruments; then hands gave cluster of jonquils out—one to each and every member in the circle. Following this came several messages, the most significant one was this from Silas Webster, Mr. J's chemist guide:

"We can see in our medium's mind a great deal of worry as to the outcome of changed conditions that he thinks he will meet in his new home. We wish him to understand that the change will be all in his favor, and that the fact of his being able to secure the house he is going to is entirely due to our efforts in balking would-be buyers through mental suggesstions. He will find all for the best."

In explanation of this note, Mr. and Mrs. J. recently purchased a home in Pasadena, where they hoped to find ideal conditions for a seance room; but Mr. J. appeared to be worrying about the length of time it would take to get the walls sufficiently "magnetized" for good results. The note from Webster soon set his mind at rest.

There were three trumpets on the table and sometimes they were all in use at once. The confusion was occasionally enough to make it almost impossible to catch more than a small part of the messages coming through. All told there must have been 30 to 40 voices. Mother spoke briefly, saying:

"Oh, son, if I could just lift the veil from your eyes so you could see the beautiful spirit forms all around the room, and all anxious to deliver a message. You could realize better what a wonderful meaning life has on the spirit side. I cannot talk much with you tonight, my boy; there are so many waiting for a chance."

I interrupted with, "Before you go, mother, were you in my room with father last night?"

Answer: "Yes, and we were with you through nearly the whole day—all of us—and did not leave you until you were asleep. But I will talk with you more at Mrs. Miller's." I asked if sister Annie was in the alcove in my room at the same time.

Answer: "Yes, she is there every night and will soon be able to materialize for you more fully in your room."

Minnie tried three times to speak, but each time the vibration was interrupted and she had to wait for a better chance. Finally she got this much through:

"I was with you all day Sunday, but I wont have time to tell you about it now. I will meet you at Mrs. Miller's and make up for it. Goodbye."

Several songs came through the trumpet, both from men's and ladies' voices—once three of them singing at the same time.

Mrs. Wheeler seemed to have been thinking seriously of making some important change in her affairs, but evidently was in doubt as to what she should do about it, when this came in from her husband on the spirit side.

"Bert, don't think about that any more. Just pass it up; because it would not be best." She asked:

"How did you know what it was?"

Answer: "You didn't send out the thought to me; but you kept it on your mind so constantly and seemed undecided, and I felt as if I wanted to help you out. It wouldn't be for the best, and I would advise you to forget about it."

The following conversation took place between Dr. Wetherby and his guide, Hester:

W: "Hester, what change took place in you since the last time you materialized previous to Mrs. Jonson closing her work for the summer?"

Hester: "In what way, doctor?"

W: "I can't exactly describe it; but there appeared to be a difference in your general form and also in the robes you wore."

Hester: "The difference was merely one of progress. I have not stood still during these months. I have continued to go on."

W: "But what was the robe made of—what kind of cloth?"

Hester: "Why do you ask? You were with me all the time I was in the seance room. You should have made a closer study. That is the way you have to develop on your plane. I turned clear around several times to give you plenty opportunity."

W: "But why can't you tell me what it was? I am only after detail."

Hester: "But it is detail of a character that you could not understand if I told you. It is not to be expressed in terms of cloth as you understand it in your life. The robes are mine by right of my advancement—not by the standard of your plane."

W: "But, Hester, I still don't understand the distinction."

Hester: "It is a distinction that could add nothing to your knowledge in the material world; but will mean much to you on this side."

W: " Well, Hester, can you tell me why it is that Mrs. Severy has not materialized for her husband for so long?"

Hester: "Mrs. Severy was in the cabinet at the time I materialized last Friday; but was not strong enough to come through the curtain."

W: "Why was that?"

Hester: "She has just gone to a higher plane. She is now on the fifth plane and has difficulty in returning for the present; but will overcome this soon."

Hester dropped the trumpet and Timothy asked Miss May

Wheeler how she was getting along with her new beau. She inquired:

"If you know so much about him, Tim, can you tell me his name?"

Tim: "I am going to call him June Showers."

May: "What a name! Why would you call him June Showers?"

Tim: "Because he comes after May."

Tim then addressed a stranger in the circle, saying:

"Mrs. M., there's an Irishman over here that used to know you."

Mrs. M: "Can you tell me his name?"

Tim: "Sure, its Tom O'Riley."

Mrs. M: "Well, bless his heart, Tim; of course, I know him; but please ask him where he knew me." The answer came:

"Marcellus, Michigan." (Correct).

One of the new comers seemed to take all messages as a huge joke and appeared to have rather a shallow understanding of the work, even when the messages came as a serious lesson. Finally Krocho took up the cudgel:

"Now, friend, let me tell you something: You haven't the right idea of spiritualism at all. That friend of yours came to this circle, and came to you, for no reason except to help you; to place you in a better frame of mind; to uplift you and turn your thoughts to higher things. Her message to you is not a joke and it is not a thing to be made light of. She did not come because she needs you. She came because you need her. What she is trying to do is to take you out of yourself and raise your thoughts to a level where your mind will be receptive and ready to grasp the great truths of the hereafter. And while she does this you laugh and make light of it. You are removing the stones she places in the brook as steps for you to cross over the waters on to the green sod to a brighter and happier path. It is no joke and it is no time to make puns. When you are alone in your room tonight you call upon your friends on the spirit side of life to give you a better understanding of these things; to place you in a more reverend mind toward spiritual things. Then when you come to a seance room again draw a straight clear line, wide enough so it can be seen, and let that line stand between the serious and the frivolous. Leave the frivolous things behind you for an hour or so and don't cross that line. You need not put on a long, blue face. That's isn't the idea at all. That isn't what we teach. We teach happiness, cheerfulness, brightness and a clean, wholesome good humor for everybody. But when your friends come to you with the message from the Master and say: "Be of good cheer I am with you," take it as it comes and follow that precept in the spirit in which it is given. Then you will come into an understanding of this great law and not until then will you know the happiness and the truth of it."

MEMORANDUM REPORT OF PHYSICAL MANIFESTATION

At Developing Class at Residence of Mr. and Mrs. Victor H. Severy, 4304 S. Western Ave., Los Angeles, Wednesday P. M. Jan. 18th, 1922.

This class is now closed with ten members. All were present. Miss McClain, medium, led in prayer; then followed two hymns. After this a period of silence. In a few moments more Mrs. Severy became entranced. We were all convinced that the trance state was much deeper than at any previous meeting and looked for something unusual to happen.

Note:—These seances are held in a small room which will comfortably seat a class of this size. The only furniture in this room besides the chairs is a small center piece on which are usually placed a few flowers. In the ceiling, about center, is a direct light with a red bulb. This light can be adjusted from within the cabinet at the will of the guides.

One corner of the room is partitioned off by a curtain of heavy material, making a small cabinet. This curtain is a mottled affair, something on the order of a Turkish portiere. Running clear across the curtain, about 18 inches apart, are parallel broad stripes, perhaps six inches wide. The curtain is in two pieces. Mrs. Severy takes a seat in front of this curtain and remains in full view of the entire class all the time she is entranced.

Big Chief, the Indian who controls her, appeared just for a moment, etherealized and indistinct; then returned to the cabinet.

Next came two transformations (or transfigurations) similar to those described in report of seance of Jan. 4th, 1922. These were merely the heads and faces of women unknown to any one in the circle. They did not speak and at the time seemed to have come for no particular purpose, unless—as we suspected—the guides were leading up to some special demonstration.

These transfigurations are supposed to be formed by the guides drawing from each and every one in the circle as much of the "aura," or "fluidic emanation," as may be required for the purpose. The formations change gradually, one disappearing slowly as the other takes its place, the new one coming as gradually as the retiring one fades away. To the sitters they seem to take the place for the time being of the head and face of the medium and her own features are not at all visible (or distinguishable) until the spirit form retires.

Then came a gentleman's head. On being interrogated by Mr. Severy he gave the name of "Dr. Grayson" and said there were a number of physicians and chemists present and that we were going to witness an unusual phenomenon—something that had never yet been tried in this part of the world.

The Doctor then disappeared leaving Mrs. Severy's face visible. Another moment and her head and face were no longer to be seen. For a time it appeared as if the guides had covered her completely from her shoulders up with a black cloth.

But on closer observation we all decided that this could not be the case, for the reason that even the outline of the form above the shoulders had disappeared. Further, the broad stripes in the curtain against which she sat were clearly visible all the way across the curtain, instead of a portion of the stripes being obstructed as would be the case if her head were in its normal position. To the observers it appeared precisely as if her head had been dematerialized. We all looked very closely, studied the conditions carefully and discussed them in detail among ourselves.

During this time her hands gradually grew smaller and smaller. For a short period—perhaps four or five minutes—her left hand was completely obliterated and the right hand partially so.

At this point we recalled writings of psychic phenomena brought about by the "adepts" or "masters" of India who produce the most startling phenomena by the aid of a certain vital force which has been known to the Hindoos since ancient days. This is some force never understood by physicists of the earth plane, but seems to be much used by the spirit chemists. It is presumed to be in the air and in and around human beings as well, and the guides are supposed to draw upon the air and upon the members in the circle for this force.

While we were discussing this subject a figure appeared above the shoulders of Mrs. Severy, announcing that he was the chemist guide; stated that we were correct about this particular force being used in our circle and he spelled and pronounced it very clearly and slowly—"A-k-a-s-h-a—Akasha."

By the aid of this force they appear to be even able to dematerialize portions of the human form. The guide stated that they were using this force for our benefit and that this was only the beginning of the phenomena that would come later.

When the chemist guide disappeared Mrs. Severy's head and face gradually returned until it was again normal and visible, although she was still in a deep trance. She then reached out her hands and her arms were nearly twice their normal length. She raised partially from her chair—more as if she had been levitated—reached toward the middle of the room again; then gradually returned to her seat.

Suddenly both of her arms, still elongated abnormally, shot up over her head as quick as a flash. There was a short metallic click (which appeared to come from the throat) and she was again conscious, with all of her faculties normal.

As a rule we all have some of our friends from the spirit side visit us at this developing class. But this was not the case tonight. None of us felt the presence of any one except the transfigurations and it was evident that the guides were conserving the strength of the entire class for this particular work.

From the various experiences of the members of the circle as to their feelings during these manifestations, they all appear to have felt something unusual—some of them expressed it as if numbness had overtaken them; one as if he were being raised from the floor in his chair and others as being chilled through. Personally,

I felt nothing unusual beyond a few moments of slight nervousness, such as might come from an excess of coffee.

But whatever the effect it was undoubtedly the result of the demand made upon our vitality to bring out these phenomena, and this seems borne out in a brief speech made by one of the guides speaking through Miss McLain in about this language:

"We wish to thank you all for your cooperation in this effort. But do not think it is for no purpose. We are leading you by degrees to higher work and you will all be greatly helped by the results yet to come. We have used largely of your strength tonight and may do so again, but it will return to you and well repay you. You have been patient; the class is harmoniously blended and there is much in each of you that we can use. Do not fear for the medium. Your circle was well attended by a school of physicians and chemists who have guarded her at every step. We are protecting her health, both in the circle and in the home, and we must not keep you longer."

Note:—The above description of this strange phenomenon may be more or less ambiguous and involved; but a study of the subject from the very few who have touched upon it at all, will convince the investigator that none of them understand it very well or know much about it. And it will doubtless always remain an obscure subject until such time as more perfect communication is established between the earth and the spirit sides of life.

FULL REPORT OF TRUMPET SEANCE

Held at Residence of Mrs. Mary Miller, Los Angeles, Calif., One O'Clock Thursday P. M., January 19th, 1922.

I stepped into the seance room alone while Mrs. M. went out to emerse her trumpet and while waiting for her stood in front of the picture of "Sunbeam" (Mrs. M's. guide at the flower message service at the church) and carried on a little imaginary conversation with her to see if she would make any mention of it through the trumpet.

As soon as the light was turned out the room became full of etheralized spirit forms and spirit lights were plentiful, coming and going in shades and sparks and flashes. Two large lights, as big as one's fist, settled down upon the floor a little to the left of my chair and remained there during the entire seance. These two lights resembled the lighted embers of a wood fire with plenty of life still in them.

Mrs. Miller began: "There is a tall, well built, handsome Hindoo priest standing at your right and just a little back of your chair. He has a beard and moustache, a white turban on his head and dresses in the robes of a Hindoo priest. He holds in his hand a pair of scales, such as you have seen to symbolize justice, and seems to be weighing out something for you."

At this point Dr. Worthington (Mrs. M's. trumpet guide) spoke up: "Well, good afternoon, Mr. Goerner; I am glad to see you again. You didn't know that I was in your office a couple of times lately. Your friend, Jim and his son John and I were all there together. We sat around and made ourselves at home and took in the general situation. You had some important business that day and we wanted to bring strength enough to give you the right thoughts and see that you were protected. You haven't had justice altogether done you and we want to right this condition for you. Jim will talk more with you about these visits. How are you today, Mr. Goerner?"

Answer: "I'm very fine, thank you doctor; and how are you—but I guess it seems foolish to ask spirit folks about their health—they are always well."

Worthington: "Yes, that's right; you know we have none of the physical ills of the body and have no worries of material things. But our hearts are often saddened, Mr. Goerner, when we look at conditions on the earth plane—the strife and ill-feeling among nations and individuals—it pains the heart and seems all so useless when just a little love all around would make the world so different. Well, I will not talk longer; the room is filled with your folks and you are going to have a wonderful chat with them. Goodbye."

Mother next took the trumpet, greeted me with: "God bless you, my son· I am so happy to be able to talk with you again. I have been looking forward to this meeting. I was with you all day Sunday and was out to the dinner party with you. We were all there and enjoyed the visit with you and your friends."

I asked: "Mother, weren't you in my room last Tuesday morning early?"

Answer: "Yes, I was; I talked with you on the pillow. Your sister Clara was also there and sister Annie. Annie wanted us to come and see her materialize in the alcove for you and she feels so proud that she can do so well."

George: "I also saw Jim Thomas walking across the room and got a very clear look at him."

Answer: "Yes, son; that was the day you had some important business on hand and he wanted to impress you while you were still asleep. He walked back and forth in your room studying it out and putting thoughts in your mind."

George: "Well, mother, I saw Clara quite clearly—where did she stand?"

Answer: "She stood leaning against the tall dresser facing you. (Correct). I am so glad that we can all reach you this way and know that you can see us and hear us. It brings us all a great deal of happiness. We didn't have much success trying to talk at Mrs. Jonsons the other night, did we? The room was so full of your friends and there were so many waiting for a chance to use the trumpets. Well, I always come when I can and when I don't speak, remember I am with you every day. Goodbye, son." Throwing kisses through the trumpet she handed it to Clara.

"Well, George, it looks as if you were going back to my old town of Philadelphia. Jim is looking after some business there for you and if he tells you to go, it will be a wise move. You wont be there long—just three or four weeks. Jim is very much interested in your business affairs and he and John are working for you. To me it would seem like going back to old friends to visit you there."

I asked: "Well, if I should go you are all going with me, aren't you?"

"Oh, sure, brother; we'll all be there and come back to California with you too. I want you to stop off in Chicago and see all the children and tell them about the talks we have had; give them the messages and show them how to get into communication with me. I am going to guide you to a good medium for them and you will be led to the right place. Make it clear to the children and once the door is opened to them it will be easy after that. Goodbye, brother."

Another voice through the trumpet called: "Its Annie, brother."

I answered: "Well, hello, sister. I'm glad to hear from you and want to thank you for the wonderful work you have been doing in my room."

Answer: "Oh, George, I am so proud that I can come to you this way and give you such strong proof that there is no death; that we do live; that we do come back and we can talk with you and guide you and help you. I am soon going to be able to materialize strong enough to walk all around the room for you and sit down and talk with you."

Question: "Sister, can you always see me when I sit up in bed and can you always catch my voice when I talk with you?"

Answer: "Why, of course, I can, and it makes me so happy to know that you recognize me and when you speak to me you will always notice my light get brighter. That's the way I answer—that's my signal. You see I am not strong enough yet to speak aloud and am too far away from you to throw my voice to you in a whisper; but if you will watch the next time you will see the light get brighter when you speak. I am going to bring a wonderful light to Mrs. Miller with me the next time we meet here, because I want you to see it; then you will know that it wont be long before I can materialize for you at will."

At this point there was a lull in her speech and I asked:

"How is little Georgie, sister?"

Answer: "Oh, he's fine and just impatient to get the trumpet and talk with you." She handed the trumpet to Georgie and the message came:

"Hello, Uncle George; I heard you ask after me. Do you know that I go down the street with you every day? When you swing your arm then I take hold of your little finger and go through the crowds with you. I went in the automobile with you Sunday. Didn't we have a nice ride?"

Minnie came in with her usual announcement: "How do, George; its Minnie. I told you I'd make up for the chat we didn't get at Mrs. Jonsons. There was so much confusion there Monday night; you know how hard I tried to reach you; but it was no use."

George: "Yes, but was that the last time you tried to speak with me?"

Answer: "Why, no. I talked with you on your pillow this morning and there is never a night goes that I don't come to your room just to be with you again. You heard my voice this morning and carried on a little conversation with me. I am always glad to confirm these visits, because I know that you are anxious to get us all identified. But you are safe against intrusions. No one interferes with our work and the way is clear for us all to reach you direct."

I asked: "Minnie, do you remember the very last time that you and I talked together on the earth side?"

Answer: "Yes, it was in the hallway in the old school; you, sister Annie and I were all together."

George: "That's right; but what I wanted to ask was this: I never saw you again after that, and I wondered so often how it happened that I never met you in Washington during all those years. How long after the talk in the hall was it before you passed out?"

Answer: "Just about four years, George; and as soon as my body was in the grave and I opened my eyes to consciousness and knew that I was still alive, I began trying to reach you. I always loved you and you were so good and thoughtful of me that I felt you belonged to me; and I waited and worked all these years to get within your vibration. I never married and I passed away very soon after brother Seth did."

I replied: "I can understand now how much happiness I have missed by not getting into spiritualism long ago. If I had only known what I know now, we could have met and talked many years ago."

Answer: "Yes, but its all right now, George. We are very close to each other and I can see you and talk with you every day; and when you come over on this side I will meet you at the border and we will go through eternity together. I am so happy at the way you have changed since you had your eyes opened to this wonderful life, and we are all helping you to live so there will be no loss of time for you when you pass over. It is nothing to fear, George; it is just going from one plane to a better and a higher one. You can only die once; but you live forever and progress never ceases. Goodbye."

I interrupted with: "If it becomes necessary for me to go east you will go with me, wont you?"

Answer: "Indeed I will, George. Just go to any medium and I will talk with you, and you will hear me in your room just the same. We will all be with you; the distance will make no difference. Soon you will be able to see me and hear me better."

I asked: "Will you still have on your little blue and white gingham apron that you used to wear at school?"

"No, George. I don't have to wear them any more; I prefer to come to you in my robes; but I could come in the little apron if it were necessary for the purposes of identification; but you can recognize me too easily without that."

Came next a strong cheerful voice: "Hello, old pal; this is Jim. See me take up your own trumpet?"

George: "Yes, I can see it moving up toward the ceiling. Glad to hear from you, Jim; and I want to tell you what a wonderfully strong appearance you made in my room last Tuesday morning. I could see you moving about the room—stronger than I can see you now. I have been wondering if you knew that I recognized you."

Jim: "Oh, yes; when you sat up in bed and looked right at me I knew that you could see me and knew who I was. That was the morning you had an important meeting and I wanted to impress you with what to say. I didn't want you to commit yourself too strong to the big fellow and the little Hebrew. I have visited the office in Philadelphia and looked the situation over. It looks good, George. I think you are going to be well pleased and get better results there. You talk to me again in about a week. I don't like the attitude the little Hebrew takes. He's too much for himself and gives no justice to either you or the company. Go slow with him and talk with me again in a week or ten days. In the meantime I'll ferret this thing out a little farther for you. But its coming out all right and you are holding your own nicely."

I asked: "Jim, if it becomes best for me to go east on this thing, I want you and John to go along; because I expect to talk with you all from there the same as I do here."

Jim: "Don't have any worry about that. We will be there and you will feel our presence every time you go into that office, and we'll stay with you until it is all over. Then when we've got you on your feet we are going to give you some suggestions as to how to use your prosperity for a good cause, and you will find more happiness in that than anything else in the world."

John followed his father, confirming the visits to the office with Jim and Dr. Worthington. I took occasion to thank him for his materialization at Jonsons last Friday, stating that I felt very proud of the fine strong appearance he made and got the reply:

"You didn't feel any prouder than I did. I worked a whole week to make that appearance and was glad that you could recognize me, because you only saw me through my photographs at home in Denver. Little Kitty did great work in helping me to get through. I'll try it again sometime when the opportunity is favorable. I am with you and father in your new business undertakings and we are going to pull this thing through. Don't worry about that."

I thanked him for his efforts and before putting down the trumpet got this: "George, I want to tell you what a wonderful spirit that sweetheart of yours is—and she's so happy when she can reach you and talk with you. We all think a great deal of Minnie and we have a little fun now and then joking with her about you. We know how proud you are of her and you have reason to be. I am going now. Mother wants to say a word to you."

Mrs. Thomas asked that I be sure and see Gordon in Chicago on my way east and show him how to get in communication with his mother. "That will make me so happy, Mr. Goerner, and Gordon is not going to be so hard to convince as you may think. He will be interested right away and will soon talk with me."

Jim again took the trumpet just to tell me that: "I got away with the mouthpiece of your trumpet."

I asked: How he happened to do that and got the reply:

"Just thought I'd take it off and dematerialize it. May be when you come back to Mrs. Miller's again I'll put it back on the trumpet. But you can look all over the room and you wont find it. Its gone for the present."

Goerner: "Jim, how is this dematerializing done?"

Jim: "Its very simple;—just the proper combination of chemicals. Kitty can tell you all about it. She dematerializes chocolates."

Next Kitty came to the trumpet laughing: "Hello, Mr. Goerner. Don't you know how things are dematerialized? We just work over the different chemicals and everything that's solid gradually dissolves. That's the way the chocolates went; but you know we get a certain food sustenance out of them."

I put in with: "By the way, Kitty; I've got a bone to pick with you."

Kitty: "Why?"

Goerner: "Somebody told me that you whispered in a fellow's ear that you didn't come out after those chocolates yourself; that you sent a substitute to get them."

Kitty: "Yes, that's what Mr. Severy said at Mrs. Jonsons; but it isn't true, Mr. Goerner. I came out after them myself and dematerialized them myself. The little bird that whispered to Mr. Severy was joking with him."

Next little Mary Ellen came with this: "Uncle George you didn't bring me any rose last Sunday night."

Goerner: "I know it, dearie; but I didn't go to church. I was at a dinner party."

Mary: "I was there with you—we were all there. I went with you and your friends in the automobile. They are nice people and I like them."

Goerner: "Well, dearie, who else was in the auto with us?"

Answer: "I sat on your knee; little Georgie sat on the other knee and Minnie stood up in front of us against the glass."

Note:—This was a Stevens car with a glass shield between the rear seat and the front seat. I sat in the back seat.

I continued: "If you will come to church next Sunday night I'll bring you a beautiful rose and mark it for you."

Answer: "I'll tell you what to do: You pick one rose out of the bunch for me; put the bunch on the table and hide my rose and see if I can find it."

Goerner: "That will be fine, dearie. Do you think you can do it?"

Answer: "I'll try. I can if there isn't too much confusion in the church."

Finally Harold Cook came in with: "Hello, George; this is Harold. Always glad to be with you, and if I don't talk often just remember there is never a day goes by that I am not with you some part of the day. Father is here today—just came in to be with you. You know he thinks of you as one of his sons. He says he is going to talk with you through the trumpet soon, but wont try it today."

Goerner: "Harold, is your mother still on the earth side, and how is brother Walter?"

Harold: "Yes, mother is still on earth. She is getting very feeble and will be out of the body before many weeks. We are preparing to take care of her here. Walter is doing fine; he has a nice law practice now and getting very prominent. I can see them all every day; but I prefer to meet them on the spirit side. The earth has no more attraction for me except to chat with my own friends and try to help them. There is so much more freedom and contentment when you are once out of the physical body and away from material cares. Well, goodbye, old pardner; I'll come again."

This from Sunbeam: "Hello, Mr. Goerner; I heard you talking to my picture and you said you wondered if I could hear you and if I would tell you about it. You know now that I heard you. I like to come to you this way; because I love all of your friends and I love your guides and I was glad to hear you chatting with me when you stood in front of my picture. Goodbye."

Dr. Worthington closed the seance with this: "You have had a fine visit with your friends and I have enjoyed it just as much as you have, and your medium enjoys having them come too. They are so considerate of her. I just want to say that your friend Jim is a strong guide for you and he is so interested in helping you along. You stick right with him, Mr. Goerner. The Hindoo priest who came in is an ancient scholar and he has been attracted to you. From now on he is going to stay pretty close to you. His scales represent justice for you and he can do a great deal to see that you get it. Goodbye, and God bless you, friend and brother."

Note:—On the Sunday following this seance, I took a cluster of roses to the church, placed them on the table for the flower service, but first pulled one out of the bunch to hide for Mary Ellen. I placed it in my right hand coat pocket and took a seat in the front row of the church. When Mrs. Miller was reading the message from the roses she said:

"A spirit child steps up and says she is Mary Ellen and that there is one rose missing. She says, Uncle George hid it. Its in his pocket—on the right side—in his coat—and I want my rose." Mrs. Miller then came to where I sat and held out her hand, saying: "Let me have it because she wants me to get it for her."

Comment:—Those who have read this record thoughtfully cannot very well question the identity of the communicators. Their intimacy of my affairs and the accuracy of their references to them are significant.

I had only told one living person of my Philadelphia negotiations and that person never visits mediums. I am the only one living on the earth plane who knew of the last meeting between Minnie and myself and those present at that meeting. My spirit friends must certainly have been at the dinner party Sunday to have known so much about it and the auto ride in the car with the glass shield.

There is also much proof in the various references to the visits to my room and my office; the important business meeting; the mention of the attitude of the "little Hebrew;" Harold Cook's remarks as to his brother Walter's law practice; mother's reference to the crowd at the Jonson trumpet seance; Kitty's comments on the statement of Mr. Severy at the Jonsons as to the recipient of the chocolates, etc., etc.

With these references in view, if the reader has kept the preceding chain of facts in mind he will find in this volume "cumulative evidence" enough to furnish all the conviction he can ask. These communicators have made good their claim . They have proven their identity—the continuity of life—spirit return—spirit communication —the survival of memory and personality.

REPORT ON PHYSICAL MANIFESTATION

At Seance Held at Residence of Mr. and Mrs. Severy, 4304 S. Western Ave., Los Angeles, Wednesday 8 O'Clock P. M., January 25th, 1922.

The phonograph was placed in the seance room as an experiment to see what results it would have on the work. But even when reduced to its lowest tones it made too much noise for the size of the room, and Mrs. S. suggested that the music be eliminated until after she became entranced; then try it again.

The result, however did not seem to meet the approval of the guides, and "Big Chief" informed us that the "noise was too big; stop it and may-be try again after a time." So the music was dispensed with for the rest of the seance.

We began with a trifle brighter light than on the previous Wednesday. Later "Big Chief" instructed us to give him less light. This was adjusted and we asked him if it was then satisfactory and received the reply, "Yes, all right now."

The demonstration throughout was about the same as reported for the last Wednesday class; although the changes in the transformations were not so many, nor were the changes as rapid. Big Chief explained this by saying that the guides had been experimenting with a new control, but that the new control "would not fit" and Big Chief had to come back.

During the transfigurations several spirit forms appeared; but only two of them spoke and this in whispers barely audible. One gave the name of "Pearl" and stated that she was a guide for Mr. McIntyre; that she did not know him on this earth and he would not recognize her last name.

For a considerable time after Mrs. S. became entranced, a bright light played about her forehead and the upper portion of her face. Finally this assumed the shape of a star and became brighter for an instant at a time, changing both in place and brightness.

Dr. G. called attention of the class to this and when some one remarked, "maybe that's what she is trying to show us" the spirit form nodded her head up and down and answered, "Yes."

Several times during the evening the whole face, head and neck, and once or twice the shoulders, were entirely obliterated and could not be seen even on the closest observation. This part of the work was practically the same as on the previous Wednesday, except that while the disappearance of the head seemed as complete, it appeared and disappeared oftener and more rapidly. Before becoming totally invisible the face would turn dark as the blackest kind of cloth, the dark shades showing first as blotches, then covering the entire face.

Both of the hands of the medium turned dark very gradually; and no less than three times the right hand was obliterated altogether. It simply seemed to have dematerialized.

Finally, the medium leaned forward and began (apparently) drawing in strength from the circle. The left hand remained stationary on the arm of the chair, while the right hand was extended slightly toward the center of the circle, and the fingers began a very unusual and very rapid motion of twisting, turning, extending forward and coming backward, folding and unfolding with some of the quickest motions I have ever seen in a human hand.

A few moments of this and the control whispered to Mr. Severy that they had already taken a great deal of strength from the members present; that the work for the evening had been of an experimental character and was merely to enable the guides to lead up to more important demonstrations to follow.

Miss McLain, the medium in charge of the class, became entranced for a few moments. This came through no effort on her part and was presumably influenced by the guides, or control, for some purpose in their work; but was the first time that this had occured at the developing class.

Before the close of the seance two of Miss McL's. guides spoke through her commenting on the progress of the work, complimented the class for its patience and assuring us of satisfactory results from the work now being done. The messages concluded with a brief lecture on the psychic law; advised perfect harmony among all members, both in the class and out of it and finished with, "God bless you all; we greet you with love and light, power and truth."

Comment:—Personally, I am still asking what can be the object of these dramatic phenomena and what special good can come of them? For the present I am trying to content myself with the assurance given us by one of the guides that we must "not think it is for no purpose; we are leading you up by degrees to higher work and you will all be greatly helped by the results yet to come."

This recalls another seance which I attended not long ago, at which the spirit control was asked why the necessity of these startling manifestations and the reply came:

"Why was it necessary to crucify Christ to bring about his phenomenal resurrection before the world would accept him? You have not changed so much during these two thousand years. You will accept the truth only through some such dynamic evidence."

MEMORANRUM ON MATERIALIZATION SEANCE

Held at Residence of Mr. and Mrs. J. B. Jonson, 855 N. Marengo Ave., Pasadena, Cal., Friday 8 O'Clock P. M., January 27th, 1922 Under arrangement with the Society for Advanced Psychical Research.

The Jonsons had just moved into their new home and were still somewhat doubtful about the results they could get under the changed conditions, until such time as the seance room and cabinet became well magnetized.

The room selected for this purpose is on the second floor of the house, away from the noise of the street and the usual flashing of automobile lights through the windows. This room is approximately 16x20 ft. and will comfortably seat the full circle of 20 members when the chairs are arranged in a horse shoe against the walls, and leave plenty space for the spirit forms to come well down into the room if they are so disposed.

The cabinet merely consisted of a commodious closet-room with drawers for storing linen, etc. At one end of this room is a door leading to an adjoining room; but no door at the front end of the closet. Across the front entrance a black curtain was drawn, the same as was done at the cabinet in the old home on Vermont Avenue. The door at the end of this "cabinet" was sealed with a broad strip of paper, extending from the door across the jamb and this strip would necessarily be broken if the door were opened.

Knowing, as we do, however, that the spirits themselves could remove and replace this strip if they so desired, we attach no particular importance to this. But rely partly upon the fact that the medium is in full view of all the members of the soceity during nearly the entire time of the seance, and principally upon our intimate knowledge of Mr. and Mrs. Jonson, their past record, their integrity and the genuineness of their work.

The light used for this occasion gave considerable trouble all during the evening. The slide door to the box in which the light is placed did not work satisfactorily and the cord leading from the light to the cabinet gave further trouble; so that we had seldom light enough to see the forms clearly except upon a very "close-up" inspection. This condition will be remedied between now and the next seance.

There was a full attendance, lacking one member. The work began promptly at eight o'clock, the seance opening with the Lord's prayer and singing a couple of hymns.

Mr. Jonson became entranced sitting on a stool in front of the cabinet and in the presence of the circle. This was evidenced first by very heavy, loud breathing, a little coughing and after this he moved about freely in front of the curtain.

"Gray Feather" made known his presence by his usual greeting to the circle with his characteristic Indian accent. Mrs. J. then asked if Gray Feather had a good hold on his medium, to which she received reply, "Oh, yes, me got good hold." She then asked if he would give Mrs. Baker a treatment for her throat and spine trouble. Mrs. Baker stepped to the center of the room; Gray Feather passed his hands around her throat and up and down the spine. Mrs. Baker's statement was the same as after the previous treatment, viz.: "I can feel the electric sparks going clear through me and feel some relief."

The first form to appear was Viola. She announced in whispers that it required more effort to materialize under the new conditions, and that the light was not conducive to the best results; required too much strength to manipulate; but she knew these conditions would improve. The light was too dim to show the face distinctly; though we have become so accustomed to Viola's appearance that we had no difficulty recognizing her from the general form.

Mr. Oaks' wife's sister was the second spirit to come before the curtain. She was unknown to any one in the circle except Mr. Oaks and he seemed satisfied with the identification said there was not much room for doubt, that to all appearances as to face and figure it was his sister-in-law.

Figure No. 3 was Mr. Baker's mother. She was greeted by Mr. B and his wife and both vouched for the likeness and the bits of identification procured in a brief conversation.

No. 4 was an unknown lady, quite elderly, who pointed to Mr. Drake, the vice president of the society, and upon his going to the curtain and asking if she was for him, received assent by nodding her head, although she did not appear to be strong enough to even whisper. He failed to identify the visitor.

No. 5 was Mrs. Jacobs' son, "Bobbie." This is always a strong, delightful character; stands erect with his head up and shoulders back and chats with his mother in a very distinct whisper which can be heard by most of the circle. He retreated to the curtain and his mother started back to her seat, when Bobbie stepped up to her, patted her on the shoulder and announced: "Mother soon I am coming right over and sit down beside you in the circle."

No. 6 was Minnie and after the usual greetings I asked if she hadn't spoken to me on the pillow early that morning and received the reply:

"Yes, I was there to tell you that I would come tonight this way. I tried to bring sister Annie with me; but the vibration is not good tonight. It will improve later. We are always happy to come to you and will do so as often as we can. Can you recognize me?"

I replied: "I certainly can; you look perfectly natural and as sweet as a rose." She thanked me for the compliment, bade me goodbye, threw out a kiss and gradually receded toward the floor until she disappeared.

No. 7 was Henry Marshall, who comes as a guide to the Lombards. The first time Marshall appeared, several weeks ago, he seemed hardly able to hold up his head and could not even speak in a whisper. Since then repeated visits have made an improvement, until he now comes as a very strong spirit, speaks in a clear, audible tone and steps before the curtain with plenty of life. This case seems to bear out the statement frequently made to us by the "other side" that they gather strength for these materializations by repeated efforts. We have seen this demonstrated a number of times in the trumpet class.

No. 8 was a brother to the Misses Worrals; stated that he could not come through the curtain tonight, but would do so another time. The Worrals have had these visits so often that they no longer question the identity. The weakness was no doubt due to the same cause—strange surroundings and vibrations not yet quite in tune.

No. 9. "Catharine," the guide to Mr. and Mrs. Majors, is always a strong spirit and seems to overcome local conditions that might usually be expected to work against good results. She complained, however, that the light was "on the bum" and said things were "mixed up." She carried on quite a conversation with the Majors and diappeared in view of the circle in front of the curtain.

At this point Gray Feather picked up his stool and went into the cabinet to add strength to the helpers, or "guides." This seemed to have its effect and the forms again began to appear more rapidly.

"Big Heart," Mr. Lombard's control, came as No. 10 and brought with him good light and strength; spoke above a whisper and had no trouble making himself heard. His visit, however, was brief and he disappeared with the curtains parted and so those close to the cabinet could see him go.

While the circle was discussing the good luck of the Jonsons in procuring the particular location which they did, Kitty spoke through the curtain with:

"I wouldn't let anybody else get the house. They came to see it lots of time but we wouldn't let 'em get it." She then gave us a pun which no one in the circle seemed to catch. We asked what she said. It was repeated and we asked for it again; then the third time and got the reply, a little out of patience:

"Oh, never mind it now."

Comment:—Those who have followed the record of past seances to date, will note that this particular seance may be called "tame" in comparison with some of the results of other meetings. There is always a reason for this. A change in the arrangement of the sitters will often influence results. Some lack of harmony on the part of any of the members will do the same thing. Illness is another cause; too much or to little light; a damp or foggy atmosphere will have its effect; the right kind of music is beneficial—the wrong kind offsetting; too much noise in the seance room is detrimental and the same thing may be said of too great silence. We are often told, "to say something—start the vibration."

Perhaps this will answer the question of those critics who persist in asking: "If a medium claims he can do these things in his own home, in his own cabinet, why can't he do them anywhere else at any time?"

He can't. He can't even always do them in his own home nor in his own cabinet. He is subject to the laws of both this earth and the psychic world, as well as his own changing temperament. I have known the medium to have to dismiss his entire circle because he could get absolutely nothing on that particular occasion. He is much like the chemist viz: he can only get the same reaction when all conditions are the same. It takes time and patience to get the best results and those who are prone to condemn all psychic phenomena because their first seance brings no evidence, had better let it alone altogether.

MEMORANDUM OF PSYCHIC EXPERIENCE

Monday A. M., 5 O'Clock, January 30th, 1922.

Los Angeles had a dreary rainy day for Sunday, the 29th, and I hesitated about taking any flowers to the evening service at the Spiritualist Church, assuming that Mrs. Miller would probably not be there to deliver the usual messages.

During the afternoon it occurred to me to try an experiment. I argued that if the folks on "the other side" were in my room as often as I believe they are, and as often as their own statements would indicate, they would be just as likely to be with me in my room as in the church, although in the absence of a developed medium it might be more difficult for them to make their presence known. From their own statements, they are usually with me when I purchase the flowers for this purpose.

I, therefore, procured half a dozen fresh carnations, embellished with a little fern; placed them in a pitcher of water on a stand beside my bed and under the pitcher a slip of paper on which I had written a name for each flower—One for mother, one for sister Clara, one for sister Annie, one for Minnie, one for little Mary Ellen and one for Mrs. Thomas.

My idea was to see whether or not they would indicate to me at the next trumpet seance that they knew what I had done and were cognizant of the presence of the flowers in my room. This part of the experiment cannot be determined until the Jonson seance tonight or at Mrs. Miller's later in the week.

I retired about 9.30. Early in the morning I was awakened with a distinct feeling that there was some one in my room. Strangely enough when these visits come they never produce a sudden awakening, nor is there the slightest fear or feeling of what might be called a "spooky" nature. On the contrary, the feeling to me is invariably one as if my mind had been put in a calm condition before waking and I open my eyes without any surprise at finding some one moving about the room.

On the right side of my bed and leaning directly over me stood my mother. Her face was within twelve inches of my own. I could see her clearly, but asked:

"Is that you mother?" and in reply she nodded her head, "Yes," very positively. I answered:

"Well, bless your heart, dear mother; I'm awfully glad to have you come this way. This is just fine. Did you come to see the flowers I bought?"

Again she nodded her head, yes. Standing at her side and a little back of her was my father. I spoke again:

"Isn't that father beside you?" and he replied with the same nod of the head. I continued:

"This is as good as a materialization meeting. I can see sister Annie in the alcove; she is doing wonderful work and I have grown to recognize her light."

Again mother nodded her head in assent and I continued to talk, trying to hold the vibration as long as possible. I addressed a few remarks to Annie:

"Don't you know I have missed you, sister, during the three evenings you didn't come; but I figured it out that you had been saving your strength for the materialization at Jonsons."

At this she threw out a much brighter light, probably in response to my question. I then asked:

"Did you know I just had a nice letter from your little daughter, Naomi?" Again the light brightened and I recalled what Annie had told me at the Miller trumpet seance, that I could recognize her answers by the light signals.

I asked mother and father if they would be with me at the trumpet seance and confirm this meeting, and again got a nod of the head, indicating, "Yes."

There was still a fourth figure in the room, but I could not see the face plainly enough to make up my mind who it could be. All I could see of this was a pair of eyes standing back of father and mother, and still a little to the right. I asked mother if sister Clara was with her, but at this she stepped a little farther back, and I supposed it was to give me a better view of the fourth figure, but I could not determine whether the reply was "Yes" or "No."

Then mother again stepped close to my bed, leaned over me again and her face was plainly seen and I would certainly recognize it as my mother. I asked if she would soon be able to stay with me longer and if I would be able to carry on a conversation with her. Again she nodded, "Yes."

Father and mother then disappeared; but sister Annie continued in the alcove for at least half an hour afterwards, and twice came within three feet of my bed. I kept speaking in a natural tone and asked if Minnie was in the room, but received no reply that I could definitely accept as "Yes" or "No."

Just at this point I dropped back on my pillow and heard Minnie calling my name and giving her own name. There was no other response and I felt that my visitors were gone.

I got up and looked at the watch. It was just 5.30 and I figure that about 30 minutes had elapsed from the time I first woke up to the time I turned on the light.

Spirit lights were plentiful in the room and I could readily see the light which most invariably comes with mother at the trumpet meetings.

During all this time I could "sense" the presence of still another spirit besides mother, father, sister Annie and the pair of eyes. This fifth party I now presume to have been Minnie, as she spoke on the pillow almost immediately after I asked sister Annie if Minnie was there.

Mother had her hair combed the same as when she was on earth —parted right through the middle and combed in waves down toward the side of the head. At her throat was a sort of a white collar, which seemed to have been made of lace and this was ruffled, after the fashion of collars commonly worn about forty years ago. The rest of her apparel I could not make out, except that the dress was of some dark material. Father was dressed in dark clothes with a "lay-down" collar, such as he often wore. He wore his beard and moustache and closely duplicated his appearance at the materialization seances. Sister Annie was in robes of white, the same as she always is when materializing.

With reference to the visits from sister Annie: These have been going on for fully three weeks, almost nightly, and they are every now and then confirmed by Annie or some of the rest of my folks on the spirit side at trumpet seances in the presence of eight to a dozen or more people.

My practice usually is, first to give the folks a chance to verify these visits themselves in the presence of others without any suggestion from me. But if I feel that they are drawing near the end of their message through the trumpet without mentioning it, I make it a point to frame a question or a comment so as to bring it out of them without directly referring to it myself. Usually this latter course is not necessary; they seem proud of these achievements and anxious for a chance to confirm them.

Again I say to the reader, I ask no consideration of the stranger who does not know me and has no means of forming an opinion as to my sanity and veracity. I write these experiences for my own record and not for the benefit of any one else. As I am always alone in my room I have no way of verifying these visits except at some subsequent trumpet seance. But to me personally they are the strongest kind of proof for the reason that I know that there is no other human being in my room, the door is locked, and these manifestations cannot come from any one on the earth side of life.

MEMORANDUM REPORT ON TRUMPET SEANCE

Held at Residence of Mr. and Mrs. Jonson, 855 No. Marengo Ave., Passadena, Calif., Monday P. M., 8 O'Clock, Jan. 30th, 1922.

The weather was disagreeable and those who would go the distance from their homes in Los Angeles to the north end of Pasadena for the satisfaction they might derive from the seance, would naturally be those who are earnestly interested in the work. There were only eight members in the circle besides Mr. and Mrs. J.

The seance opened at 7.30. Father was the first one to speak through the trumpet and when I asked where I had talked with him last he replied:

"We were with you in your room this morning, George."

George: "That's just what I wanted you to confirm. Who was with you?"

Father: "Your mother, sister Clara and sister Annie and Minnie."

George: 'Did you know that I had recognized you?"

Father: "Of course; we couldn't help knowing it when you sat up in bed and talked with us."

George: "Did you know what I had placed on the table beside the bed?"

Father: "Yes, and in the future put your flowers in your room. Don't take them to the church. They belong in the room and will help us to reach you. They give cheerfulness to the room and give us strength. Wasn't it wonderful that we could come to you that way?"

George: "That's what I've been thinking all day, father. I didn't think you could do it without the presence of a medium."

Father: "We didn't; you are the medium. We are developing you for this work so we can get close to you, and these meetings at the Jonsons are a great help to you and to us as well. It will be easier for us the next time."

Sister Annie later took the trumpet and confirmed her visit to the room in this way:

"Brother, you remember what you told me in your room this morning about getting a letter from Naomi?"

George: "Yes, I remember telling you about it, sister."

Annie: "Did you tell her about talking with me?"

George: "I merely opened the way, by hinting at it to see first how she would take it; so I could tell her more the next time."

Annie: "What I want to say is this: You don't need to be as careful about that as you think. Naomi will be interested in every detail and she will believe what you tell her. You will hear from her very soon again."

George: "All right, sister. The next time I write to her I'll give her some pretty strong evidence. And, by the way, dearie, you are doing wonderful work in the alcove in my room and getting stronger all the time."

Annie: "Yes, that's what I want to do. I want you to tell Naomi about it; let her know that there is no death: that I still live and love her and walk beside her every day and I put many thoughts in her mind to make life pleasanter for her. Tell her she can talk with me and I will give her proof that I still live and can come to her and that I am even closer than when I lived in the flesh."

After two or three other voices had spoken to other members in the circle, mother came with this:

"Thank you for the flowers, dear son. I looked at every one of them and knew they were for us and it made me so happy that I could come to you in this way and to know that you could see us and talk with us. The flowers were beautiful and they add so much of cheerfulness to the room. Isn't it wonderful that we could appear to you in that way and make known our existence in the life beyond the veil? But we are lifting the veil for you and you are getting closer to us all the time. I will enjoy meeting you at Mrs. Miller's. You are developing along the right way. We have guided you to good mediums and that helps us as well as you. Goodbye, son." She patted me on the head with the trumpet, then placed it on the table.

Minnie's appearance can never be mistaken. She seems to have adopted a sort of password as a greeting and this is always the same.

"George, this is Minnie. I was glad that you could hear me on the pillow this morning."

George: "I knew you were there, Minnie; but wanted you to confirm it, and I am waiting for the time when I can see you as clearly as I do mother and father and sister Annie."

Minnie: "You will, George. You give such a good vibration and make right conditions and it takes less effort now than it used to."

Then followed a few reminiscences of school days and she seemed greatly pleased at being able to discuss these things again, enjoyed a good hearty laugh over them and put down the trumpet with: "Don't you realize that it is easier for me to see and talk with you, and come to you, than it used to be when I lived on the earth? I will talk with you again at Mrs. Miller's."

Then came a lull and the room was quiet for a moment. I broke the silence by asking:

"Krocho, have you seen my sweet sister Clara anywhere in this room this evening?"

Krocho: "Certainly she's here right now and standing at your chair. She has been here all the time."

Goerner: "Well, if she will just take hold of that horn and give me a little message that's what I've been waiting for."

Clara then spoke, confirmed the visit to my room and said Mary Ellen was looking forward to the next meeting at Mrs. Miller's. I told her that I would be just as pleased as Mary and that I wanted to compliment her on finding her rose at the church a week ago. The reply came, "she felt very proud over that and is so pleased that she could show you that she knew where it was."

Crystal, the little 12 year old guide to Mrs. Majors, came with this request of Mr. M., whom she calls papa:

"Papa, I want you to put up a swing on the porch at your house, so I can come over and swing in it with the little white dog."

Majors: "Well, Crystal, we are thinking of moving to another house soon."

Crystal: "You can take it down then and put up one at the new house. Don't you see the little white dog running around and barking, bow-bow-wow? He's playing with me when he does that; —we have become great friends."

Goerner asked: "Crystal, can the dog actually see you and hear you talk?"

Crystal: "Why, yes, better than the folks can. He knows me as soon as I come out to play with him."

Note:—Mr. and Mrs. Majors have a little white dog. Crystal was never known to the Majors on the earth side and it is hard to deny a pretty strong evidence of spirit intelligence here. If we attempted to argue telepathy, then the telepathy would have to come from the spirit side and would prove spirit existence whether the identity of the spirit were involved or not.

Crystal seemed so happy at being able to talk to us that she expressed herself by saying that she felt "like busting." Then turned the horn toward me and asked:

"Mr. Goerner, was it right for me to use that word?"

I replied: "Yes, its all right, dearie. You talk in a perfectly natural way and that's the way Mr. and Mrs. Majors want to hear you talk."

She thanked me and dropped the trumpet. Following came Timothy and I put this question to him:

"Tim, I am going to ask you a question that I presume has been put to you before, but I didn't happen to be here. At any rate I find none of the scientific writers who have answered it very satisfactorily:

"I am talking about what we call 'spirit cloths.' My father appeared to me at a materialization seance dressed just about as I saw him in life more than 40 years ago. Where did he get the clothes —or how?"

Timothy: "Where did he get the materialized body in which he appeared?"

Goerner: "I understand that is derived by properly combining atoms of physical matter taken from the medium and the rest of the circle."

Timothy: "Correct, and that's exactly the way the clothes are procured. It is nothing but taking advantage of a natural physical law. You know but little of chemistry on your side. You will learn that when you get over on this side. It is no more difficult to produce the clothes than it is the materialized body; in fact, projecting a body in materialized form is the more difficult of the two."

Some one asked: "Tim, do you know whether or not the planet Mars is inhabited?"

Timothy: "I do not know of my own knowledge; but I have been told by some of our higher instructors that it is and that they are far more advanced than your earth; that they are a much older civilization, and that when communication is established between your earth and Mars it will come primarily through the efforts of the Martians. Some of our teachers here seem well advanced on information regarding life on Mars and when the way is clear can give your earth much new knowledge; but you must first be ready to receive it and accept it."

Krocho then spoke; said the vibration was getting low and that Mrs. Jonson had prepared a treat for us and she thought it time to go home. Some one asked if spirit folks can read the minds of earth people and the answer came:

"They can if their minds are worth reading. Many people keep their mind so full of trash that it would not pay to try to dig into it. But if your thoughts are high and your lives as high as your thoughts the spirit side will come to you often and help you to keep that way. Good influences will come to you and surround you on every side and when you are in trouble and everything looks dark around you, if your mind is clean its like an open door and good forces can take hold of you and lift you out of your despair. When you come to the spirit side you will find that our lives are an open book and you will enjoy the free and honest thoughts by which we live. We have no secrets on this side except such as make for love and happiness and charity and lead you on to higher and greater things. Keep your minds sweet and clean friends; look always to the highest standards and the best that's in you, for as you think, so you will live. Goodnight friends and God love you all."

REPORT ON TRUMPET SEANCE

Held at Residence of Mrs. Mary Miller, 1512 Magnolia Ave., Los Angeles, Cal., One O'Clock P. M., Thursday, Feburay 2nd, 1922.—Sitter, G. F. Goerner.

As I entered the seance room I stepped before the picture of "Sunbeam" hanging on the wall. Sunbeam is the spirit guide who controls Mrs. Miller during the "flower service" at the spiritualist church. I again carried on an imaginary conversation with Sunbeam, as I did on the previous visit, to see if she would mention it when speaking through the trumpet.

In the meantime, Mrs. Miller (the medium) had gone out of the room to emerse her trumpet. When she returned I commented upon a recent materialization seance which I had attended at the home of Mr and Mrs. Severy and mentioned the fact that Mrs. Severy was being controlled by an Indian whom we call "Big Chief" because of his huge size, and spoke of the previous night's seance having been postponed on account of Mrs. S's. illness.

Mrs. Miller then closed the door, with my chair close enough to it so that it would have been impossible for any one to have entered the room without my knowing it. The light was turned out and the room in darkness.

Mrs. M. then described a large, heavy set Indian, dressed in the regalia of a chief, and I asked if it was "Big Chief" who controlled Mrs. Severy. He took up the trumpet and spoke in a clear, full voice in broken English with an Indian accent:

"Yes, me hear you call my name. I am chief that controls Severy squaw. Me been with her today. She better now and hold seance next Wednesday. You got nice circle there and me like you and all circle. Me go now. Goodbye."

I thanked him for his visit, assured him that he would always be welcome and to come whenever he felt so disposed. He dropped the trumpet and disappeared, his etherealized form retreating toward the door; then upward as near as I could visualize it.

Dr. Worthington, the spirit control who acts as trumpet guide to Mrs. Miller, and usually opens and closes the seances, gave me the usual greeting: said he was glad to see me looking well and smiling and advised always bringing a cheerful disposition into any seance room,—"by so doing you clear the path for your friends from the spirit side and make it easy for them to reach you." He continued, "your guides and friends have already assembled in the room and are anxious to have another chat with you. So I will bid you good-bye for the present and God bless you, friend and brother."

He was followed by mother and I extended the usual affectionate greeting, the same as any son might extend to his mother on returning home after an absence. She answered:

"My son, I am so happy to be able to come to you in this way and to prove to you again that I still live and that there is no death. I am always happy that you have taken up this wonderful study and made it so easy for us all to come to you and communicate with you.

We are still with you a part of every day and when you go to your room at night I am there. But you know this, son, and it pleases us that you can see us and recognize us and talk with us. Do not be downhearted if business matters drag. Do not get worried. Keep your mind clear and bright. Do not allow depressed feelings to darken the aura that surrounds you. To do so is to make it difficult for the higher forces to reach you within. Hold only good thoughts and keep a high principle. This will bring good influences to you from the spirit side and they will guard you like an armor that cannot be penetrated by evil forces. Let truth, integrity and harmony prevail and keep your eyes on the Master's light. Think on these things and live by these thoughts. Do not be downcast by the disasters of the day. They are part of the discipline that brings strength and character. They bring light after death and open the door into the hereafter. You have a long life on your side yet and can do much good. We are helping you to live that your coming to our side may be a day of rejoicing for us all."

I thanked her for her materialization in my room Monday morning and remarked that I did not think it possible for her to do this without the presence of a medium, but she replied:

"You were all the medium that we needed. We have been developing you for this purpose and much happiness will come to you through this work. Goodbye, son—goodbye." Throwing kisses through the trumpet she passed it on to sister Clara.

After greeting I suggested this: "Sister, it looks as if I will not get east as soon as I had expected and in order to reach the children I think I will write Alton a letter about these visits you and I have had, so he can show it to the rest of the children."

She replied: "I would be so happy if you will, brother, and give him this message from me: Tell him his mother still lives; that I am still with him and all the children; that I still love them and that I am watching over them day by day. Let them know that death does not end all and that life is eternal. Tell them how often I have talked with you and show them how they can talk with me the same as you do. Tell Alton not to worry; to keep cheerful; take care of his health and do not be annoyed over business matters. If you will get this message to the children, brother, I will be so happy. God bless you, George; goodbye."

Next came Minnie with her unmistakeable greeting:

"George, this is Minnie. I am so glad to be with you again. I have waited for this hour and have been with you all day and I am happy that you can come and talk with me. We have no mixed vibrations here and it is no trouble to get the voices through to you. You make conditions favorable for good results and we are all glad to meet you here. I spoke to you on your pillow this morning and was so glad when I heard you answer."

I thanked her for her materialization at the Jonson seance and for her visit to my room the evening before and asked:

"Minnie, are you going to be able to come to my room soon so that I can see you clearly and talk with you as I do with mother and father and sister Annie?"

Answer: "Yes, George. We are all working to bring this about and you are becoming more mediumistic as you get farther in the work. The trumpet is not idle; you will hear from us in that way before long. I always look forward to these meetings and to the day when you will come to this side and there will be no more parting. You cannot in your world know what a wonderful life the spirit world is. . . . . . Goodbye, George; I will materialize for you at Jonsons Friday night if the opportunity is right. Goodbye."

Little Mary Ellen spoke up, all bright and sunny with laughter: "Hello, Uncle George. I am so glad that you came today. Didn't I tell you that I could find my rose if you hid it in the church?"

"Yes, dearie, you did and I think its just wonderful that you could prove to all that crowd that little girls don't die, but that you just go from the earth plane to a higher plane and can come to us and prove your identity. That was wonderful work, Mary."

"Well, Uncle George, I was glad for a chance to show that I could find it and you saw how it affected everybody in the church."

Answer: "Yes, I did; it was a wonderful test. But let me ask you, sweet soul; when are you coming to my room to see the pretty flowers I put there for you?"

Answer: "I have already been there. I was there with grandpa and grandma early Monday morning. We were all there and picked out our flowers from the vase on the table."

Little Georgie came with this: "Say, Uncle George, you know about two weeks ago I came to your room with Mary Ellen and held the big end of the trumpet in front of your eyes when you woke up and sat up in bed and I peeped through the little end with my eye. Do you remember it?"

Ans: "I certainly do, because I spoke of it to my friends in the office the next morning." He continued:

"Mary Ellen was with me and she looked through it too. Then mamma told us to put the trumpet down and said we were always up to some mischief."

My old friend Jim Thomas took up my own trumpet and spoke through that instead of through Mrs. Miller's. I still have the aluminum band with the radium paint on the trumpet and could see it move around the room and clear up to the ceiling. Jim's figure was just barely visible and I could not see him as plainly as on the night he appeared in my room. He greeted me with:

"Hello, old pal. This is Jim. Follow me closely and you can see the trumpet move up to the ceiling. You know when I used it two weeks ago I told you that I would dematerialize the rubber mouthpiece that belongs to it. Well, you have missed it for two weeks and I have brought it back to you. I didn't altogether dematerialize it—just partly so. In fact, I hid it in the room here where no one could touch it until you came back."

I replied: "Jim, I understand pretty well how the spirit side dematerializes objects, but to re-materialize them again is a harder nut to crack."

Answer: "In the first case, George, the dematerializing is simply a matter of bringing together the proper combination of chemicals. To materialize again is a matter of re-assembling them by magnetic attraction. There is no mystery about it. It is a natural law. But you are soon going to get speeches in your trumpet in your room. It won't take long now. The walls in your room are well magnetized and so is your trumpet."

I asked: "Jim, were you in my office last Tuesday morning?"

Answer: "Yes, and I am there every morning between nine and ten o'clock, and you can usually sense my presence. But I wanted to impress you last Tuesday to come and talk with me. We have not made much headway the past two weeks and there is a reason for it. You have taken on considerable anxiety about business matters and have allowed yourself to become worried over the delays and setbacks. This you must not do. Preserve a cheerful expectancy and let your hopes be just as buoyant as you please; but do not allow it to take the nature of worry. Worry closes the door to our work and makes negative your own efforts as well as ours. Keep the aura about you radiant and cheerful; that makes it easy to reach you. Free your mind of its uneasiness. Matters will turn out better than you think and there will soon come a change. It will come as quickly as is possible consistent with permanent benefit . By all means hold no thoughts of failure. Rid your mind of anxiety and relieve yourself of any semblance of worry. Others around you may worry and fret; but you must be negative to these impressions. Do not permit them to come within you. This may at times make you appear unsympathetic. But in the end it will be best for your associates and you too. We know what you are contending against. We know what you are trying to accomplish and we are opening the way so that it can be done. One of the old mines in your district will open up soon and this is going to be a great help to you."

I thanked him and asked if Mrs. Thomas was in the room. He replied: "Yes, and she will talk with you in a few minutes. John is going to say a few words to you; then his mother will give you a message for Gordon. Goodbye, old timer. Call on me whenever you get in a tight corner and I'll be with you."

John Thomas spoke mostly of the cooperative work which he and his father and friends were doing in regard to certain business matters in which I am interested, and spoke of some greater work of a psychic nature which they wished me to do after these entanglements are out of the way. They seem perfectly familiar with my affairs, with my office surroundings, the location of my mining interests and even of private correspondence carried on with parties at a long distance.

John was a mining engineer and a good chemist in life on the earth and I asked him if he was engaged in chemistry on the other side.

Answer: "Oh, yes; that is principally my work."

Goerner: "Harold Cook was in the same work in Denver. Is he in chemistry on the spirit side?"

Answer: "Yes, we both work together."

Goerner: "John, is it a fact that the spirit side is so far ahead of us in chemistry that our knowledge of this subject is actually crude and rudimentary?"

Answer: "Yes, George, that is true. The earth side is yet in its mere infancy in chemistry and when you get over on this side you will find out that all the chemistry which the earth has came to them from this side, and they will understand higher chemistry when they are able to receive it and apply it as we do here. I may explain it this way:

"Imagine a child building a crude figure with its hands full of coarse clay. Now, put this figure beside the pure white smooth marble statue of a finished sculptor and your earth is farther away in chemistry from the spirit side than the clay figure is from the marble work of art."

He continued: "We have a little surprise for you. We have lately arranged for the cooperation of another chemist guide, who is one of our instructors, to help you with your treatment problems at the mine. You would be surprised if I told you who it is and you couldn't guess."

Goerner: "No, John, I am afraid I could never guess who it could be."

John: "Well, it's old Ben Franklin. He has been attracted to you and you are going to get some good help from him and we are all cooperating to bring better results. Goodbye for today. You will hear more about this later. Mother is going to talk with you."

Mrs. Thomas announced: "Mr. Goerner, this is Mrs. Thomas. I heard you call my name and I am so glad to be able to talk with you."

I answered: "Well, Mrs. Thomas, I am going to write to Gordon Sunday, and I know you would like to send him a message."

Answer: "Yes, Mr. Goerner, I am happy to get the chance. Give my love to my son, Gordon. Let him know of the talks you have had with me and with his father and his brother John. Let him know that there is no death; that we still live and that consciousness is not buried with the physical body. Tell him to cheer up; take care of his health and don't worry. Tell him his latest undertaking will be all right; take a firm stand and keep working for the best that is in him. Tell him we are with him every day; that I still live and love him and watch over him. Let him know how to reach me. I know he will come. He will not be so hard to convince as you may think and I will hear from him soon after he hears from you. Give my love to my boy, and God bless you, Mr. Goerner."

Kitty spoke next independently of the trumpet. This is the cabinet guide at the Jonson materialization seances. She is presumed to have been a New York street waif who was frozen to death in a dry goods box in an alleyway. She is a strong spirit, always comes with a cheerful laugh and is always ready to help some one else manifest themselves to their friends on the earth side. She volunteered the information that she was in my room last Monday morning when the folks materialized and seemed proud to have given them assistance in building up.

Next came "Sunbeam" and confirmed the imaginary conversation which I carried on with her picture on the wall and asked:

"Did you notice my picture shaking its head when you spoke to me?"

Goerner: "Why, no Sunbeam, I didn't."

Answer: "Well now, you listen: The next time you come to see Mrs. Miller if you will talk with my picture on the wall and watch it closely I will nod my head to you so you can see it. Now remember and watch closely."

Note:—I will look out for this. I do not know just how she intends to produce this phenomenon; but certainly it can be no more difficult than materializing the full face and figure as in life; or speaking and singing through the trumpet; dematerializing solid materials; producing pictographs on cardboard, etc., etc.

I asked: "Sunbeam, is my sweet sister Annie in this room?"

Answer: "Yes, she is here and will talk with you now."

Then came a voice: "Brother, this is Annie." I greeted her with:

"I didn't want to miss talking with you today, sister; because I have decided to write another letter to Naomi Sunday after talking with you the other day, and I know you would like to send a message to her."

Answer: "Yes, brother, I want you to tell Naomi not to look so sad. Tell her to cheer up, for I am with her every day. I walk by her side I talk with her and love her and watch over her. Tell her that I still live. Tell her that I can come to her and talk with her and I want you to show her how she can communicate with me. Tell her that I will give her proof that I still live and that there is no death. Tell her she can talk with me just as you do. Thank you brother, for giving her this message. Tell her I send a mother's greeting of love and happiness. Goodbye, George, and God be with you."

During these conversations the usual "spirit lights" hovered about the room. There were the usual two stationary lights on the floor; also two in the ceiling and others moving about here and there. Mother's light and sister Annie's I can always recognize and they are always present.

Dr. Worthington concluded the seance by informing me that father was in the room during the entire time; also young Harold Cook, but that both of them wished to let the rest of the folks speak and they would talk with me at another time.

Note:—Both sister Clara and sister Annie commented upon the fact that they and brother George are so much nearer to one another since they passed from the earth than when they lived here. This is a fact, as we have had many chats together, and many visits, in the past twelve months. These are all my closest relatives and friends. They have come to me often and identified themselves in unmistakable ways and given the most convincing proof of their continued existence, the survival of consciousness and personality. These proofs have not only been given to me individually, but have been manifested time and again in the presence of ten to 30 others just as intelligent, just as sane and just as truthful as the average American citizen, and entitled to just as much consideration and respect.

REPORT ON MATERIALIZATION SEANCE

Held at Residence of Mr. and Mrs. J. B. Jonson, 855 No. Marengo Ave., Pasadena, Cal., Friday P. M., February 3rd, 1922, by L. A. Soc. for Advanced Psychical Research.

Two members were absent on this occasion. All those who could attend (eighteen) being present at 7.30 the work began at that time, starting with the usual prayer. Mrs. J. impressed upon the circle the advantage of the members all taking the same seat for each seance and holding the same position with one another regularly.

The red adjustable light controlled by the guides in the cabinet had been improved upon in the meantime, worked well and gave a very satisfactory result. This light is adjusted in the cabinet by a cord leading from the slide door of the case in which the bulb is enclosed, so this door may be raised or lowered as required. (Some of the visitors need more light than others).

By the time prayer was over the medium, Mr. J., was under control of Gray Feather. This was unusual, as he does not as a rule become entranced until after we have had a little music. There was, however, a good feeling in the circle, the vibration appeared strong and every one was expecting good results.

Gray Feather voluntarily asked Mrs. Baker to step to the center of the room and said he would give her another treatment for her throat and spine trouble. Mrs. B. stated to the circle that she felt a permanent benefit from these treatments so far as she could tell up to this time; that the good effect appeared to remain with her and that her general health was better than before taking them.

Mr. Baker's mother was the first spirit to appear before the curtain. Both vouched for the identity (Mr. and Mrs. B.) and both claim there could be no mistaking the characteristic personal traits which she always brings.

Viola came next; walked well down to the center of the room; talked with us in whispers clear enough to be heard by all the members; extended a greeting to the circle and disappeared.

Then came Mr. and Mrs. Baker's son. This was a young chap who passed out of life at the age of 17 with bronchitis and heart trouble. He had never been a very strong lad, always had poor health, but was generally known in life as a lad with an entertaining gift of speech. These traits he brought with him, doubtless for the purposes of identification—his appearance of delicate health and a voluable flow of language.

Dr. Wetherby was invited up to meet him and on asking the lad if he had been to see his sister since he passed out and where he saw her, he seemed to evade the question by answering:

"Yes, I have traveled a good deal—been to the moon." (Whatever that may mean, we did not then understand).

Mrs. B. then tried a test by asking if he knew what became of the tree at the ranch where he used to carve names. He replied:

"It was struck by lightening a few days ago and washed down the stream after the heavy rain." This was precisely correct.

She then asked what names he had carved in the tree and received the correct answer. Why he should have answered these questions so correctly and readily and evade the Wetherby question is open to conjecture. Our experience in the circle has been that it is always best to put these questions tactfully, because anything that sounds like an effort to "corner" the spirit will most invariably be ignored. This lad has been on the spirit side for four years, but seemed very familiar with what had happened to the tree during the past two weeks.

The "Star of Hope" came radiant, cheerful and beautiful. She was robed in what we all pronounced a "wonderful gown." It was by all means a thing of beauty. She was asked if she could come down into the center of the room and replied that she could with a little stronger vibration. So Mrs. J. stepped beside her on the left and requested Mr. Lombard (who is very mediumistic) to walk on the right side. This seemed to give her strength and she walked slowly to the end of the room, turning to the right and left, extending her arms to the circle and all the time delivering a message of cheer and hope. Her language was well chosen, her speech came slowly and clearly and every syllable came as if from an effort at clear enunciation. Moving about in the room, as she did, while speaking, it is doubtful if any one caught the full text of the message. The general theme, however, was "love, truth, light, harmony, cheerfulness, charity and helpfulness to one aother," and the concluding sentence was, "love God, for God's love is with you all and in you all; strive for the best that you may come closer to the Master and live for the good that you can do. I bid you good night and the peace of the angels be with you."

She then retreated slowly, moving backward toward the curtain, extending her arms first to one side, then another, as a farewell salutation.

The next figure before the curtain announced to Mrs. J. that she came to see George. I stepped up and received the greeting:

"George, this is Minnie." I replied:

"Yes, I recognize you, and am awfully glad to have you come."

The answer came: "I was in your room this morning at half past five and tried to tell you that I would materialize tonight."

Answer: "Yes, I knew you were there, Minnie; I heard your voice on the pillow and answered you. Could you catch my voice?"

"No, not this morning, George. The vibration didn't last long enough."

Minnie: "Well, I am coming to you tomorrow morning again at half past five."

George: "All right, Minnie; I wish you would, and if I am not awake you put your hand on my head and wake me up, will you?"

Answer: "Yes, I will. Do you recognize me?"

"I certainly do, Minnie you look perfectly natural and as sweet as a rose."

Minnie: "Thank you for that George. I'll see if I can't materialize a rose for you for the compliment."

Note:—I did not at the moment understand just what she meant by this and returned to my seat as she disappeared. I had no sooner reached my chair when she again came to the curtain—perhaps a minute had elapsed. I stepped up to the curtain and she handed me a large, luscious pink rose, damp and fresh. The rose was as large as the palm of my hand and very fragrant. I will ask at the next trumpet meeting whether she brought this from "the other side" or from some of the neighboring gardens. Those familiar with the neighborhood informed me that there were no roses of that kind to be found in that locality.

Following came Mrs. Lombard's mother. She needs no identifying tests; her own personal appearance, her characteristic style of wearing her glasses; her speech and general mannerisms are sufficient. I stepped up to her and spoke to her and had a good view of her.

"Crystal," the little guide to the Majors, came as usual in bare feet; perfectly at home in the circle and seemed to have plenty strength. She is very enthusiastic about that swing which she requested Mr. Majors to put on the porch and said she and the little white dog were going to have some good times in the swing."

Mrs. Majors asked: "Crystal, who were your father and mother?"

Answer: "I do not know. I wasn't raised with a father and mother. I came to you because you didn't have any little girl and I wanted you and daddy for mother and father."

"Well, dearie, why do you always come in bare feet?"

Answer: "I never had any shoes when I was on the earth and my teachers on the spirit side say I don't need shoes now."

Question: "Why do you love our little dog so?"

Answer: "Because he's so white and clean."

Crystal is becoming a favorite with us all; seems pleased to come to the circle either by materializing or through the trumpet; has recovered from her fear of Gray Feather and stated that her teachers had taught her that it is through Gray Feather that she gets the strength to materialize for us.

Note:—I asked Mrs. J. why the voices from the spirits all seemed to have a certain resemblance to one another. She replied that this is because they use the vocal cords of Gray Feather (or Mr. J.—the medium) to a large extent. This is also true in trumpet work—whether the medium is entranced or not—and it is true to some extent when my own folks speak with me on the pillow, although neither I nor the medium may be at all conscious of this use. The same thing will happen even though there are two or three voices coming through the trumpets at the same time, and it may also happen even though the medium may be in conversation with some one else at the same time.

Came also Stella de Lucca, the Italian girl, who appeared at a previous seance at the Vermont avenue home. Stella appeared in some dark costume with bright colors after the dress of the Italian peasantry; sang for us in Italian, but did not come up to other voices we have heard from the spirit side, and we concluded that Stella had not been a singer of high order on the earth, although those who understood something of the strength required for these efforts, will give her credit for raising her voice as loudly as she did and carrying the tune for so long, without any accompaniment to strengthen the vibration and help her on. She spoke freely in Italian and also in broken English. She is decidedly Italian in appearance and manner, with a very pretty face.

Then came our old friend, Krocho—Mrs. Jonson's trumpet guide. She had been promising us this visit at a number of trumpet seances, and told us that when she came she was "going to walk right straight down the room so the whole circle could see her." This is just what she did. She had told us that we would recognize her, because she would "have two long plaits hanging around her shoulders, but no head feathers and that she would dress in very ordinary clothes, but nothing fancy." She carried out her program to the letter; we congratulated her and she came back with:

"Didn't I tell you I would come just this way?"

"Yes, you did, Krocho, and now that you've got started we expect you to come often."

Answer: "You can't keep me away now." She bowed to everybody; waived her hands in farewell and stood right before the curtain and dematerialized in full view. Some one asked if she brought the "bug" along and the answer came: "No, I wouldn't give Gray Feather a chance to use it on me."

An incident crept into the circle that gave us all a chance to choke in the throat a little and put the handkerchiefs to our eyes:

An elderly lady, perhaps 65 or 70 years of age, with a good, refined face came before the curtain. Mrs. J. did not seem to be able to locate any one for her and I stepped up to the old lady asking if she was for me. The reply came:

"I am for any one who can help get me in communication with my dear ones on earth." I aked for her name, which she gave as "Aunt M——B." I asked who she wished to reach on the earth side.

Answer: "My nieces by the same name at La Jolla, California. I am in their home every day; but they close the door on me and I can't get near them. Will some one tell them that I still live; that spiritualism is true; tell them not to close the doors on me that I still love them and want so badly to help them. Please get the word to them. Ask Miss B——; she knows them. But please do this for me. Tell them not to be hard; the way is open for them to eternal life and they must not deny me longer."

Note:—Inquiry developed the fact that these people at La Jolla always loved old Aunt M., but the whole family belong to the orthodox religions, have no consideration for anything resembling spiritualism, and will not even discuss the subject, or listen to any suggestions from their closest friends. Thus the door remains closed.

Mr. Lombard' sister, Agnes, came in with a rose for Mr. L. This was a cream rose, very fragrant and still damp and fresh. Like the rose given me by Minnie, it had no thorns anywhere on the stems or branches. Agnes stated that she had brought "it from the other side as a demonstration."

Chief "Big Heart," the guide who comes to Mr. Lombard, came in citizens clothes, as usual. Mr. L. called me up and introduced me, and brought this from Big Heart:

"Yes, me know you,—you be chief of this camp." (This was his way of referring to the presidency of the circle). Mr. Lombard had been showing some of the members of the circle (before the work began) a newspaper clipping with some historic data relating to Chief Big Heart. The chief seemed to know all about this, spoke of some of the incidents in the article, said the fellow who wrote it (calling him by name) was on the ground in the early days and knew what he was talking about.

At this point Gray Feather said: "Me hear somebody in cabinet say something about taking rubber mouthpiece off somebody's trumpet. Me know nothing about that."

I replied: "It must be some of my friends. Jim Thomas took the mouthpiece off my trumpet at Mrs. Miller's two weeks ago; then put it back yesterday, and that's probably what he is referring to."

Note:—Minnie made good her appointment to come to my room the following morning at 5.30. I awoke with a distinct feeling of a hand on my head; heard a voice speak and answered it; but received no further reply. It sometimes seems strange that performances which to us might seem trivial and so easy, nevertheless appear very difficult to the "other side," such, for instance, as carrying on a lengthy conversation; and yet the same spirit will perform phenomena of a startling character that will baffle the most astute scientific investigators and which simply cannot be accounted for by any known physical laws.

Take the case of Minnie procuring the rose for me: Regardless of whether she got it from the neighboring gardens or from "the other side," it was first necessary for her to materialize in the form of a human being, a perfect resemblance of her earth self in every detail—with robes, head dress and veil, voice, smile, complexion, color of eyes, etc. Then she had to dematerialize, or etherealize, in order to go out after the rose. Then to re-appear and present me with the rose she had to again materialize and then dematerialize to return to the spirit side. All this was done within a space of scarcely three minutes—most of which was taken up in conversation with me.

Those who have followed these records will have observed that the majority of our visitors at these seances are "repeats." This is so because the circle consists of practically the same members every time. The visitors are the close friends and family members of the "sitters," and their identification has long ago been established. There will, however, every now and then come a stranger, unknown to any of us. From these we get just such information as we can as to their identity, but in most cases have no opportunity of checking them up; so the record is merely carried in the secretary's minutes as an incident of the meeting.

REPORT ON TRUMPET SEANCE

Held at Residence of Mr. and Mrs. Jonson, Pasadena, Cal., 7.30 P. M., Monday, February 6th, 1922.

There were only eight members present including Mr. and Mrs. J. The seance opened with prayer and music from the "Orechestrion." This has to be wound up about every thirty minutes and after the voices began coming through the trumpet the music box "ran down." We then heard some one winding it up. All members were in their seats around the table, close enough to one another so that no one could have left their place without its being known by other members.

Finally the music began and Crystal took the trumpet and upon being asked advised that she had wound up the music box. This was later confirmed by other communicators through the trumpet. Those of us who have wound up this box know that it is not a trick that any child can perform and takes quite a little strength and care in keeping the "crank" in place.

Sister Clara came with this: "Brother, I couldn't get in that vibration at the church where you went Sunday afternoon. The message you got from the platform was not from us; pay no attention to it."

I answered: "I had no more than got inside, sister, when I felt out of place and could see that there was nothing to be gained there; but merely remained through the service to try it out. But, when did I hear your voice last, sister?"

Answer: "On the pillow in your room this morning. I woke you up. We were all in the room during the night and were so glad when you sat up in bed and spoke to us. We are always happy when we know that you can recognize us. We admired the pretty roses that you brought and they helped us all to make a good vibration."

George: "Clara, I sent your message to Alton and am sure he will read it to the rest of the children. I enclosed a full record of the last meeting we had at Mrs. Miller's; told them how to reach you and how to form a weekly class so they can all get together and talk with you the same as I do."

Clara: "Thank you brother. I will be very happy when I can see them all together around the table and talk with them and make myself known to them. Oh, if every one would just give out what they get through spiritualism as you do, how much good it would bring to the world. So many on this side are trying to reach loved ones on the earth side and just have the doors closed on them day after day. I know Alton will soon talk with me now that you have pointed the way. We all love you, brother, and it will come back to you and you will be repaid for the pains you have taken. Goodbye George, and God bless you."

Mary Ellen asked: "Uncle George, why do you open your eyes so wide when we all come into your room?"

Answer: "I do that so I can see you all."

Mary Ellen: "I know it; I know it; I know why you do it, but I just asked so you would know that I was there. We were all there. You didn't see me, but I was there and picked out my rose. Let me tell you what I want you to do for me: Will you get me a little bunch of violets and put them on the stand, and I will take one out and put it on your pillow so you will know that I was there. Will you do that?"

Answer: Why, of course, I will, dearie. They will be there tomorrow night and when I wake up I will look for the violet on the pillow."

Had a longer chat with Minnie than usual. I thanked her for the rose which she gave me at the materialization Friday and asked where she got it. The reply came:

"Perhaps I had better not tell you, because I didn't get it from the other side."

I suggested: "Well, you might get arrested some time and suppose they put you in jail?"

Answer: "I am afraid they would have a hard time keeping me there. But I like to do these things for you and I hope to bring you many more roses in the future. Don't you want to do something for me, George?"

"Of course I do, Minnie. What is it?"

"You get a fresh white Easter lily and put it in the vase with a little water and set it on the stand beside your bed. The lily stands for purity, uprightness and life eternal. It is a symbol of the resurrection of Christ. I will pass through the room and put a blessing on the flower and a thought in your mind that will help you to the higher life you are striving for. The thought will come to you often through the day. It will be a precept to you. And before you sleep at night look again at the lily and give me your thoughts just for a moment; put your mind on the Master and visualize to yourself the day of the resurrection. Keep this up while the lily is fresh and full of life and beauty. I will work with you and this will bring you the things you seek—a high purpose, psychic success, desirable companionships, the visits and the voices from the spirit side. These things will mean so much to you and to us too, for they enable us to get closer to you and bring you strength. Never mind what some one else thinks about it. Your earth has scoffed at the truth for ages and millions have had to pay for it on this side. Good night, George; your mother has a message for you."

Mother followed the same trend of thought: "My son, you could not very well expect to get within our vibration where you went last Sunday afternoon. Did you not see the commercial side to all their work? They were not true spiritualists. They have a certain psychic talent, but have stunted their best impulses and given their work over to material gain. There was not a message through the entire meeting that didn't carry the imprint of money. My prayer for you is that you keep within the spiritual path—separate the world of materialism from the world of spiritualism and keep them apart. Those who seek to do good will find in this way the real truth. We love you and are working with you every day. We wanted you to take the flowers to your room, because as long as they last they bring you a good vibration and assist us in getting near you. The flowers mean light, truth, strength, beauty and harmony. They send forth these influences to all who come near them and will open their ears to the voice. They will take from you what is left of selfishness and displace it with charity and kindness. Look upon them and study them and they will carry to you the light that is within them. I send you a mother's love and greetings of peace and happiness. Goodbye, my boy."

I asked Krocho if sister Annie was in the room and received the reply: "Yes, and just taking up the trumpet to talk with you."

Annie: "Brother, I want to thank you so much for the letter you wrote to Naomi. I know it will do her a great deal of good. She will think about it; she is going to be very happy to feel that I still live and that she can really talk with me again."

I interrupted with: "I do not expect to have any trouble convincing Naomi, because she has confidence in me. But how about the doctor, her husband?"

Answer: "He wont be very stubborn about it. He will not think much of it at first, but when he finds that it makes Naomi happy he will be satisfied and will not oppose it."

Crystal spoke to Mr. Majors in a very knowing way about the cold and headache that was bothering Mrs. Majors and which kept her away from the seance; seemed to know more about it than Majors did, as he came to the seance direct from business without going home first. She closed with this: "Papa, I am going from here to see mamma and will stay with her until you get home." (I think it safe to say that she went and made known her presence to Mrs. Majors).

At this point we had some violent table tipping. The table swayed from side to side and end to end, and two or three times turned completely over into my lap. Then Catharine came with:

"That's the way two of the members of your research society feel. They are discordant and some one will have to talk them out of their skepticism. They have been in this work too long not to know that any lack of harmony is detrimental to good results. They mean well, but have taken on the wrong way of thinking. They believe the visits of their own people from the spirit side are genuine; give them to understand that if they will ask their own spirit friends they will get all the assurance they want and get it direct from the lips of their own loved ones."

Timothy announced that if we had any questions to ask let him have them, because he was going to return in a few moments with a little charity work for us to do. I asked:

"Tim, in what way do the spirits use the vocal cords of the medium, or sitters, in expressing themselves?"

Answer: "We don't exactly use the vocal cords. We simply

draw strength from them. This we do without producing any physical strain on the medium. If the medium were conscious of it he would be coughing all the time he tries to talk. You see that when Gray Feather is leaving and the medium is just coming out of the trance; he generally comes out coughing. In trumpet work the use of the medium's vocal cords is usually not necessary. The trumpet then acts as a cabinet to the voice. But it is often a great benefit."

He dropped the trumpet and Santa Fe John came whistling in, bright, chatty and full of life and good wishes. He remained less than a moment, but it was enough to show a big improvement since Timothy first brought him to us.

Then came Tim again. "Friends, I wanted Santa Fe John to come in to show you how much good you can do by just laying aside now and then your own pleasure in the seance, and turn your thoughts to a little charity. I am going to bring in a lady who deserves your help, your good thoughts and efforts. She is not a stranger to Los Angeles and this is the place, and this is the circle for her to come to, and I feel at liberty to ask you to open your arms and give her your help. The earth was not very kind to her in life and from childhood on she walked with fate against her."

We assured him that the door was open and our arms extended. An attempt was made to take up the trumpet, but it fell to the table. A second attempt and again it fell. A third attempt and a voice, just barely audible came through; then the trumpet fell. Once more it was taken up and we caught this:

"Rappe! Rappe! Its Virginia—Virginia Rappe." Again the trumpet fell and silence followed. I asked:

"Krocho, can you help Miss Rappe to get back to the trumpet?"

Krocho answered: "No, not tonight, friends. Miss Rappe has gone for the evening. She tried hard to make it, but didn't have the strength. She will try it another time. But there is a worthy case friends,—a fine girl more sinned against than sinning. She did not come to this world with a silver spoon in her mouth and all she ever got out of it was a bitter fight. She had talent, yes; but it was talent that brought her under the show and tinsel of a false life. She fought against evil force, and there were none in her world brave enough to help her to better things. They worked with her, yes—but to her undoing. She paid the price with her life, while those who planned the sorry deed fight for freedom with money. But the law of compensation will have its day. You might fool the courts, but you can never fool God on high. When she came into the world, the day had gone when the law of the home was the law by which your earth lived. The day when parents tapped their fingers gently on the table and the children followed in loving obedience, had already given place to the cold and workaday world that cares not for your honor just so it uses your talent—that day found her fighting her way in the world without a guiding hand to help. What was the end? What can be the end of a people who can never spend money enough, can never wear clothes enough, can never be amused enough and who live only by the light of vanity and false show? Her lot was among those who didn't care. She fought an uneven fight and found her rescue only in death. But she will live to pass judgment upon those who seek victory in her defeat, for her triumph is just beginning and we want you all in this circle to send out to her your loving thoughts and give her Godspeed in her new life. Good night friends and God love you all."

Before giving her chance to get away, I asked:

"Krocho, what did Mrs. Baker's son mean by telling us at the materialization seance Friday that he had been to the moon?"

Answer: "He meant that he had been there. He was not just talking. We can go to the moon if we want to. We have instructors on this side who have very high knowledge of conditions on distant planets. It is no more difficult for us to visit the moon than it is to visit the earth. This young man has an exploring mind. That is his strong point and he will be given an opportunity to develop it here."

NOTES ON MATERIALIZATION SEANCE

Held at Residence of Mr. and Mrs. Jonson, Pasadena, Cal., Friday P. M., Feb. 10, 1922.

The work on this occasion was a repetition of previous seances in that the visitors from "the other side" were entirely confined to the close relatives and friends of the circle—those who have been coming to us regularly from week to week.

There were no sensations and no new visitors. The singers and dancers were absent and the only unusual occurrence was the appearance of ex-President Wm. McKinley. He had appeared to us once before, stood in front of the circle and made a few remarks in a loud whisper that was easily heard. On this particular evening, however, he stepped before the curtain, bowed his head, waved his hand and was gone. He did not speak and was in the room not more than a moment. It was at any rate a very good resemblance and a close reproduction of the former visit.

All told there were some twelve or fourteen figures to come through the curtains, instead of the usual twenty or more. One of the visitors, a sister to Mr. Lombard, advised us that we were all in too tense an attitude—too anxious about what was going on back of the curtains, and suggested that we relieve our minds of the strain, enter into conversation with one another or sing. In the meantime Mr. J. (now Gray Feather) went into the cabinet and this seemed to bring the forms out more rapidly.

Minnie was the fourth visitor. The theme of her conversation was mostly with regard to the lily plant which I had placed in my room at her request. She asked if I had received the flower message which she gave in my room. I replied:

"I am not sure, Minnie. I received a very distinct message that came from the pillow and it came twice." She answered:

"You received it. I impressed it on your mind."

George: "Will you confirm it at the trumpet meeting; then I'll know that I didn't make any mistake."

Answer: "Yes, I will give it to you again through the trumpet. But you didn't make any mistake about it; it is still in your mind. I put it there."

George: "What do you think of the lilies?"

Answer: "I think they are beautiful; that is what I wanted you to get. Mary Ellen wanted the violets and she told me to tell you that she hasn't forgotten the one for the pillow. She will put it there. George, I want you to know how glad I was to hear you make that speech to the circle tonight and tell them what Krocho said about the boy's trip to the moon. You don't know how many doubts that removed. Keep giving out what you get—that's what helps."

I asked: "Are you going to help me take care of the lily plant?"

Answer: "Yes, I'm watching over it. All you need do is to give it a little water every day. If you will step back a little I will come out into the room."

I stepped back and she came down into the center of the room; placed her hand on my arm, then on my hand, then on my face, moved back to the curtain and disappeared.

Note:—In Minnie's trumpet message of Monday, Feb. 6th, when asking for the lilies, she stated that she "put a thought in my mind which would come to me often through the day." The lily plant was placed in the room on Tuesday evening, the 7th. Wednesday there was nothing that came to my mind that I could connect up with a message from Minnie, except that she spoke on the pillow in affectionate and appreciative tones for the plant and her manifestations of appreciation were very marked.

Thursday morning I was awakened and heard (or thought I heard) this upon the pillow:

"Gaze often upon the lily. When a wrong thought comes to you visualize the lily. Think of its purity and beauty. Notice how slender yet how straight the stem is. Its uprightness is its strength."

To those who insist that I merely dreamed this, or that it came from my subconscious mind—I am willing to let it go at that. The fact is the same thing was repeated on my pillow the following morning (Friday) with a change of two words in the message. Friday's voice gave it this way:

"Gaze often upon the lily. When a wrong thought comes to you visualize the lily. Think of its purity and beauty of life. Notice how slender yet how straight the stem is. Its uprightness is its strength." The only change was in the addition of the words "of life" at the end of the third sentence.

On both occasions I immediately wrote the message on a slip of paper and returned to bed. You may also argue that the second message was likewise from my subconscious mind. Perhaps so. I will, nevertheless, wait for the confirmation from Minnie through the trumpet. But whether it was a dream, or from the subconscious mind, the original message from Minnie, its partial confirmation at the materialization seance and its later verification at the trumpet meeting would all confirm the doctrine of spiritism regardless of whether this particular message and wording came to me through a dream or from my subconscious mind.

During these materializations there occasionally come apparent contradictions in the personal appearance of the visitors which might bring a doubt as to whether or not they were actually the spirits they claimed to be, were it not for their own readiness to give the necessary identification. This doubt could be brought about by reason of the fact that a spirit well known to those in the circle will come several times a perfect image of their earth self as to height, figure, mannerisms, method of combing the hair, and even complexion and color of the eyes. Then later this same spirit may appear with some change in figure or facial expression that brings out a question as to their identity.

Two such interrogation points could easily have been raised at this seance had it not been for the readiness of the visiting spirits to prevent it. Minnie came in larger form than usual and there was a decided change in the shape of the face. But her reference to the lily plant in my room, the message on the pillow, the violets requested by Mary Ellen, all identified her sufficiently for me in the light of past visits.

The same thing happened with "Hester"—Dr. Wetherby's guide.

This has been explained to us in two ways: First, they sometimes fiind it easier to materialize in one form than in another and may adopt the appearance which brings them most easily within the vibration. Apparently some such necessity existed at this particular seance.

Secondly, the development, or what the circle unually terms "the make-up" of the spirit is more complete at one time than at another. When the vibration is just right the development will be right and the reproduction perfect. If the vibration is not just right there is likely to be a change in the "make-up" and the general appearance.

I have seen cases in the seance room where the face appeared in what might be called a "semi-solid" condition for a few moments; it then gradually dissipated and scattered until the entire figure disappeared, forming into the shapeless mass of a cloud and finally vanished. In the meantime the body might be solid and well made up, with the face and head cloudlike, or unassembled.

We have seen what appeared to be the spirit form of a woman start to come through the curtain, but could not come within the vibration with strength enough "to make it", and suddenly the figure would change entirely and a complete, well developed spirit of a man would take its place.

REPORT ON PHYSICAL MANIFESTATION

And Trumpet Seance at Residence of Mr. and Mrs. J. B. Jonson, Pasadena, Cal., 8 O'Clock P. M., February 13th, 1922.

Seated in the kitchen, waiting for two belated members of the Monday evening circle, were five of the members including Mrs. Jonson. The conversation had been mostly of psychic phenomena and most of us agreed that there was "some one present from the other side"; when the kitchen door suddenly opened and closed rapidly three times. Mrs. J. went to the adjoining room, looked to see if there was any one there and if the windows were all closed. She returned and sat down again. In a few moments the same thing occurred.

We then went up to the seance room—which is not used for any other purpose. A cabinet was arranged by stretching a black curtain across one corner of the room. On a chair behind the curtain were two small silver table bells; a child's rattler, a small music box, writing paper and pencil.

In front were three chairs for the "battery." Mr. J. took one of the end chairs; I (Goerner) took the other one and the third, or middle, chair was occupied by Miss Worrall. We all clasped hands after the usual manner, so that no one could release a hand without its being known.

The vibration was strong from the beginning and both Mr. and Mrs. J. expressed themselves as sensing a new force, some one from "the other side" who had not before attached himself to either of the Jonsons. It was a new impression which they could simply describe as being "different" from that brought by their usual guides.

The action behind the curtain was lively, no time being lost putting the bells, the music boxes and the tambourine into vigorous service.

We called for various friends,—Timothy, Minnie, Mary Ellen, etc., and from the responses (three taps on our shoulders or heads for "yes") it seemed that the cabinet was well occupied, and all appeared anxious to furnish some sort of demonstration.

Mary Ellen raised her hand above the curtain two or three times and twice passed it right through the curtain, tapping the three members of the battery on the face and arms or shoulders.

Then there came a larger hand, like that of a woman—a hand which we all admired and complimented as the most beautiful hand any of us have ever seen. To women who admire beautiful hands and arms this would certainly have been a revelation. It was delicately slender, beautiful in its tints of pink and marble. We called for the other hand and both of them were held up before us, exposing the arms to the elbow.

These hands indicated that we had a materialization, or several of them, in the cabinet, and these materializations took place while the medium was in his normal condition—wide awake. Those acquainted with these manifestations will understand that this required an unusual draft upon his strength, and in fact upon the entire battery.

Then came small bunches of violets, damp and fresh as if just picked. There was a bunch for each member in the circle and on inquiring if Mary Ellen had given them, three raps on my shoulder indicated "Yes."

Timothy wrote a brief note calling attention to the unusual success of the cabinet on its first trial in the new home and predicted even greater things to follow.

Later, at the trumpet table, Viola appeared as the first speaker and informed us that the beautiful hands and arms which attracted so much attention belonged to "Alice," a guide who comes to Mrs. Lombard.

Before the cabinet work closed I asked Mary Ellen if she could tie a knot in my handkerchief if I passed it over the curtain. The answer came "Yes." I had Mrs. J. take the handkerchief from my coat pocket, pass it over the curtain and in another moment it was handed out tied in three knots to represent a "rag doll baby." Others then handed over handkerchiefs; they were all rapidly fastened into knots and either thrown or handed over the curtain.

Vola's talk was entirely independent, and she described the new force behind the curtain as a Hindoo scholar from East India, with very dark skin, a black moustache, a gotee and white turban. Said he came with a great deal of strength and would appear often in the future. It was he who had opened and closed the kitchen door.

Mary Ellen took the trumpet with: "Oh, say, Uncle George, didn't we have lots of fun in the cabinet. There were so many of us." I asked if she had been to my room to see the violets I placed there for her and got the reply:

"Yes, that is why I brought you the violets tonight. Did you know we were all in your room last night?"

I answered: "Yes, and sat up in bed and talked with you. Didn't you see me open my eyes real wide, so I could get a look at all of you?"

Minnie was the third speaker. I told her that never in my life had I ever received a letter from her and asked if she couldn't get me one from the cabinet at the next meeting, so I could retain it among my memories. The reply came:

"You do this, George: Bring an envelope and a sheet of paper; put the paper in the envelope and leave it on the chair in the cabinet. I may not be able to write the letter the first time, but I will magnetize it and try it again at the next meeting."

George: "All right, Minnie; I will do that. Are you going to meet me at Mrs. Miller's, so I can chat with you?"

Answer: "Yes, George, wherever you are, and whenever you call, I will be there. Whenever you open the door and there is the slightest chance for me to get within the vibration, I will be with you. I will be with you to the end and when you are through with your world and pass out of the body, I will be at the border to meet you and will go the rest of the way with you, united froever. Keep before you the vision of the lily; let it guide your thoughts with its wonderful beauty and purity, its uprightness and its strength. This is my message to you. I do not want you to know any darkness on this side."

I asked if she would tell me what her favorite hymn was, and sing it for us if I put it on the Victrola.

Answer: "Select any of the old familiar ones we used to sing in the chapel—Jesus Lover of My Soul is a good one."

Note:—The above is doubtless Minnie's way of confirming the message on my pillow of February 9th and 10th. The wording is merely a revision of exactly the same theme and thought and can leave little doubt as to the origin of the pillow messages.

Viola called for "Whispering Hope" and sang it for us.

Alice sang "Abide With Me;" said she would sing "Ben Bolt" for us as she used to sing it on the stage if we would procure it for the Victrola. (Will do this at the next meeting).

Timothy was asked: "Just how does an undue anxiety in the materialization circle affect the work in the cabinet?"

Answer: "It will be detrimental most every time. Always avoid a too tense or anxious frame of mind at any manifestation of this character. You must keep your minds open, relieve yourselves of any anxiety of what is going to take place behind the curtain. Whenever the work lags enter into conversation with one another, or sing something. Never mind the curtain. That will take care of itself. The less you think about that the better results you will get. When you become impatient and anxious you place a barrier between yourselves and your spirit friends."

Jim Thomas came in with a strong voice and a hearty greeting; said he had been to my room with the rest of the folks the night before and wanted to help me develop. "I want you to be able to help Mrs. Severy in that little class all you can and I am going to help her too. She's a fine little woman. We all think a great deal of her; we are working with her and she has the making of a wonderful medium."

Crystal came for Mr. and Mrs. Majors; said she had been having a lovely time in the swing. On being asked if she had been able to get the dog in the swing, she replied:

"Yes, but he won't stay in the swing. If you will get me a little basket to put on the seat I think I can keep him there." They promised her the basket. She then continued:

"Papa, didn't I tell you a week ago that I would go right over and stay with mamma until you got home? Well, I was there and she knew I was."

Note:—Mrs. Majors confirms this by stating that several raps on the walls and doors took place and these were carried on in response to her inquiries as to whether Crystal was in the home.

Sister Annie picked up the trumpet as the vibration was getting very low and her voice could just barely be heard. She promised to continue the conversation at Mrs. Miller's and said little Georgie was waiting anxiously for the meeting; also that he had been peeping through the trumpet in my room at night and woke me up on one occasion in this way. (I can confirm this).

Father tried the trumpet following Annie, but the force had given out. A little music revived it. In the meantime, Mr. Jonson told us that he could plainly vision a narrow strip of black cloth being drawn before him across the corner where the cabinet had been formed, and this piece he could see as being fastened toward the top of the cabinet curtain.

Mr. J. remarked that he did not understand what this meant; but Timothy explained through the trumpet that this was a suggestion from "the other side" for him to follow at the next meeting—place a narrow strip of curtain in front of the cabinet curtain, toward the top, so as to subdue the light which sifted through the thin curtain into the back of the cabinet. On discussing this after the seance we could all see the advantage in this change.

Krocho closed by thanking me for giving out to the Friday evening class the message regarding the Baker boy's trip to the moon. Said it was the proper thing to do and that "whenever any of you get a message from the spirit side that will help some one else, don't keep it to yourselves; give it out and spread the good work. Don't be afraid to repeat it. It may be just what some inquiring soul needs. It will be like spreading butter on the bread of some hungry person seeking the truth. The more you give out to others the more benefit you will receive yourself. It is doing good for others that makes you strong on the spirit side. Death is nothing. It is not the change that hurts. It's just that little temporary let-down out of the physical body into the spiritual. When you know that you are going just relax and close your eyes and when you open them on this side you will know that your real life has just begun.

REPORT ON TRUMPET SEANCE

Held at Residence of Mrs. Miller, No. 1512 Magnolia Ave., Los Angeles, Cal., one O'Clock P. M., Thursday, February 16th, 1922.—Sitter, G. F. Goerner.

In report of Miller seance of Thursday, February 2nd, 1922, reference was made to "Sunbeam's" promise that she would nod her head at me on my next visit if I would again address her picture on the wall. Before opening today's seance I stood before the picture and reminded her of this promise, but inadvertently called her by the name of "Blossom." There was no motion to the picture. Mrs. Miller was in the hall, overheard this and corrected me. I then greeted the picture by the name of "Sunbeam" and the picture and frame both moved perceptibly back and forth—outward from the wall and back. I asked "Sunbeam" to stop it for a moment while I closed the door so as to be sure there was no breeze coming into the room. After closing the door I addressed her again and the picture once more began moving back and forth.

I thanked her for this demonstration; took my seat before the table; the light was turned out and Mrs. Miller spoke:

"I see a strange looking wheel, something like what you would call a chance wheel with numbers on it, and the numbers are all small except the number four. This stands out larger than the other numbers. I do not know what it means. Perhaps you do."

I replied: "I think I understand the wheel, but not the number. Perhaps it will come through the trumpet."

She continued: "Now, the wheel is moving around, crushing and grinding into the earth and rock and I see it moving very rapidly, crushing at a great rate and there is water being poured on it from somewhere above, as if it might be run by water power."

I again replied: "Yes, I understand it all—except the figure four. That may stand for the number of days, weeks or months."

Then Dr. Worthington, trumpet guide, greeted me with his usual hearty welcome and followed with:

"Your friend Thomas was showing the medium some piece of machinery you are interested in and I see you understand what it is better than she does. He will talk with you later about it."

Note:—This was a good piece of pictographic work in which Thomas sought to impress me through the medium with the idea that he wished to talk with me regarding a patent shaft and drift boring machine of my own design.

Mother followed Dr. Worthington, spoke briefly and turned the trumpet over to sister Clara. Clara's theme was principally her joy at the prospect of soon speaking with her children in Chicago through a letter which I had written them for the purpose of opening the way.

Minnie came third and, like mother and sister Clara, seemed to feel that she should shorten her conversation to make way for a business conference between Mr. Thomas, his son and myself. She confirmed the suggestion made by her at the Jonson trumpet seance of Monday, February 13th, that I place a sheet of paper and envelop in the cabinet at the next Jonson seance and she would write me a letter later. She seemed anxious to make this demonstration. Also confirmed recent visits to my room, conversations on the pillow; spoke again of the lily plant which I had there and concluded by saying:

"I wish you could have seen the pretty lilies I brought to the room from the other side. But it wont be long before you can see these things yourself. You are very close to it, both clairvoyance and clair-audience, and you will soon be independent when you wish to send and receive messages. Remember, you have not been in this study very long; but you have worked hard and earnestly."

My old friend, Jim Thomas, confined his talk mostly to business matters, saying: "Conditions are really better than you think. The little Hebrew and his friend are doing some figuring now. They have reached the conclusion that you are not so easily handled as they thought you would be. In a few days they are going to be willing to talk concessions. But you hold out for just consideration for your company and yourself. If they do not come to your terms, do not be afraid to go east with it. Money conditions throughout the country have not improved much lately; but you are able to offer a better proposition now than when you went east before. You are going to lock horns with the Hebrew and his friend and they are going to do some bullying; but stand pat and hold your own.

"If you go east you will not be gone long; but you can keep in touch with us there just the same. Use your horse sense. We do not mean to dethrone your reason. If we give you a suggestion which you know to be at variance with the facts, then you may know that it is only our view as it appears at the time we give it, or it may be that our message to you is relayed through several instrumentalities before it reaches you. But we can see both your side and the other side too, and by mental suggestion take advantage of this condition and give you the advantage of it to.

"You will miss the psychic work to some extent east. Los Angeles is right now attracting the attention of the world in psychic matters. Your atmosphere here is favorable to good results and your city is rapidly becoming a wonderful psychic center. A few years more will see some fine buildings dedicated to spiritualism and psychic research."

At this point he moved the trumpet all around the room, up to the ceiling and from corner to corner. With the aluminum band on it I could clearly see these movements. He finally tapped me on the head with it and I remarked that it was almost hot and asked how this happened. He replied:

"That comes from the electric heat in the horn. We use a good deal of electricity in this manifestation."

As soon as he had finished talking and returned the trumpet to the table I took hold of it, but it had cooled to its normal temperature. Before bidding me goodbye he thanked me for the letter to his son,

Gordon; said he stood beside me when I wrote it and followed it east until it reached Gordon in Chicago.

His son John announced: "This is John and I am going to talk to you a little about the boring machine. That is why I gave the medium a picture of it. The figure four represents four months and it looks as if by the end of four months you will have the mine under operation and the machine completed. Put it in use at your property; watch for any defects, then correct them after you have made a practical trial of it. They can be improved and your best success will be in using electricity for power. But by all means hold on to this machine. Keep it well under your trumb. You are going to have some offers for it after it is once demonstrated and there will be schemes to get an interest in it. But you either sell for your own price or else keep the absolute control. You are on the right track there and with a few changes you will have a boring machine that will do what you want it to do. Goodbye, George. Harold is here and he's right on the job looking after you."

Mrs. Thomas again thanked me for writing to her son Gordon; said she believed he would later decide to change his location and come to California, and she hoped he would do this.

Mary Ellen came in, all breezy and full of laughter with: "Oh, Uncle George, I am always so glad to meet you at Mrs. Miller's. Isn't it wonderful that we can talk this way? And didn't we have lots of fun behind the cabinet at Mrs. Jonsons Monday night. Did you know we were all materialized and the new guide from India was so strong, he gave us such wonderful help. Do you know what happened to your handkerchief?"

I asked: "Do you mean at the cabinet?"

Answer: "No, you put it on the table a few minutes ago, just as I tied it at the cabinet. There were three knots in it then; so I got busy and put another knot in it. When you turn on the light you will see it has four knots in it instead of three." (Correct).

She continued: "You know, Uncle George, Viola was bossing the work behind the curtain last Monday, but Kitty just went right along the way she does at the Friday class and didn't pay any attention to anybody else. Wasn't it wonderful that we could put our hands through the curtain. We did that for a test. If there had been any holes in the curtain some one might have been suspicious; but we just dematerialized a part of it." (See report of seance of Monday, February 13th).

She closed with this piece of information: "I wanted to tell you about the violets. I did put one on your pillow the first night, but you knocked it off in your sleep. After that you got so anxious about it that I couldn't hold the vibration long enough to get it over. Just forget about it for a few days till it gets out of your mind; then I'll try it again."

From Sunbeam then came this: "Didn't I tell you two weeks ago that I would nod my head if you would talk to my picture? You first called me 'Blossom' and I didn't answer, because that isn't my name. That's Mrs. Wagner's guide. Then when you closed the door I wanted to show you that it wasn't any breeze that shook the picture and I nodded to you all the time you stood there."

Note:—This was substantially correct. "Blossom" is the guide who speaks through Mrs. Wagner, pastor at Mrs. Miller's church.

Father came with: "Say, George, I thought I had better make myself known to you again, because I haven't talked with you for some time. But you must'nt think anything of that, because I am only making room for the girls; they get so much happiness out of these chats and look forward to them with a great deal of pleasure. I heard John talking about the boring machine. Machinery was never my work and I don't understand much about it, but I am going to have John explain it to me because I want to be where I can help you all I can."

Finally, Dr. Worthington started to give me the farewell greeting and I broke in with:

"Doctor, before you put down the trumpet, I want to give my love to my sweet sister Annie and little Georgie; because I know they are in the room."

The answer came: "Well, Mr. Goerner, I just can't refuse him. The little fellow is here pulling at my sleve for a chance to say a word; so I'll let him in."

Then came this from Georgie: "You know, Uncle George, I was in your room this morning. I pushed your pillow up against your head and rapped on the pillow until you answered me. (Correct). Wasn't it good of the Doctor to let me talk to you before the vibration gives out?"

"Spirit lights" were again plentiful. There were two large white lights on the ceiling; another one across the ceiling up in the corner of a bright, electric green, and on the floor a light resembling a live coal about four inches in diameter. These lights moved about from place to place, but were visible during the entire seance.

MEMORANDUM OF MATERIALIZATION MEETING
Held at Residence of Mr. and Mrs. J. B. Jonson, Pasadena, Cal., Friday 8 O'Clock P. M., February 17th, 1922.

No attempt will be made to go into full details of this evening's seance. To do so would be merely to repeat the work of the previous Friday's meeting. There were just about the same number of appearances answering to the same description, names and identity.

Mr. Jonson was indisposed from a slight case of influenza and the vibration throughout the evening showed its effect behind the cabinet. His control, "Gray Feather," made it clear that it would not be wise to hold the medium too long and all told there were not over fourteen or fifteen spirits before the curtains.

The object of this memorandum, therefore, is simply to report for my own record two pieces of evidential matter coming from Minnie which are in themselves valuable as connecting up the intelligence of the visiting spirit.

The reports of trumpet seance of Monday, the 13th, at Mrs. Jonsons and again at Mrs. Miller's on Thursday, the 16th, both made reference to Minnie's suggestion that I place a sheet of paper and envelope behind the curtain at the cabinet seance of next Monday, the 20th, so she could magnetize it and later write me a letter with this material.

At this meeting (Friday, February 17th) she again impressed upon me not to forget her former requests for the paper and envelope, and she would endeavor to write the letter.

There is close enough connection here between these three seances to check up the visitor and connect her with this instance.

The second reference is this: Minnie and my sister Annie were always very close friends at school in Washington, D. C., years ago and this friendship was never interrupted until Minnie passed out of this world. At this particular seance she gave this:

"I am going to try to bring your sister Annie with me tonight."

Sister Annie, however, did not materialize, due probably to the lack of strength in the medium to hold out longer under his illness. The message, however, forms a connecting link between Minnie and Annie which has at least a small value as evidential matter.

Another instance worth recording is the following: Doctor Peebles, so often referred to as the "venerable father of spiritualism," passed out of the body on Wednesday, the 15th of February. The littl cabinet guide, Kitty, called Mrs. Jonson to the curtain with this:

"Auntie Jonson, I've got a new grandpa, now."

Mrs. Jonson asked: "Who is it, Kitty?"

Answer: "Dr. Peebles, of course—who else could it be? He's here; but he is not going to materialize for a few days yet. He will soon."

Note:—At the time of Dr. Peebles death he was within a month of being 100 years old; had been actively engaged in spiritualistic work for more than fifty years, and had many times asserted his belief that he would appear before his friends in Los Angeles frequently after leaving this world.

It is reported, and generally accepted among spiritualists locally, that in the afternoon of the day of Dr. Peebles' death he appeared clairvoyantly to Mrs. Wagner and Mrs. Miller, psychics, at the Peoples Spiritualist Church, Los Angeles, and also appeared at Mrs. Velasic's church the same evening. In one of these appearances he is said to have been supported by the late Andrew Jackson Davis, a co-worker and close friend when on earth.

"Billie," Mr. and Mrs. Baker's son, spoke briefly with his parents, clearly materialized, and said he could not remain long because of weak vibration; but that he intended to come again with strength enough to give some definite information relative to his trip to the moon and the instructions he had received from the teachers on conditions there.

Before Mr. J. became entranced this evening, Mr. Lombard had made some comment about feeling uneasy over a sore finger which he had bandaged, when some one suggested jokingly that he try Christian Science on it. Mr. L. replied that he didn't think there was very much to this doctrine.

At this point three of the clairvoyant members remarked that Mrs. Mary Baker Eddy had stepped into the room, and some of the clair-audient members repeated a message from Mrs. Eddy as follows:

"It is true—it is true—if you educate yourself to it properly. It is a valuable form of healing, but you must believe it and live it to make it effective."

The form remained visible for perhaps half an hour and repeated her message a number of times. In a class of 18 or 20 members who have followed spiritualism, some of them, for many years, there will always be some who are well advanced psychically and have the clairvoyant and clair-audient sense well developed. It is from among these that manifestations of this character come to the circle.

About four years ago the Worrall sisters lost through death a friend who was a devout Catholic and bitterly opposed to spiritualism all his life. This gentleman materialized on this evening and upon being asked by the Worralls whether or not there was anything to spiritualism, he replied:

"Yes, girls, there is; there is everything to it; it is all true. Don't wait until you get over here before you accept it."

MEMORANDUM OF PSYCHOMETRIC READINGS

At Peoples Spiritualist Church, 12th Street and New Hampshire Avenue, Los Angeles, Cal., Sunday P. M., February 19th, 1922.

The occasion was the visit to the city of Mr. John Slater, regarded as one of the best psychometrists in America. He has been actively gaged in spiritualist work publicly for many years; has traveled extensively and has an international reputation. It is stated that his work has been under the investigation of such men as Sir Oliver Lodge, Sir Arthur Conan Doyle, the British and American Societies for Psychical Research, etc.

As might have been expected, the church was crowded; every seat taken and many people standing up. Automobiles began to arrive more than an hour before the opening of the service and the church had to send outside for additional chairs.

Mrs. Mary Carpenter delivered the address of the evening, taking her text from the 14th chapter of St. John, and emphasizing Christ's commentary that "the things I do shall ye do, and greater things than I do shall ye do."

Mr. Slater preceded his work with the statement that he was a delegate to the coming International Spritualists Convention to be held in London in May or June, and that he was going there to "prove spiritualism to the world."

Messages had been placed on the table in large numbers—perhaps a hundred in all. There were no pre-arranged writing boards or pads provided by the church; each visitor wrote his or her message independently, sometimes on a sheet of paper which was folded over and marked with an identifying figure or letter; some of them were sealed in envelopes; some were written at the church and some were prepared at the homes of the writers and brought to the church guardedly.

In some instances Mr. Slater called off the identifying marks on the message before he even found it in the pile. In other cases he would call the identification off while holding the message in his hands and look at it afterwards, and in still other cases he would first give out the message, then call the identification.

He could not in the course of a single evening have read more than a third of the messages on hand, and all told he probably delivered 25 or 30 messages to the congregation.

I did not put any message on the table at all, because I am not very keen about public readings and would just as soon that those who are more eager for this kind of work should have the benefit of the medium's talent. Mr. Slater is something of an egotist and insists that the message is correct, even when it isn't.

I did not, therefore, expect any message from Mr. Slater. But he spoke up with this:

"There is a band of five spirit friends here for a Mr. Goerner. The name is spelled Gaerner—G. F. Gaerner. (This is wrong; should be Goerner). Is there such a party in the house?"

I answered: "Present," and the message continued:

"In this band I catch the name of Mary Ellen, Annie, George and others whom I need not mention. But these friends are here to tell you that they are helping you in certain material affairs in which you are interested. I am not going to call any names, but they want me to say that you are right in your suspicions regarding the actions of two certain business associates, and this has something to do with a gentleman connected with the Hebrew race. You cannot expect much in the way of justice and fairness from these parties, and you are cautioned to go very slowly with them.

"They impress upon me that this enterprise in which you are concerned will work out to your satisfaction. You have a journey across the continent ahead of you and you are going to accomplish what you go after this time. Hold tight and do not be in any hurry about signing any papers before you leave here.

"There are important papers awaiting you in the United States Patent Office in Washington, D. C. This patent has to do with a machine for boring through the earth and solid rock, and there are forces on the other side who are capable of assisting you in the development of this machine and they are working with you. You are told that this will work out to your satisfaction, and to hold on to it by all means.

"Does the message fit you, Mr. Goerner? and is it correct?"

I answered: "I understand the message fully, and it is correct so far as I can tell to date."

He then asked: "Do you know me?"

Answer: "I do not."

Slater: "Did you ever meet me before in your life?"

Goerner: "I did not."

Slater: "Would I be likely to have had any means of learning these details previous to tonight?"

Goerner: "I do not think so."

He concluded with: "You seem to be interested in a Collie dog that crawls up beside you, are you not?"

Answer: "No, I cannot locate the dog."

Slater: "Perhaps not, but he seems attracted to you; he is crawling right into your lap, and I think you'll locate him by turning it over in your mind a little."

The only dog that I could fancy being in any way attracted to me, sufficiently to come within the psychic's vision, would be the one which belonged to the Thomas family, and which was seen and described at Mrs. Miller's trumpet seance Thursday, Nov. 29, 1921. To date, however, I have not been able to learn whether this was a Collie dog or not. In any event, I cannot fancy any dog trained by Jim Thomas crawling into a stranger's lap, least of all a big dog such as his was presumed to have been.

The rest of the message is very good and I make the record merely because it is in its essential features another check-up of one medium against others and adds another link to the chain of evidence, and it is, after all, the cumulative evidence which affords the strongest foundation for spirit return and spirit communication.

During the evening many pieces of evidential matter appear to have been brought out, and many who had been longing for months and years just for one word of consolation from friends beyond the grave received their first proof of the continuity of life. For instance:

One lady was asked to step to the platform, with this: "Your dear husband comes to me and asks that I take your hand for him. He says you have come many miles to get this message, and he will not disappoint you. He says tell Margaret that I still live; that I am with her daily; that I still love her; to take off her mourning robes; put on the bright colors of a happy soul, for I am helping you to forget. He gives his name as Henry and says that during all the four brief years we were married I never left your side and death has not broken that tie, for I am nearer to you now than ever before, and when you pass out of your world I will be on this side to meet you. I will again take you into my arms and we will go the rest of the way together." He concluded: "There is much that I could tell you, lady, that would be of comfort to you; but it is too sacred for a public message."

The lady confirmed the names, the number of years of their married life and that she had come miles for the message.

I have concluded that it is messages like the one just above written, more than any business aids, that make spiritualists—the reunion of family ties, the comforting messages from departed friends and the small bits of personal proof that strike home and make a deep seated conviction that lasts. It may sometimes be only a word, but it is enough for those who understand it.

Ninety percent of Mr. Slater's messages were given over to matters of dollars and cents. The sooner the church eliminates this commercial feature the sooner will spiritualism rise to the high dignity which I believe to be its destiny and command the attendance and reverence of thinking people.

MEMORANDUM OF TRUMPET SEANCE

Held at Residence of Mr. and Mrs. J. B. Jonson, Pasadena, Calif., Monday, 8 O'Clock P. M., February 20, 1922.

There were present the usual members of the Monday evening circle. All arrived early and had assembled in the seance room discussing various subjects at random, when I made the following statement in the hope of eliciting opinions from the more psychic members:

"About two o'clock last Sunday morning, February 19th, I awoke and saw a bright light above my pillow against the wall. I sat up and turned around to get a good look at it. It consisted of a hand pointing downward toward the pillow, with all fingers and thumb strung with small lights of various colors clear to the tips. The back of the hand was also studded with lights like jewels. It was a very pretty phenomenon and I watched it closely; heard Minnie's name called on the pillow and asked if it was her light. I received no reply, but thanked her for the manifestation and commented upon its wonder. By this time the lights had all gone, but the hand was still there luminant. I put out my hand to touch it, but it had disappeared. It was a very vivid and beautiful manifestation—to say nothing of its strangeness as a phenomenon."

I continued: "Personally, I know that I was wide awake and that it was no dream; but I am in hopes that some one from the spirit side will verify it through the trumpet in the presence of the circle, in order to relieve further doubt."

A few moments later Mr. Lombard, who is quite psychic and subject to rather precise impressions, remarked:

"The impression comes to me that you will hear something about that hand in a letter from Minnie from the cabinet tonight; I get the impression that the hand was either hers or sister Annie's, and if it doesn't come from the cabinet you will get it from the trumpet."

I accordingly placed on the chair behind the cabinet the sheet of writing paper and envelope which Minnie requested at two previous circles, to give her a chance to write me the promised letter.

The work behind the cabinet started with lively demonstrations from the tambourine, music box and rattler. Materialized hands of little Mary Ellen and "Alice" came over the top of the curtain and through the curtain and tapped the members of the battery on the face and shoulders.

A note came out from Timothy thanking us all for our efforts to bring about the right conditions for the work of the two mediums, and predicting that we would some day "find this the banner seance room of the Golden State."

Silas Webster, chemist guide, wrote this:

"Friends, one and all, for such we deem you all to be, we greet you kindly and are using our best efforts to make this truly a banner seance room, and your sincere efforts to assist us are duly appreciated by our band of workers, as it should be."

Kitty handed in one of her usual humorous scrawls, written in circles. Henry Marshall, an old friend and guide to the Lombards, handed out one to the L.'s, and Dr. Franklin, guide to the Majors, indicted one for them.

Then came this note from Minnie: "My dear Sweetheart: I cannot write much, but I am so happy to come to you in this way. I will try and talk to you later on. Please excuse writing. Will see you in the morning. Minnie."

Then came the trumpet work. At the table I had been discussing a point which came to me through the trumpet at Mrs. Miller's as to Los Angeles becoming a psychic center, when father gave this through the trumpet:

"That's all true, my son. You are going to have some wonderful buildings erected to the perpetuation of spiritualism and psychic research, and you are going to have schools that will be dedicated to this purpose. Wasn't it a wonderful meeting that you had at the church Sunday night? You had a chance to see there what can be accomplished when the forces are in harmony and all sending their strength to the workers on the platform."

Sister Annie spoke briefly, but with unusual strength, and explained the difficulty in the way of her appearance with Minnie at the last Friday materialization class, and stated that this was due partly to illness of the medium and partly to the changes in the circle, which had a tendency to cause breaks in the contact and thus weaken the vibration. I replied that in asking her to materialize I did not wish to be unreasonable, nor appear to ask for recognition which may merely take the strength of the visitors.

The answer came: "No, you must not misunderstand me. We are always pleased when you ask us to do something for you, and the way in which you cooperate with us gives us both strength and happiness in working with you."

"Santa Fe John" paid us another visit and promised to materialize for us if we didn't mind his coming in his old clothes, saying: "You will know me, because I'm coming in whistling my old tune—just to let you know how much you have all helped me in my efforts to get ahead on this side of life. I could never come this strong if it hadn't been for your help." He dropped the trumpet whistling just as he did the first time he ever appeared to us, and was gone.

Minnie then came and confirmed the lighted hand which appeared above my pillow on the previous morning—Sunday—and explained:

"It was my hand, and I thought I would have a little fun with you when you tried to reach it. It gave me a great deal of happiness to make this demonstration for you. But you will see another one more wonderful than that. This is what I meant in my letter by telling you that I will see you in the morning. These are the things that help you to realize the truth of our life on the spirit side, and every such manifestation removes your doubt and confirms your belief."

She then verified Miss McClain's statement made at the previous Thursday evening class to the effect that Mary Ellen was in the center of the room dancing, and when I asked what Mary Ellen was saying on that occasion, the answer came:

"She was singing: "Mary, Mary, Quite Contrary." Couldn't you see her? You heard her."

I replied: "Yes, I did hear her, but I am not clairvoyant enough to have seen her. I wish I were that well advanced."

In this she encouraged me by saying: "You will be very soon now. I am going to write you another letter and give you some instructions that will be of help to you in cultivating clairvoyance and clair-audience both. It is easy for me to help you, because you are willing to make the conditions right."

Note:—Miss Mary McClain holds a small developing class at her quarters in the Richmond Apartments, and on last Thursday at this class I remarked that I could hear a voice in the room repeating "Mary—Mary" with something to follow, but could not make out what it was. Miss McClain replied: "It's Mary Ellen in the center of the circle, looking into my face and singing "Mary—Mary—Quite Contrary." Minnie's message through the trumpet confirms this.

I asked Minnie if it would not be easier for her to write from behind the cabinet if she placed the paper against the wall, so as to have a smooth surface. She objected with:

"That would only be overcoming one trouble by substituting another. We draw considerable strength from the members of the circle in writing, and can get this strength better by writing against the backs of the members in the battery."

The phonograph then started and Minnie sang "Aloha" for us. Following this we put in "Jesus Lover of My Soul," and both Minnie and Agnes (Mr. Lombard's sister), sang this as a duet. The voices were very clear and loud enough to have been heard by any ordinary-sized church congregation.

This hymn seemed to bring a wonderful vibration. "Fleet-foot," the Indian guide who comes to Mr. and Mrs. Majors, spoke with a strength that could have been heard clear across the street had the windows been open. He certainly proved to be a "real live Indian."

Then came Mr. Blinn on the same vibration, giving a wonderfully strong imitation of his train arriving at the depot; spoke to us a moment of his work as an engineer on the "Clover Leaf" route, and when asked if Fleetfoot had come in on his train, he answered, laughingly:

"No, he didn't have any ticket and the conductor wouldn't let him ride."

Crystal, the child helper, who comes to Mr. and Mrs. Majors, remarked that it was still raining in Los Angeles. Mr. Majors asked if she brought any rubber shoes along with her, to which the answer came:

"No, I don't need them. Mamma has a new pair which she can use."

Majors: "How did you know mamma has a new pair?"

Crystal: "I was with her when she bought them—today.'

Majors: "Well, if she's spent her money for rubbers I can't buy a new hat."

Crystal came back with: "You don't need a new hat. You just bought one a few days ago."

Note:—The fact is that Mrs. Majors did buy a new pair of rubbers that day, and Mr. Majors likewise bought a new hat just a few days before. No one in this circle knew of this except Mr. and Mrs. Majors. Can we doubt that Crystal was present in spirit and knew of these events?

Timothy then gave us an opening for questions and some one asked if there was any difference between a Helper, a Guide and a Control. The answer came, briefly but sufficiently explanatory:

"Your control will necessarily guide and help you in every way possible in order that he may the better control you when you are entranced; but your helpers and guides may not necessarily be controls. The helper and guide may be one and the same, despite the writings of earth psychologists. They draw too fine a distinction."

Goerner asked: "Tim, what do you think of our admitting the two latest applicants to the Research Society?"

Answer: "If you want to bring discord and trouble into the circle, let them in. But my advice would be to pass them up for the present. You will have trouble with them if you don't. Let me make another suggestion: Keep your classes together. Don't allow them to change from one to the other at will. Every change breaks the contact. You must not allow this. If you do you all suffer in a weakened vibration."

Krocho followed with this: "Say, Irish, are you ever going to get through talking?"

This brought forth a little repartee, in which both held their own with amusing tact—Timothy ready with Irish wit and Krocho just as quick and snappy with bad grammar and slang befitting the occasion. Then suddenly she changed like a quick turn around a sharp corner and went into a beautiful sermon on the lesson in "Jesus Lover of My Soul," saying:

"Friends, I asked for that hymn a second time—Jesus Lover of My Soul—because I love every word of it, and because I want to impress you all with the wonderful love that Christ has for you—that He loves all of you—every one of you—that His work here, as on earth, is to help you to live—to prepare the way for you—so that when you to come to this side you may know no darkness—that the way may be open and the gates to eternal life lifted for you. And how His brow is saddened when you turn your backs on Him and will not listen to that wonderful message of love and truth. If you could only realize what it means to be prepared. Some day dear old Dr. Peebles will talk with you and confirm this truth. Then you will hear it from one you all knew that Christ does live and that He labors for every one in His vineyard. Dr. Peebles accepted that love, that light, that truth and that helpfulness so freely offered by the Master and he knew no death. He has had no set backs and no delays. He came at once to his reward and the full measure of happiness that was his. He understood the spiritual life on earth. He believed it and he lived it. He met with no darkness in the world of spirit, but stepped right out of the body into full consciousness. He will come to you many times in the future to bring you the proof of everlasting life and spirit return, that you may know these things for yourselves and walk with Dr. Peebles in the paths of the Master. Good night friends, and the peace and blessing of the Father be with you all."

Note:—Minnie carried out her promise to see me the next morning after this seance and bring to me even a greater manifestation than the lighted hand which appeared on Sunday morning. I returned to my room after the Monday meeting and retired about midnight. I was awakened shortly after one o'clock and saw a number of lights moving about the room. I sat up in bed and watched them flying from place to place; small green lights, blue lights, red lights and white lights. They were numerous and beautiful and very much resembled "shooting stars." I caught the name of Minnie on my pillow, answered and thanked her for the demonstration. Then followed long streaks of light—perhaps a dozen of them—extending down the walls in parallel stripes almost from the ceiling to the floor. There was the same variety of colors, but the flashes of light were more lurid than the "shooting stars." For an instant a glow of violet filled the room.

I again thanked Minnie and remarked that she had certainly made good her promise to outdo the phenomenon of the lighted hand. This demonstration did not last more than one minute, I should judge; then all lights disappeared very quickly, one after another.

There were more folks in the room besides Minnie, as I caught the name of Clara, Mary and Annie.

For this statement I ask no consideration from the skeptic. Neither do I expect to receive any. But those who do not care to accept it as a fact can remember that this record is written for my own memorandum alone. It is not for the purpose of convincing any one else or making converts to spiritualism. The reader can "take it or leave it," just as he pleases.

Nevertheless, I confidently expect to have this confirmed at some seance in the near future in the presence of others who have gone far enough with psychic investigations to know what usually constitutes evidence and the case can rest upon such confirmation.

DID THIS COME FROM GEORGE WASHINGTON?

February 22nd, 1922.

The Wednesday evening class met at the usual hour, eight o'clock, and proceeded to work with one member absent. This did not appear to make any particular difference in the atmosphere and there was a general feeling that the work would bring forth a satisfactory result, but in just what way is always a matter that cannot be determined in advance.

There was, however, nothing of an unusual nature in the way of physical manifestations. A few transfigurations took place; there was an evident strong demand on our forces for strength for some purpose, and there was an occasional total obliteration of Mrs. Severy's head and face as at previous sittings.

Mary Ellen seemed to be enjoying the flowers on the center piece, handled them and made it known that she realized that the violets had been placed there for her benefit and that "Uncle George brought them."

Voices could be plainly heard throughout the evening and I remarked to Miss McClain that I had a strong impression that she was going to get some special message for me. She answered:

"Yes, Minnie says to tell you that at the first favorable opportunity she will give you a message through the trumpet and will also write out some instructions that will be of help for you when you go east."

A good part of the evening was taken up in inspirational messages through Miss McClain while Mrs. Severy was under trance. Friends from the "other side" gave out greetings and suggestions to members of the circle and there were some demonstrations in the way of etherealized forms—Mary Ellen, Minnie and my mother being all three on the floor at the same time.

The inspirational messages were more lengthy than usual and consisted mostly of instructions for the class to follow in its work. Also compliments and thanks to Mr. and Mrs. Severy for their earnest efforts in holding the class together, and for their harmony in the home as well as in the seance room.

As this was George Washington's birthday, someone remarked that they wished he would step out of the cabinet materialized, as it is reported he once did at Mr. and Mrs. Jonson's. Later a voice speaking through Miss McClain in a man's tone said:

"You ask for an appearance of General Washington. This gentleman cannot materialize for you tonight, but he will be pleased to address your little band of workers briefly."

Then came the following inspirational message. Whether or not it came actually from George Washington I do not attempt to say. All I say is that I know Miss McClain well enough to know that it was neither her voice nor general style of speech and in my opinion it did not originate with her.

"Dear Friends: It is indeed both a privilege and an honor for me to greet the friends of earth who are gathered here this evening. You are to be commended for your patience and devotion in this great work, and it is given to me to say that your efforts will be richly rewarded at no distant time.

"It is to be regretted that the constitution of your country has been grossly misinterpreted in regard to the matter of religious liberty. There is even in your advanced day bitter antagonism toward the principles of light and truth for which you have so earnestly met tonight. But those principles come to you from high authority and they will stand the test of time.

"Twenty-five years more will see this great truth rising with a force of fact and numbers that will command and obtain the recognition which is due it.

"You have in your dear country today many factions and many perplexing problems and there is much work to be done to clear the mists and bring you out into the full realization of that marvelous development of which you as a nation are capable. There is much dissension among your leaders and the path to further difficulties with neighboring peoples is fraught with danger. You will need a strong guiding hand and power from on high to aid you in overcoming the forces which tend to becloud your future.

"And, my dear friends, I pray for you and your country that wisdom and sustaining arm which will guide you into the light and the truth, and bring to you that deep and growing patriotism which has made you strong, has made you great and will lead you on to higher freedom and independence as individuals and as a nation.

"I bid you good night and God's blessing."

Note:—With the investigator, or psychical researcher, the question is not so much whether this came from Miss McClain or from the spirit of George Washington. Rather the question is, was it from the spirit of George Washington or from some interloping spirit claiming to be George Washington? Or, whether or not the speech was relayed through several instrumentalities on the spirit side between George Washington and the medium on the earth side—Miss McClain.

On this point it is possible to get at least some light by making inquiry of Minnie, or my mother, or both, who were doubtless present in the seance room at the time the speech was being delivered.

Those who argue that the message could have come from Miss McClain's subconscious mind, would first have to prove that she had ever at any time in her life heard such a message, because unless she had it could never have entered her subconscious mind. To furnish such proof would doubtless be even more difficut than proving that the message was, or was not, garbled through intereferences on the spirit side.

Most all of George Washington's public utterances have been published in one form or another many times. If any one can give evidence that any such speech was ever delivered by him on earth, it would be sufficient to establish the subconscious or telepathic theory. If not, they will have to fall back on the spiritistic hypothesis.

MEMORANDUM FROM TRUMPET SEANCE

Held at Mr. and Mrs. Jonsons, Pasadena, Cal., Eight O'Clock, Monday P. M., Feb. 27, 1922.

Five strangers came into the circle last evening and this, together with a few colds and an evident feeling of antagonism on the part of one of the visitors, gave the regular members a suspicion that there were too many "curiosity seekers" for good results.

This memorandum is, therefore, written merely to keep a record of two confirmatory messages from Minnie, which I desired for my own satisfaction.

The first was with regard to the lights which appeared in my room on the morning of Tuesday, February 21st, as noted at the bottom of report of Feb. 20th. A description of this demonstration of lights will be found at the conclusion of the report of Feb. 20th.

At the seance on Monday, the 27th, Minnie brought out a confirmation of this in the following language:

"George, this is Minnie. Didn't I tell you last Monday night that I would appear to you the next morning with a greater demonstration than the lighted hand, and didn't I tell you that I would not disappoint you?"

I replied: "Yes, you certainly carried out the plan to the letter and I want to thank you for it. It was beautiful and just as wonderful as it was beautiful."

She then asked: "You didn't try to count the lights, did you?"

Answer: "No, I didn't; there were too many of them and I was too much interested in the phenomenon to try to count."

This coming in the presence of thirteen witnesses was sufficient, and hoping to get an expression on the George Washington speech before she put down the trumpet, I asked:

"Minnie, you were in the room at Mr. and Mrs. Severy's when we got the inspirational speech that was supposed to have come from George Washington. Was that really from Washington or was some one else on the spirit side delivering it in his stead?"

Answer: "I prefer not to say, George."

George: I just asked the question because we had all discussed it among ourselves, and were all equally in doubt. Miss McClain would not feel in the least offended if she thought we questioned the real source of the speech."

Minnie: "I know it, George; but no good can come discussing it now, and it is sometimes better not to commit oneself."

Note:—My own impression is that if the speech had come from George Washington, Minnie would have said so. But these folks on the spirit side are usually very tactful when it comes to mixing in matters that may only hurt the pride of some one on earth or cause ill-feeling among friends or associates.

Many voices came through the trumpets and on a number of occasions both of them were being used at the same time and there was considerable confusion.

Sister Annie confirmed a materialization in my room early that morning, and stated that she had done this merely to give evidence of what can be accomplished when we on this side cooperate with the spirit side. I remarked:

"There were three or four times, sister, when I thought you were just going to walk right out of the alcove into the middle of the room."

She replied: "I will do so before long. Say, George, I was with Naomi when she received your letter and was so pleased that she felt so kindly toward your suggestion. The letter made her very happy."

Note:—I did write such a letter and sister Annie must certainly have been there to have known anything about it.

Krocho addressed me, with: "Goerner Chief, you've got it up in the head, haven't you?"

Goerner: "What is it I've got in my head?"

Krocho: "That cold—the sniffles. You wont get the flu; it will be better tomorrow."

Goerner: "How did you know I had a cold in my head?"

Krocho: "How could I help know it? Do you know, chief, that when we come to the mediums we take on all the aches and pains that they have got. We feel them just as they do when they are wide awake, but when we have possession of their bodies they don't feel them—but we do. When I control Auntie Jonson I feel all the hurts of her physical body until I get out and give the house back to her again."

Mrs. Jonson had evidently had some sorrow during the past few days and Krocho followed up her little speech with:

"Do you know, friends, there are times when we feel that it would be better to bring Gray Feather's medium and my medium over on the spirit side with us?"

At this some of them gasped in astonishment, but she kept on:

"No, you needn't gasp for breath, because I mean it. My medium and Uncle Joe have worked hard for many years to bring this great truth to the people of earth and God gave them a wonderful talent to do it with. And how have the folks of earth received it? Do you know how many mean things—wee, small, little bits of spite and trouble they have made, and how many heart aches and days and nights of sadness they have caused my medium? Of course, you don't. Do you think my medium is afraid to die? Not for one minute. Many a time she has asked me to bring her and Uncle Joe over to our side, to open the path so they can come—to put my little canoe at the bank where they can step in and be with us. Then I snug right close up to her and talk encouragement and tell her to hold on just a little while longer; that there is still work for her to do, and when that is all over with we will give her the signal and she can come right over and receive her reward. The little canoe will be there, all decked with roses and pretty flowers, and across the little river will be the shining lights and the smiling friends, and we will all be happy—so happy—then."

Catharine, who has been coming as a guide to Mr. and Mrs. Majors, gave this: "I will not be with you very much in the future. I go to a higher plane and my new life will keep me farther from the earth contact than heretofore. I know you will not mind this, because it means progress for me and higher duties."

Mrs. Majors: "No, indeed, Catharine, we would not want to stand in the way of your advancement. We will miss you very much. Does it mean that we will not see you or hear from you any more?"

Catharine: "Not exactly that. My work will lie in higher spheres, where I can do more good. I will come to you now and then and I will often watch over you, though you may not be so well aware of it. I can really aid you more though you may be less conscious of it."

Mrs. Majors: "How does it happen that you can help us more if you are farther away from us?"

Catharaine: "The vibration is better as we reach the higher planes; because then we work more under the psychical law and less under the physical law."

Note:—During the cabinet work a chair was handed out over the top of the curtain, very slowly and carefully. Then Mr. Huber, who sat at one end in the battery, had his chair lifted from the floor and rocked from side to side while he sat in it. He would weigh, I should judge, at least 140 pounds.

Every one in the circle noticed the demand on their strength and all spoke of it. This was, of course, greatest on Mr. Jonson, although it might have been less had it not been that two members in the battery were apparently not of very strong constitutions and could not give much support to Mr. J.

MEMORANDUM OF PSYCHIC EXPERIENCE

The skeptic who is looking for evidence will find plenty of it streaming all through these records. One of the most convincing proofs to me of the continuity of life beyond the grave, the truth of spirit return and spirit communication, came to me this morning,—despite the scientists who insist that materializations prove nothing. They do if the identification is good.

I retired at about 9.30 last night. A little after one o'clock I was awakened with a feeling that there was some one in the room. I opened my eyes and saw father standing at the right side of my bed. He was facing the table which stands at the head of the bed, but with his face turned toward me. I called: "Father, is it you?" and he answered, "Yes," by nodding his head.

There was no mistaking the features. He had the scant hair, quite bald toward the front, as in life; his moustache and long parted beard of reddish-brown. He spoke only in the merest whispers, and I kept on talking with a view of holding the vibration as long as possible and keeping him there.

Just back of him, and on his right, close to my bed stood another figure, which I took to be my mother, as she invariably comes with father on these visits. I could not make out the facial features of this second figure, nor could I see more than the etherealized form. I asked father if it was mother and he answered: "Yes." I asked if sister Annie was in the room, but could not make out whether the reply was Yes or No.

Father remained visible for fully a moment, clear enough for me to study his features, the style of collar which he wore and the familiar black string necktie such as he used in life. Finally he gradually disappeared and I turned over again and went to sleep.

At about five o'clock I was again awakened with a feeling that there was a hand on my head. I sat up in bed and saw Minnie on the right hand side. I did not have to ask for identification, although I did so, for I recognized the features at once. It was certainly Minnie. All I could see was the head, face, shoulders, arms and hands. She appeared to be kneeling beside the bed with her elbows resting on the bed and both hands clasped together with her right cheek resting on her hands. I called:

"Is this some one I know?" She smiled distinctly and replied in a whisper: "Its Minnie."

I then asked: "Are you going to chat with me a little?" and the answer came: "Yes" with a nod of the head.

In order to assist in keeping up the vibration and holding her I continued to speak:

"Well, sweetheart, this is just wonderful—for you to come like this. I didn't think it possible. I can see you as clearly as I ever did at Jonsons. This is so much better than a public materialization. Are there any difficulties in the way of your being able to speak when you come in this way?"

For answer she nodded her head, "Yes" and I could catch in whispers: "Its hard now—you talk."

So I discussed her appearance at Jonsons and it occurred to me to ask: "Have you been trying to impress me that you can come just as well here as at the materialization meetings?" (This was suggested by a remark along this line made to me by sister Annie at the Jonson trumpet seance Monday, the 27th). Minnie confirmed this by answering:

"Yes, in some ways easier." I then asked if she would be at the Miller trumpet meeting with me and got the reply: "I am always there." (Correct).

Note:—The statement that it is "in some ways easier" to materialize before me in the room than at the public materialization seances I assume means that there is not the chance for "cross vibrations" that there is in a circle of eighteen or twenty people, most of them strangers to one another and really having but little at common.

In the seance rooms we go upon the theory that "the other side" lives by the law of love and kindness, and it is our custom to use a great many terms of endearment and tenderness when conversing with spirit friends. I applied this to Minnie and she showed that she was wonderfully pleased. I caught the remark: "I am so happy that you recognize me."

I answered: "I couldn't help it, dearie; you are so perfectly natural and as sweet as a rose, as you always were when I knew you in life."

The face was Minnie's without a doubt—narrow and slender; hair brown and combed just as was her custom at school years ago. Her face was beautifully rosy and I suspect that there was some careful attention to detail here for the purposes of identification, as Minnie and her family were victims of tuberculosis and she had in life what is called "the hectic flush" of those afflicted with this trouble. She brought with her light enough to make the face clearly visible and it was easy for me to study it in detail. I could even see the amber-brown eyes which was always an outstanding feature.

In a meeting like this there will come during the brief period bits of conversation which are too sacred to place in a written record: they concern no one else, and yet they are usually the things that are most evidential in character. To me, personally, there can be no doubt as to the identity, both because of the resemblance and little stray remarks of by-gone days that could not possibly have been known to any one except Minnie.

She remained at the side of my bed for fully three or four minutes; then slowly began to etherealize, the face growing darker; the figure more obscure, until it disappeared altogether.

During all the time Minnie was present sister Annie was in the alcove of the room building up a materialized form, which, however, did not come into the main portion of the room. I recognized Annie's light and asked Minnie if it was Annie, to which she replied: "Yes." After Minnie left I carried on a little chat with Annie, although her only mode of reply was by light signals, which flashed up brightly for "Yes" and darkened for "No."

Note:—To me there was nothing of the "hallucination," "imagination" or "dream" about these visitations. They were real and I was wide awake and "possessed of my right mind." But those who have gone this far with these records know by now that my friends on the other side have a faculty of confirming these phenomena from time to time in the presence of other visitors and I shall be surprised if I do not get the verification of these manifestations at a very early date.

Wednesday night, March first, 1922. Confirmation of the above visits to my room came sooner than I had expected. The regular Wednesday evening developing class took place at the home of Mr. and Mrs. Severy, 4304 So. Western Ave., Los Angeles, with eight members present. Mrs. Severy was entranced and Minnie appeared as a transfiguration; that is, she displaced the features of the medium with her own and spoke through the medium's vocal cords, announcing:

"This is Minnie, George. You did not make any mistake this morning. I was there and was so pleased that you recognized me. I will be with you again tonight, as I always am. Goodbye."

This appearance has the marks of having been made for the express purpose of confirming her visit of the early morning, as she merely remained long enough to do this and disappear.

She said nothing about father's visit; but as he came to the room at about one o'clock and Minnie at five, it is possible that she knew nothing of his visit. Father may confirm this at the next trumpet meeting. To me personally it needs no further confirmation, as I have had too many of these visits not to recognize them.

Thursday P. M., March 2nd, 1922. Father's materialization was also unexpectedly confirmed at an early date in the following manner: It was Miss McLain's Thursday Evening developing class at the Richmond Apartments. My niece, Mary Ellen, stood in the circle etherealized for several minutes then crawled upon the lounge and sat beside me. Next she went to Miss McLain and began tugging at Miss McLain's sleeve and I remarked that I believed Mary Ellen wished to give a message. Miss McLain leaned over and got this clair-audiently:

"Tell Uncle George I am going to materialize in his room just like Minnie and grandpa did, and it wont be long. Tell him I saw the violets in the room today."

Note:—About five o'clock in the evening I purchased a small bunch of fresh violets and put them on the stand in my room. Looks very much as if Mary Ellen was certainly there, for I said absolutely nothing to any one about the violets. When placing the violets in the vase on the stand I carried on an imaginary conversation with Mary Ellen and she no doubt understood they were intended for her.

Throughout the messages coming to me from my own folks on the "other side" there is a consistency that is difficult to get away from. Minnie's truthfulness at school was a distinguishing virtue and her messages from the spirit side are characterized by the same trait. She may decline to answer a question, but she will never distort it.

The same is true of my mother, father, sister Annie and sister Clara. Jim Thomas was in life well known for a high regard for his word. That always meant more to him than anything else in the world and his messages from the spirit side bear out that same determination to adhere to the truth. It would be exactly like him and Mrs. Thomas to have raised their son John with that same regard for honor.

I, therefore, hold that truthfulness throughout this entire band that comes to me is a sacred thing and its absolute reliability may be depended upon. I would have readily accepted the word of any one of them on this earth without question, and I have just as much reason—perhaps more—for doing so now than then.

This seems to me the rational answer to the question as to the reliability of "spirit messages." If the message is relayed and distorted in the repetitions, then the blame cannot be laid to the original communicator. So far I have not often met with this difficulty.

Another interesting incident brought out at the McLain class was this: Mrs. Hill remarked that she saw clairvoyantly a large Collie dog walk through the circle and sit near me. I asked for a description and she replied:

"He is sitting up on his haunches with his forelegs propped up their full length. He has a white spot in his face and his tongue is hanging out of his mouth. He is a very large fine-looking dog."

I then said: "Watch him closely when I call a name and see what he does. Is this Rover? How are you Rover, old fellow?"

Mrs. Hill answered: "He shakes his head and his tail as if he recognized the name."

I have not yet been able to get information on the Thomas dog through their son Gordon at Chicago. But this is the third time this same dog has been seen clairvoyantly near me, each time by a different medium, no two of them being present at the same time or having any previous knowledge of the dog. They all give the description of the Thomas dog as first seen by Mrs. Miller and confirmed by Jim Thomas in the seance room.

MEMORANDUM OF TRUMPET SEANCE

Held at Residence of Mrs. Mary Miller, 1512 Magnolia Ave., Los Angeles, Cal., Tuesday, One O'Clock P. M., March 7th, 1922.—Sitter, G. F. Goerner.

I again carried on a conversation with Sunbeam's picture while Mrs. Miller went out to emerse her trumpet. The picture distinctly moved back and fortth as before, and there seemed something unusually animated about the face while I spoke. I dismissed this from my mind as probably imagination and perhaps would not have thought of it again had it not been for the reference made to it later by Sunbeam in her conversation with me through the horn.

She asked if I had noticed her smiling at me. I replied:

"No, I didn't, Sunbeam. How could you do that?"

Answer: "The next time you come you take good notice—watch closely—and see if I don't smile at you."

Here is another mystery yet to come. Will look out for this next time. In talking with Sunbeam, I remarked that from the view which I had of Mary Ellen when she came to my room last Saturday morning, I believed Mary Ellen and Sunbeam looked very much alike. She answered:

"Yes, they call us the twins on the spirit side." I followed with:

"Sunbeam, you know that dear sweetheart of mine, Minnie? I have never in my life had a photograph of Minnie, and I want to know if you will tell Minnie sometime how you made this picture for Mrs. Miller and see if Minnie can make one of herself for me, and get Mary Ellen to make one of herself too."

Answer: "All right, Uncle George—you see I call you Uncle George the same as Mary Ellen does. But Minnie and Mary Ellen and I will all get our heads together and see if we can't make the photographs for you." (Another interesting experiment).

In talking with Jim Thomas I asked what kind of a dog Rover was—whether Collie or Newfoundland—and was told:

"You might say he was both, George. He was really part Newfoundland and part Collie. When Mrs. Miller described him for you she spoke of his black and tan coat. He got the black from his Newfoundland ancestors and the tan from his Collie blood."

Goerner: "The reason I asked, he was described to me again the other night at Miss McLain's class."

Jim: "Yes, I was in the circle that night, George, and Rover was with me."

Changing the subject I said: "Jim, I suppose it will be all right for me to talk with you just as I feel and, as you used to say, 'like a Dutch uncle' without any fear that I am taking undue liberties."

Answer: "You talk right from the shoulder, old pal, just as we used to do in the office in Denver—just come right out with whatever you've got on your mind."

Goerner: "Well, you know, Jim, I have always tried to avoid using my friends on the spirit side for business purposes."

He interrupted with: "That's why we like to help you."

Goerner: "All right and thank you for it. Here's the point: Every now and then we get suggestions and advice from the spirit side on material affairs. How far is it wise for us to tie to this advice?"

Answer: "If you were not properly protected the advice wouldn't be of any value to you. But your band of protectors is formed on our side, and this holds good with the class of mediums you associate with. If I advise you in a certain direction it is just as if you had come to my office in Denver—I could only advise you within the scope of my vision and knowledge, with this advantage: From the spirit side I can hear and see your point of view and I can also sometimes be present when your opponents are discussing it and can give you the advantage of this information. I can sometimes warn you in advance.

"What you get from me in the way of a prediction is based upon conditions as I see them at the time. There may be sudden changes and if you were sensitive enough I might impress you as quickly as they take place and protect you. But if not the information may not reach you in time to be of help."

Goerner: "In other words, a man must use judgment and horse sense in any case?"

Jim: "Exactly. If you could depend on the spirit side for your thinking where would you get your development? If the conditions as you know them on your side conflict with the advice I give you, think it over cautiously and study it out; then if you can do so talk with me and I may be able to straighten things out—may be not."

Goerner: "Then the principal advantage you have is in your broader view of things from your plane and the fact that you can be present to both sides of the controversy?"

Jim: "That's right, and it will also explain why it is that our advance information on matters of great national and international concern is more likely to work out correct than if we attempt to predict the outcome of affairs among a handful of people. In the first case, big affairs in the making are not so likely to be upset by the whims of one or two people; but where a small company of business men are concerned one man may undo the best efforts and plans and change the program very quickly.

"We can help you many times, but the thing to remember is that the better you understand the law the closer we can get to you. You are on the right track and will soon be able to get your information direct. Don't be discouraged; you are becoming more clairaudient every day.

"One thing more, George: Take as an illustration your Research Society: The guides will come to the seance room and give you suggestions as to how to conduct the meetings to get good results. Then some of the members immediately turn around and insist on doing something different. You have seen the effect. Men will do this repeatedly in both spiritual and material matters.

"We can often do a good deal to help you in the way of mental suggestion, planting the right thought either with you or with the opposite side and in this way help both sides. We have done this twice recently where you were concerned, as you know." (Correct).

Father again confirmed his materialization in my room (as he did at Jonsons Monday night) and asked if I had observed the clothes he wore.

I told him: "Yes, father, I did, and I noticed particularly that you seemed to be dressed just about as I last saw you in life here; I noticed that you had the same style of collar and necktie that you have in the photograph which I keep in my room." Then I jokingly added:

"I am wondering how I can make a suit of clothes last me forty-one years."

He laughed and replied: "Well, my son, you will have chance to make it last you a thousand years."

Note:—I interpret this to mean that it would be just as easy to return with the same clothes for identification at the end of a thousand years as at the end of forty.

I asked little Georgie if he still took my hand occasionally when going through the streets.

"Yes, nearly every day," came the reply.

Goerner: "Don't you ever get afraid of being run over by the street cars?"

Answer: "Oh, no; when you get on the car I jump on with you, and you know when you wait for the cars to pass sometimes I stand there and wait with you; sometimes I go through the car and sometimes I go right over the car and then wait for you on the other side."

Dr. Worthington, trumpet guide, stated that the big Indian chief who had been in the room on several occasions was there and just wanted to greet me. Then came a strong, deep voice, loud enough to be heard on the sidewalk:

"Mr. Goerner, me one of your guides. Me big and very strong; me help you great heap. Me name Big Oak because me big and strong. You hear from me often in time to come and me help you many times."

I thanked him and assured him of a welcome; suggested that he talk with me whenever he could find the door open and that I would cooperate with him in every way so we could work together to good advantage.

Other speakers were my mother, sister Clara, sister Annie, Minnie, John Thomas, Mrs. Thomas, Mary Ellen and Dr. Worthington. These were mostly brief greetings or little personal chats.

Mother made mention of the strength furnished by the flowers which I placed in my room and called off the different varieties correctly—mentioning the lilies, the violets and the roses. She asked if I missed any of the violets from time to time. I replied that I knew some one had been taking them, but supposed it was the domestic who kept the room in order.

"No," she answered. "Mary Ellen knows the violets are for her and she goes in once in a while and takes a few out of the vase."

I asked her to tell me why it could be easier for the folks to materialize for me in my room without a medium than at Jonsons with Mr. Jonson in a trance. She explained it this way:

"In your room, my son, you are always asleep when we come, and we can draw upon your strength more freely than if you were awake, even though you are mediumistic. Then when we have all the preparations made we wake you up, and after we leave the room you can go to sleep again and get your strength right back. There are no conflicting currents for us to overcome, and no one present except those who belong within our own vibration."

MEMORANDUM OF TRUMPET SEANCE

Held at Residence of Mr. and Mrs. J. B. Jonson, 855 No. Marengo Ave., Pasadena, Cal., Monday, 8 O'Clock P. M., March 13th, 1922.

It was another evening of confusion. There were 21 people present including Mr. and Mrs. J. With three trumpets on the table and sometimes all of them going at once, with now and then an independent voice trying to speak or sing.

The cabinet manifestations consisted of notes from spirit friends behind the curtains; flowers for the circle and materialized hands. During this work a pair of dark hands, those of a colored person, were held well up to view. Mrs. J. asked if this was for some one in the circle and received three raps on the chair with the tambourine, indicating "Yes."

Mr. Baker then asked: "Is it George Rogers?" to which the reply came wth three raps, "Yes." Asked if he was awake to his new surroundings, he said "Yes." Asked if he had met Billie (Mr. Baker's departed son) he gave the same reply.

Note:—George Rogers was a colored boy who worked for the Bakers around their home. On Saturday, March 11th, he passed out of the body and at the time of this appearance his earthly remains were lying at the undertakers in Los Angeles. Just previous to his death, Mr. Baker assured him that he would wake up in a few hours after leaving the earth, alive and happier in spirit land. He (Mr. B.) asked his son Billie on "the other side" if he would make himself known to George before George passed out. Later George stated to Mr. Baker that Billie had come to him and assured him that he would meet George at the border and take care of him. Baker says George then resigned himself and seemed anxious to go. At the trumpet table Billie confirmed the arrival of George on the spirit side; said he was at the border to meet him, opened his eyes and assisted him in making himself known behind the curtain.

The sensation of the evening came with a most mournful, plaintive voice calling through the trumpet, like the wail of a soul in distress: "Oh, my! Oh, my! Oh, my!" We asked:

"Who is this?"

Answer: "Kennedy—Kennedy."

Question: "Is it John Kennedy, for Mr. Lombard?"

Answer: "No, No; Kennedy, the one they are trying Madalynne for."

The Circle: "Well, Mr. Kennedy, we are glad to greet you. Is there anything we can do to help you?"

Answer: "No, no; don't try to help me. Give your help to Madalynne."

Question: "Was Madalynne responsible for your death?"

Answer: "No, no; Madalynne did not commit this crime. She should not be made to suffer for it."

Question: "Would you care to tell us who did commit it?"

Answer: "No; it would do no good. It would avail nothing. Just help Madalynne. She is wrongly accused, friends."

At this he dropped the trumpet, as the voice had grown very weak and hardly audible. Later Timothy confirmed the Kennedy message, saying Madalynne was not guilty and asked that we give her our best thoughts to help her through her trouble; said her spirit friends were working with her and were with her daily in court; said at heart the authorities and jury did not believe her guilty, and that much could be done by mental suggestion.

Raymond Lodge spoke briefly to Mrs. Murray, a psychic who has received frequent automatic writings from one purporting to be Raymond.

During the cabinet work Silas Webster, Mr. Jonson's chemist guide, wrote this:

"Dear friends:—As a practical chemist in life, I never realized the necessity of conditions so fully as I do now,—where the vibration of a combative thought even has a bearing on results wished to be attained; but we are fairly satisfied and wish to do better."

Note:—The reference to counter-vibration because of a combative tendency I take to be in regard to myself. Some business matters had not gone right during the day and I went to the circle in a resentful frame of mind. I felt that I had no right to go, but went because I promised Mrs. J. that I would do so.

Mary Ellen wrote a cheerful little note commenting upon her love for the violets which I usually keep in my room for her. And when she spoke through the trumpet indicated that she realized that I was not in a very cheerful mood.

Minnie handed a note over the curtain enclosed in an envelope which I had placed on the chair, merely stating: "I cannot write tonight." Speaking through the trumpet she stated that it seemed that the pencil would not remain steady while she tried to write, and that she had to give it up.

I replied: "I think that was my fault, Minnie. It was my frame of mind and I soon saw that you would not be able to talk tonight unless I got out of it. I realized that you could not get within my vibration while I held to the thoughts of resentment and ill-will, and I have been sitting here getting rid of them so you could come."

Minnie: "I did not say, George, that it was any fault of yours."

Goerner: "I know you didn't; you are too generous to want to blame me for it; but I want you to know that I realize where the blame lies."

Minnie: "You will feel better after talking with me. It is a part of the earth life that these setbacks and depressions must come. There would be no chance for advancement on your side were it not so. There are times when it seems almost necessary to take what may appear a wrong step in order to right greater wrongs later. It will work out better in a day or two. Your father will talk with you about this when you are next at Mrs. Millers. Goodbye. I will come to you in the morning."

The following Thursday, March 16, at Mrs. Miller's, father came with this: "George, take the scowl off your forehead; throw up your head; raise your chin and straighten out the drooping mouth; put a smile on it."

George: "I know that's what I ought to do father; but up to now I didn't seem to find it very easy. Talking with you and Minnie has helped. There was too much disturbance within."

Father: "That is because you have not yet got control of yourself. You must get the mastery of both your mental and nervous forces. Then you will understand what is meant by inward harmony. A master is one who has learned to control himself. Here is a method that will help you wonderfully, and if any one thinks perfect control is impossible they can prove it to themselves if they will try this for just one month:

"Go to yourself every day and sit for half an hour quietly, in perfect control of your mental and nervous forces—in full possession of yourself. Say to yourself, 'Peace, be still' and repeat it whenever you find that you are not concentrating and that your mind is wandering. Hold your nerves under restraint; don't twitch and fidget about. Peace, be still. Drive out all worry and anxiety. Determine that you are too big for material disturbances.

"When you have mastered yourself you will find success will come to you by natural right—by natural law. You will find happiness, contentment, harmony and the spiritual gifts unfolding quietly and beautifully before you. The master stands near to the Christ and near to God. When you have conquered yourself you will feel and know and understand what Christ meant when he said: 'I and the father are one, and ye are one with God.' There's the power of the Trinity. It makes man one with God.

"Try this for one month, my son, and if you go at it earnestly and patiently you will learn that perfect mastery, perfect poise, is a truth and that it can be acquired. Once you have acquired it you have opened the door to all material and spiritual help and your psychic forces will multiply rapidly. You will be as an armor against attack—you will be a master, holding within yourself that peace of mind, that calmness of soul, that poise and power that passeth all understanding. This is my message to you today, son. Goodbye and God bless you."

Note:—I have included this discourse from father with the Jonson report in order to keep the record intact, although it took place at the Miller seance.

FULL RECORD OF TRUMPET SEANCE

Held at Resdence of Mrs. Mary G. Miller, 1512 Magnolia Ave., Los Angeles, Thursday One O'Clock P. M., March 16, 1922. Sitter, G. F. Goerner.

Mary Ellen was the first one to take the trumpet and began with: "Hello, Uncle George, I just sneaked in first before anybody else got a chance." I asked:

"Mary Ellen, what were you and little Georgie doing in my room this morning?"

Answer: "Oh, we were having just the most kind of fun; we played hide and seek and hid under the bed, annd behind the chairs and behind the trunk."

Goerner: "Well, I thought I saw you racing around the room about half past four. Sometime I'm going to get up and play hide and seek with you."

Answer: "Oh, wont that be fine. But you couldn't catch us."

Goerner: "No, I suppose not, because you'd be hiding in the ceiling, and I'd have to get a stepladder to find you."

At this she laughed and answered:. "By the time you got up the stepladder we'd be somewhere else. We could go through your trunk and hide inside and you couldn't see us."

I asked if she had talked with Sunbeam about making a photograph for me and she replied:

"Yes, Sunbeam and Minnie and I have been talking it over and we've got it all figured out how we are going to do it, and we'll make the pictures for you—one of Minnie and one of me."

I then asked—to see if she could connect up the incident: "Who taught you to whistle, dearie?"

Answer: "Oh, I just did that for fun. I couldn't pronounce that big word at Mrs. Jonsons and somebody said to whistle it and I thought I would just show you that I could."

Note:—At Mrs. Jonsons trumpet class last Monday night, the 13th, Mary Ellen tried to tell me that Mr. Thomas intended to materialize for me, but she had difficulty in pronouncing this word, and one of the circle suggestetd: "Maybe you can whistle it, Mary" and she answered by whistling through the trumpet.

Next mother spoke briefly, saying: "My son, we all want to thank you for the beautiful flowers you have placed in your room for us. You don't know how much they help us to come to you. They add strength and beauty and light, and they bring a spiritual significance that enables us to draw near to you. You make the conditions and we take advantage of them and it helps us in developing you so you can come in closer communion with us. We all love you and we find much happiness in these visits to your room and the talks through the trumpet. There are many others who want to chat with you today; so I will be brief. Goodbye, my son, and God bless you."

Sister Clara came third: "George, I leaned over the beautiful flowers in your room this morning, and sent a prayer up to the Master, grateful that you had found the way to this great truth and are so willing to open the door to us, so we can come to you and make known our continued existence; to tell you again that there is no death and that the grave means nothing. I know what trouble you are having trying to reach my children; they do not see these things as you do and cannot understand how it would be possible for them to talk with the dead, as they call us. But when you pass through Chicago, I know you can show them the way and the plan you have will be the means of opening the door to them. Thank you again, dear brother, for your efforts, and we will help you to bring them to us. Goodbye and when you see the children give my love to them all; tell them of the wonderful results you have been getting; let them know how the truth may be unfolded to them, and they will soon find by experience how wonderful, how beautiful and how sacred it is. Goodbye."

Grandmother Fowler (my sister Clara's mother-in-law) followed Clara. This was the first time she had ever attempted to use a trumpet and she seemed greatly pleased at being able to manifest herself in this way. During life she was always a very religious woman, a dear sweet old Methodist soul whom everybody loved. She had when in life given me many a religious lecture and it seemed natural to hear her say, in reply to my thanking her for her care of me during my childhood:

"You don't have to thank me, George. What I did for you I did because I loved you and because I found happiness in trying to help you. I did the best I could within my talents and God has richly rewarded me. I knew nothing of the great truth which you understand so well; but I followed the best light I had. I clung to Jesus on the cross; I accepted God the father, the son and the Holy Ghost, and Christ has bestowed upon me his smile. Is that not reward enough. I am happy; I am content in the world of spirit. I love you now as I did in your childhood. I am here to deliver to you the blessing of the Father and the peace of heaven. Goodbye, my boy; I will talk with you often until we are united on this side and there will be no parting. God bless you again and goodbye."

Then came: "George, this is Minnie. I stood with you beside the flowers in your room. I heard you name the lilies after me and call them 'Sweetheart.' I knew you felt my presence because you answered when I called your name. Whenever you are alone just call for Minnie and I will come to you. The lilies are a great help. They take you out of yourself and give the spiritual world a chance to get within. I tried so hard to write you from the curtain last Monday night; but it was necessary first to overcome your unusual frame of mind. I did not want the evening to go without talking with you and I was so glad when I at last reached you through the trumpet."

I replied: "I realized that I had placed a door up between us and worked hard to tear it down, but it seemed difficult to do until I felt you working with me."

Minnie: "Always take an account of yourself before you go to the psychic; rid your mind of everything in the way of resentment, envy or ill-will, because these things are not spiritual—they are material—and they obstruct your path to the higher law. But its all right now, George. The way is clear and I am happy to be close to you again. Goodbye; I will be with you in the morning."

Sister Annie confirmed her recent visits to the room; stated that the little alcove was becoming more sensitized and more magnetized all the time; that during my absence she and the folks would go to the room often, so that when I returned from the east I would see some startling materializations take place. Annie was certainly in the room the morning of this seance, because she mentioned the fact that she had seen on the table beside my bed a photograph of herself, of father and mother which I had placed there.

Little Georgie followed his mother and took great delight in confirming Mary Ellen's statement with regard to the fun they had in my room, playing hide and seek and I tried to draw him out as to how much he knew about the arrangement of things in the room by suggesting that sometime I would leave my trunk open so he could get into it.

He replied: "You don't have to leave it open. We hid in it this morning and it wasn't unlocked either. We went through it." (The fact is, the trunk was locked; but that means nothing to spirits).

Kitty, the cabinet worker at Mrs. Jonsons, just dropped in to say that she had been to my room that morning and had helped the folks to materialize; said she found pleasure in coming in and intended to talk to me on the pillow before long. Then she closed with, "There's a big Irishman standing here that wants to butt in to your circle."

Suspecting this was Tim, I answered: "You just tell Tim to come right in; that he's always welcome—any time, anywhere and everytime.

Tim: "Oh, I just wanted to say howdy, because I like you and I like your friends, and they are all my friends, and I like Mrs. Miller. She's a wonderful medium and you know I like to be with good people. You will notice the change in my voice: I'm using Mrs. Miller's vocal cords today instead of Mrs. Jonsons. It makes a very noticeable difference. Well, goodbye, friend; I'll see you at Jonsons Monday night."

When Jim Thomas appeared he took up my own trumpet; moved it up very slowly; waved it around the room; tapped the ceiling with it and all the time I could see it plainly, as it still has the aluminum band on it. He stated:

"I am going to use your trumpet today George, because I want to get it well magnetized for you. The last time you were here I used Mrs. Miller's, because she had not been well and I did not want to draw too much strength from her. You know, her trumpet is much more highly magnetized than yours is."

I asked: "Jim, were you in the office this morning?"
Answer: "Yes, and you knew I was there."

Goerner: "How do you know I knew it?"

Jim: "I heard you tell the young lady at the desk that you felt my presence." (Correct, I did so state to the lady in the office).

He continued: "I am in your office nearly every morning, very often with John and Dr. Worthington, and sometimes with your father. I materialized for you in your room yesterday morning, and was glad you recognized me. I did that to impress you, because I wanted to give you strength for the day's work."

Goerner: "Well, Jim I want to thank you and the folks for the work you did the past week and the help it gave me. It just seemed that previous to that it was almost impossible to get anything started my way."

Jim: "Well, we knew it would give you a little lift and you needed it. We picked the man who could do that work for you. We knew it would create a little feeling with your associate, but it was for his interest in the end as well as for yours. You will find the way clear when you get east and I am going to be right with you wherever you go. You will find me at every conference you hold. If things don't go right at the start, pay no attention to it. Just go right along, because we will look the situation over and weed out those who can't do you any good and pick those that will stand by you and that you can depend upon. We are glad you eliminated the Hebrew and it is well that you did; because you would simply have to be in trouble with him all the time."

I asked: "Jim, you know my business associate, M———, don't you?"

Answer: "Yes, I think I understand the relations between you very well."

Goerner: "What do you think of M———?"

Jim: "We like him; but he would get better results if he had better control of himself. He needs the lesson your father gave you a few evenings ago—needs it more than you do, because you are by nature of a more quiet disposition than he is. But it is a good lesson for 99 percent of the people on the earth plane. Your friend M——— must become the quiet master of himself and he will save his health and his mind from much worry. He has great energy and wonderful ambition; but he must look out for his health."

Goerner: "Jim, will he be able to pull out of his financial troubles?"

Jim: "He will if he takes care of his health. When you return from the east his troubles will be mostly over; that means as much to him as it does to you."

John Thomas surprised me with this: "Well, George, I am glad you got the patent on the boring machine. I heard you talking about it; but I knew it before you did. Your idea about getting out the second patent is good. Take advantage of it, because it will add strength to the invention and give it higher value to you. Then when you come back from the east, have the machine set up and tried out and I will be there to show you what changes to make. Then I'm going to connect you up with a manufacturing concern that will put it on the market for you better than you can yourself. I am often in the office and in your room with father and I am keeping a close watch of things for you."

I asked: "What do you think of Gordon not answering my letter with regard to communicating with you and his parents?"

John: "Well, George, you don't know Gordon the way I do. If some one tells you something wonderful, you'll investigate it even if you don't believe it. Gordon wont. If he don't think its possible he wont spend any time on it. He's hardheaded, and when you go through Chicago you will have to see him and talk with him yourself and we'll be there to help get him started."

Mrs. Thomas followed with a sweet little message, thanking me for the flowers in the room and my efforts to interest Gordon in communicating with her; then passed the trumpet on to father, who only passed a greeting. Then came Sunbeam:

"Hello, Mr. Goerner. You know Minnie and Mary Ellen and I have all worked out the plan for making the photographs. We are going to work on them while you are east and we are all going with you. Whenever you go to a strange medium call my name, so I can get within your vibration, because we will have to do this to make the photographs. Did you see me smile at you when you spoke to my picture? I winked my eye at you too."

Goerner: "Yes, I did, very clearly. I watched for it; but I don't yet understand how it is done."

Answer: "Well, I stood right there and placed my hands on the picture and sent out the thoughts that would produce the effect to impress you. But don't think the picture didn't smile, because it did."

Note:—So far as I could determine the picture did smile and there was a perceptible twinkle about the eye. I asked to have it repeated and it was done several times while I stood before the picture. To me the smile and the twinkle of the eye were as real as if they had been made by a human being. I do not, however, attempt to account for how it was done, and am not yet sure that I understand it. So the critic who wishes to argue that it was my "imagination" is entitled to his opinion for all I am concerned.

Dr. Worthington ended the seance by saying: "Mr. Goerner, that father of yours is a very wonderful man. He and I have become well acquainted lately. We were both physicians and surgeons in the earth life and have much between us in common. From him I have learned your history; I know the struggle you have had and we are all going to help you to forget it. We are interested in you and now that you have opened the way for us to get through and cooperate with you we can do you much good. You are sincere in your spiritual efforts and that means a great deal. Your father tells me how he has guarded your health during all these years. You have been very fortunate in that respect and you have a long life ahead of you. But after you get back from the east life will have a higher meaning for you and you will gain much of what you have lost in past years. The friends and guides who surround you from the spirit side are very strong for you and they can aid you a great deal both materially and spiritually. Do not worry about your trumpet. Keep it in your room. The voices are coming through very soon in a way that will surprise you and you will sit in your own room and talk with us just as you do here at Mrs. Miller's. Goodbye, friend and brother. We have all had a wonderful afternoon with you and have enjoyed it as much as you have."

MEMORANDUM FROM MATERIALIZATION SEANCE

Held at Residence of Mr. and Mrs. J. B. Jonson, Pasadena, Cal.,
Friday P. M., March 17th, 1922.

No attempt will be made to detail the work of the cabinet. The physical phenomena were all repetitions of those which have appeared to the circle a number of times before. There were twelve or fourteen visitors from the spirit side, all of them familiar to us and all recognized as friends, relatives and guides to various members present. No new materializations took place and the manifestations were all in the nature of those recited in previous records of this volume.

Not the least interesting feature of the evening was the recital by Mrs. Sarah Flint as to a miraculous operation performed upon her by spirit physicians and guides for an abnormal growth in the throat.

Mrs. Flint resides with her brother, Mr. Melvin Severy, an electrical engineer by profession, an inventor of ability and a retired business man, at No. 341 So. Berendo St., Los Angeles.

This story will naturally be discredited by those not familiar with psychic phenomena and not acquainted with the character of the people who vouch for its truth.

This throat trouble had been a source of much annoyance to Mrs. Flint for nearly three years and throat specialists whom she had consulted insisted that an operation under the knife was the only way to overcome it. It was this operation which she dreaded and had repeatedly asked her guides and friends from "the other side" to assist her out of the difficulty.

As Mrs. Flint related the story, she was visited at her home by friends from the spirit side who took possession of her and first gave her vigorous massaging around the throat, neck and chest. Then twisted, turned, raised and lowered her head repeatedly—first while she sat in one position, then another. Part of the time they had her on her knees; part of the time sitting in a normal position in a chair; part of the time with her body twisted and distorted in various positions lying in bed, and part of the time she stood erect upon her feet.

These manipulations kept up from about eight o'clock in the evening until nearly one o'clock in the morning. Finally, she felt something in her throat snap, as if a cord or a muscle had given away. Then she suddenly realized that the trouble had left her throat; there was a clear passage and she could breathe, swallow and articulate naturally. There was no blood and no pain except some slight discomfort from the violent movements of her body and head. She states that for a few days after the operation the muscles of her throat and neck felt sore, as if from some unusual exercise. But so far as she could determine up to this date (a week after the treatment) the operation was a complete success; the growth has disappeared entirely and there seems not even a trace of it left.

Mrs. Flint was not in a trance during this work, but remained fully conscious and wide awake the entire time. She could only see the forces that were working upon her dimly, as if in the etherealized form, but felt the pressure of their hands and arms as plainly as if they were earth inhabitants.

Mr. Severy, her brother, vouches for the truth of this story, so far as the results are concerned, and states that to his knowledge there was no one from the earth side in the home during the treatment but Mrs. Flint and himself, and that he is convinced that the trouble in his sister's throat—of which he had known from the time of its first appearance—is certainly no longer in evidence.

Note:—A week later, viz.; Friday P. M., March 24th, Mrs. Flint stated to the writer that the treaments had been continued and that during the intervening week the operations consisted mostly of massages by her own hands under direction of the guides from "the other side;" that the improvement was very noticeable and that she is still enjoying great relief as a result.

MEMORANDUM OF TRUMPET SEANCE

Held at Residence of Mr. and Mrs. J. B. Jonson, Pasadena, Cal., 8 O'Clock P. M., Monday, March 20th, 1922

The cabinet work dragged and the manifestations from behind the curtain were "tame." I suspect this was partly due to the fact that Mr. J. was unusually tired and not very keen about this part of the evening's work.

At the trumpet table some one asked Krocho (Mrs. J.'s trumpet guide) if that was really Belton Kennedy who came to us on the previous Monday evening and the reply came:

"Friends, I have never deceived you about anything and I am going to talk straight out, because there's a lesson here for you all to learn: That was not Belton Kennedy. No one asked for any identification. If you had he could not have given it to you. Mr. Kennedy did not come to this room on that night."

Some one asked: "Then who was it, Krocho?"

Answer: "Just a new soul who had lately come over to our side and was looking for an excuse to get back to the earth plane."

Goerner: "But why should any one want to come into the circle by claiming that he was Belton Kennedy when he wasn't?"

Krocho: "There's the point. You had a couple of strangers in the circle that night. One of them is mediumistic—and not particular about what sort of spirit she allows to take possession of her. That voice through the trumpet did not come to you through my medium. It came through this stranger, and the lesson I want you all to learn is that you must not lend yourselves to every influence that is willing to come in for the sake of giving manifestations. Go slowly, develop under good, sincere spiritualist mediums only, and do not be anxious to go under control until you learn who is going to control you. The Master said: 'Try the spirits whether they be of God.' That's the thing to remember. Be on your guard; trust to your own dear folks on the spirit side and you will have no need to fear anything. They have your interests at heart and they are guarding you like angels with two-pointed swords. No, that was not Belton Kennedy. You can just dismiss that little incident from your minds now that you have had the lesson; but it will do you good to know it, because it will teach you the value of going into this work cautiously, sincerely, in deep earnest and with a prayer for guidance in your hearts and on your lips. If you desire good influences, you will get good influences. If you don't care what you get, you will not get much of anything. Think only good and only good can come to you."

"Billie," Mr. Baker's departed son, advised his mother that Sir Oliver Lodge's family had heard of Raymond Lodge's manifestations at the Jonson home and that they (the Lodge family) were discussing the plan of sending Raymond's brother to Pasadena to witness these demonstrations; that the plan had not been definitely decided upon, but that the family were thinking it over.

Billie also stated that George Rogers (the colored boy who formerly was employed at the Baker home, and only recently passed out of the body) wished to know if he could have a chance to talk with his auntie in Los Angeles.

Krocho put in the reply without waiting on the circle: "Yes, friends; don't be selfish. This boy's aunt is an intelligent, well bred colored woman. She is a close follower after Christ and a real spiritualist. It would help George to advance on our side and would be a great comfort to his auntie. Don't be selfish—let her come in. When you reach the spirit side you will find that there is no color line, and kindness and charity on the earth side to the meek and lowly in life is what the Master taught, and we ask you to follow Him; don't shut yourselves up in your own tight little coat; but tear off the buttons and throw the coat wide open, so God's blessed influence can get way down deep into your hearts. Let George's auntie come in and talk with her boy; it will do him good, do her good and do all the rest of you good."

Next a trumpet patted me gently on the arm. This was followed by a voice, saying:

"Brother, this is sister Annie. I want you to hear what I am saying: When you reach Chicago go to a trumpet medium and talk with me. I will have something to say to you then. I know you will not forget it."

I answered: "Rest assured, I will not forget it. I have two or three good names which I got here at Jonsons and I know anyone they recommend will be all right."

Annie: "Yes, you can trust to that. We will help you to pick good mediums while you are away, and you will have means of knowing the ones which have our approval."

I thanked her for her materializations in my room and she again assured me that "it is our happiness as well as yours to come to you; we all love you and we want to help you in every way we can. Goodbye; we are looking forward to another talk with you at Mrs. Miller's before you leave."

I asked: "Did you know I intend to be at Mrs. Miller's again?"

The answer came: "I knew you had thought of doing so." (Correct).

Sister Clara made a similar request, saying:

"I will want to talk with you in Chicago, too, George, because I have something to say to you about the children. We can help you to make it easy for them to reach us. Did you know I was in your room this morning?"

George: "Yes, sister, I did and sat up in bed and answered your call. For a time I couldn't make out whether the name was Clara or Harold; finally I seemed to sense your presence and when I asked,

Clara: "Well, I only dropped in to say 'good morning,' and let 'Is it Clara?' I caught your answer. Then you disappeared. you know that I was there.

Some unseen hand tapped me on the shoulder and arm. I raised my head, saying: "Thank you for the greeting, dearie. I believe I can guess who that is."

The voice came through the trumpet: "You know who it is, Uncle George. It's Mary Ellen. I am going to sit on the seat beside you on the train when you go away, and I don't want you to be reading that book all the time."

George: "What book do you mean, dearie?"

Answer: "The book you bought Sunday."

George: "How did you know I bought a book Sunday?"

Answer: "I was with you when you bought it, and I was with you when you bought the flowers and helped you to pick the violets. Say, Uncle George, what am I going to do for violets when you go away? You'll have to get out of the train and pick some for me."

George: "I'm afraid if I tried that I'd be picking flowers outside and the train would be going on with me out on the desert."

She laughed at this and answered: "Better let me get them for you. I can catch up with the train. When I sit up and talk to you if you do all the things I want you to do the rest of the people in the car will think you are daffy."

George: "I have a suspicion that the folks who have the rooms on either side of me suspect that when they hear me talking to you during the night."

Answer: "No they don't Uncle George. I know what they think. I'll tell you: They think there's some one in there who talks in his sleep a good deal."

George: "Listen, dearie: Will you make your presence known to me on the train, so I will know you are there?"

Answer: "Yes, I'll impress you so you wont have any doubt about it. You will know I am there with you."

The evening was getting well toward the end and I asked Krocho if Minnie was in the room.

Answer: "Yes, and you needn't be afraid you are not going to get any mush, Mr. Goerner Chief, because she's picking up the tooting horn right now to talk with you."

Minnie came in throwing kisses through the trumpet and asked:

"Could you hear me answering you when you spoke to the flowers in the room this afternoon?"

George: "Yes, I did, Minnie. That was an experiment I tried and want you to know that I appreciate your coming to me and felt mighty well pleased to know that you could hear me and answer so quickly."

Minnie: "Did you know who woke you up this morning?"

"George: "Of course I did, because I caught your name as soon as I realized that I was awake."

Minnie: "Well, I want to say this: Before many days I am going to have a long talk with you through your own trumpet. I want to finish the talk we started at the materialization Friday night; the vibration became weak and I couldn't tell you just what I wanted to say. I will wait for the chance until I can tell you myself without having to talk through any other instrument.'

George: "That will be fine. I am going to look forward to that talk with a great deal of pleasure.'

Minnie: "The pleasure will be as much mine, George. But don't be puzzled about cold hands. They mean nothing of importance and there is no significance attached to that. It is the things I wanted to tell you that will help you to live that count, and I do impress you often when wrong thoughts come to you. You will not allow them to dwell with you, because I know you would not wish to put any sadness in my heart—and we are all saddened when we see our friends on the earth side do wrong or think wrong. Yes, this is the only sadness we know on the spirit side. Our life here is made up of happiness and contentment and kindness. Nothing can take this from us. But wrong acts, unkind thoughts and ill-will sent forth by our friends on earth are things that hurt, and I know you do not want to hurt or sadden any of us. I talk to you this way because I want to help you live, that you may know no darkness on this side. You have our good thoughts always—your mother, your sisters—all your friends and we want to help you. Good night; I am always with you and you will hear from me often."

Note:—The reference to the "cold hands" goes back to the materialization class of Friday, March 17th. I stepped into the cabinet with Minnie. She placed her hand in mine and I noticed that it was as cold as death, and said, "Minnie, your hands are cold tonight. Last week they were almost as warm as mine. How does that happen?" She replied, "atmospheric conditions have something to do with it; also the vibration is not so good tonight."

Krocho suddenly burst out laughing and then gave us a humorous recital of Mrs. Jonson's efforts to run an automobile for the first time. During the past week Mr. and Mrs. Baker had loaned their spare car to the Jonsons and they started out to learn how to drive it. Krocho described every movement in that undertaking. In speaking of the filling of the inner tube she said: "The first thing they did was to blow me up." She evidently was in the car, for she did not overlook one detail of that dramatic effort and it was as good as a specialty act in a vaudeville to hear it. We asked where she sat and she replied:

"All over the car. It kept me guessing to see which way my medium was going to jiggle the thing."

Some one asked: "Did she try to back up."

Krocho: "No, sir; my medium never backs up; she only goes forward. That's her style."

On being asked where Gray Feather was during all that time, she said: "He didn't do anything but sit right on the front of the car over the engine, expecting to see the buss climb a telegraph pole any minute."

She saw all the comical phases of the incident and seemed to have had a great deal of fun out of it. Finally she finished with this:

"My medium is no longer sixteen. But she learned to swim after she passed fifty and she's going to learn to run that car. I taught her to swim and I'm going to teach her to motor, and I am going to see that nothing serious happens while she's learning."

The circle then sang, "Nearer My God to Thee," and Krocho concluded the seance with:

"Friends, right here is a good place to leave you, so that you may all take to your homes the words of that beautiful hymn, 'Nearer My God to Thee.' You will never know how near you can get to the Father until after you reach this side and realize that you are after all one with God. Do not shudder at death or look upon it with fear. It is nothing of that sort at all. When the Master decides that he can no longer use you on the earth plane, and that you can do more good on this side, he will ask for the body. Do not stand back; just step out and let the elements take possession of it. It is of no further value to you. You can then enter into the joy of thy Lord and receive your reward on the spirit side of the river. Then life will have a newer meaning, a more real meaning, and you will for the first time know what true happiness, true harmony and true peace hold for you . You will know what it means to throw off the old physical coat and step into the spiritual body and life everlasting. Good night, everybody."

Note:—On Sunday morning previous to this seance I purchased a volume on psychic research in order to have something to read on the train going east. I also purchased that day some roses, lilies and violets and took them to my room. This will confirm Mary Ellen's remarks as to being with me when I made the purchases, as no one at the Jonsons knew anything about my having procured either the book or the flowers, and it could not have been a case of her overhearing any comments from me on these subjects; but looks very much as if she had gotten direct from my mind the thought I had of reading the book on the train.

But there is evidence enough through this volume to identify Mary Ellen many times over. The same thing may be said of the rest of my folks and those who comprise the band of friends who have made numerous appearances to me in the past twelve months.

"WOUND UP IN A COIL OF TECHNICAL RESTRICTIONS, DELICATE DETAIL, COLD RESERVE AND UNCOMPROMISING ROUTINE."

Memorandum from Miss McLain's Thursday Evening Developing class, Richmond Apartments, Los Angeles, Cal., March 23rd, 1922.

There were only seven members present, including the medium, Miss McLain. After the usual work was finished a discussion took place among us arising out of a statement made that most of the mediums appeared to be uneducated people, frequently very illiterate, and that poor English, both in the seance room and on the platforms of the spiritualist churches, seemed to be the rule.

(This does not, however, apply to Miss McLain. She is a woman of refinement, well educated, a painstaking student and uses excellent English at all times).

Our comments were confined largely to attacks on the ignorance of the spiritualist mediums and speakers. Our remarks were evidently overheard on the "other side," for Miss McLain suddenly went into a trance and we were gently "called down" by the controlling spirit in the following manner: The language is not exactly that given by the control, but is substantially correct, as the leading points were taken down in shorthand at the time they were delivered:

"Friends of the earth: Education, culture and the refinements of good training are all desirable qualities and without them progress would be slow and the enjoyment of material life unsatisfactory indeed.

"All people have the germ of mediumship within them; but how rarely do we find it well developed in the educated. Why? Education as it is forstered in the material world schools the mind to question all things not readily discernable by the physical senses or easily understood. The scientifically trained mind becomes an inquiring mind to the degree of skepticism. It is not an open mind. It is not often receptive or passive. Your scholar in the sciences will not humble himself as a child. Unless he be as a child he cannot enter the kingdom of heaven,—by which we mean the realms of progressed spirit land—the clasps which open the book of knowledge—which bring the spiritual gifts, clairvoyance, clair-audience, the phenomena of the trumpet, materializations, healing and other forms of mediumship.

"To develop these gifts requires a receptive mind—a passive mind. You here this evening know from experience that you cannot enter the seance room opinionated, clouded in doubt, criticism and condemnation and still get results. Your experience has taught you that it does not come that way.

"Investigating all your life and never living the life will get you nowhere on the spirit side.

"Your humble woman, humbly born and living humbly, uneducated likely by necessity rather than by choice, has not developed the mind to the point where it loses its receptivity or passiveness. She is usually nervous, because she is sensitive; but the inner being is alive to the knocking of the spirit on the door. The spirit enters, finds a welcome and an instrument that can be of service in bringing conviction to the seeker after truth. Those who visit the medium may be superior in education; but they lack the wonderful satisfaction, the wonderful enjoyment that comes with mediumship—clairvoyance, clair-audience, the beautiful lights, the whispering voices, the forms of dear departed friends and the music heard only by the ear attuned to it.

"Your sceientific investigator too often approaches the medium with a feeling of mistrust and even contempt for the undertaking. It is a frame of mind that can lead him nowhere. You here tonight, though but novices in the work, know that it cannot. Your man of science has not learned that he cannot fathom spiritual laws by material methods. He often becomes by nature of his training involved in a coil of what may be called technical red tape which works against him when he enters the spirit world.

"Many of your profound scientific investigators have left the earth plane under a compact to return to their colleagues, identify themselves and unfold to them the secrets of the psychic world. But, alas, how illy prepared they were to meet the conditions of the great beyond they only learned when it was too late. Not one of them has been able to keep that compact in any very substantial manner, and almost to a man they have failed to come to consciousness within the normal length of time. They are still in a daze, wound up in a coil of technical restrictions, delicate detail, cold reserve and uncomprising routine.

"It may be said that each and every one of you present tonight became interested in the beauties of spiritualism through some personal experience with a medium who could bring you once more in the presence of some dear departed one whom you had supposed dead beyond recall. Perhaps it was only a word, but it was all that was needed for you. You understood more of spiritualism from that one word of comforting reunion than from volumes of scientifically written matter on the subject of technical evidence. It brought more proof of the continuity of life and of spirit return and spirit communication.

"But do not think the present untutored condition of the medium will always remain, for it will not. The spirit forces are even now cooperating with the earth forces to prepare the sensitive for that efficient work which finds itself first in spiritual development, then in a trained mode of expression, platform delivery and well chosen diction. Your psychics of the earth are keener to take advantage of this schooling than you have here given them credit for. But we need not hold a dispute over such a slight difference. You have meant well and have only expressed sentiments borne of an inadequate knowledge of the progress so far made in this regard.

"But the scientific investigator must also change his method if he would achieve success both on the earth and spirit sides of life. Technical methods of investigation alone, rigid exactions demanded of the medium, criticism and cold reserve may bring you an indifferent result on the earth side, and still leave you in darkness when you reach the spirit side.

"Live the life, or the learning of scientific facts will avail you nothing beyond the material world. God is the ruling force and God gives to the inhabitant of the earth world as likewise to him of the spirit world, that knowledge which is best for him and gives it at the time and in the manner which is best, and no attempt to reconcile earthly facts with spiritual truths will change even the smallest of God's laws. Since you cannot change the law, you must seek to understand it. How? There is but one way, **and that is to live it.**"

INSPIRATIONAL MESSAGE

The following message was delivered inspirationally by Miss Mary McLain at her Thursday evening developing class, Richmond Apartment, Los Angeles, March 16th, 1922, eight o'clock P. M.

Miss McLain went into what is called an "inspirational trance" and seemed to be very deeply under control. After returning to her normal state she knew nothing of the nature of the message and could not even tell what the subject was.

The speaking guide was presumed to have been "Alice," the spirit who usually controls Miss McLain in trance. Her remarks were taken down in shorthand just as delivered, and are reported in full for the benefit of those who hold themselves aloof from the seance room for fear they may hear something that will offend their orthodox ears.

"Unto this circle of silent investigators we come tonight to bring the blessing and the unfoldment so much desired. It is a long way for some to travel, but once started on the road there is no turning back. Even if you so desired you could not, for the urge is within and you would have the will to go onward, forward and upward until you are into the relization of your oneness with the Father.

"You are, each and every one, a part of the great source of all wisdom, all power and all love. Go forth and express in every word and every act of your life your oneness with this great fount of eternal truth. You each one have a work upon this earth to do and the sooner you prepare yourselves for the beginning of that work the purer you will be, the more powerful you will be and the greater will be your success in both the spiritual and material things of life.

"It is a mistake to think that we of the spirit side do not realize the necessity of material things and material surroundings, for we do. We realize the contentment, the satisfaction and the health it brings to you to have comfortable and harmonious homes. We realize that you cannot be used by the higher forces until the physical body is strong, clean and pure. Work and live so as to bring yourselves into these higher vibrations, not only mentally and physically, but spiritually; for as you breathe and live and become one with the Father, so can we bring to you a perfect and harmonious body, and as long as you inhabit that body treat it well; take care of it as you would of a valued garment. But when the time comes to lay it aside, grieve not, remembering it has served you well and its use is over.

"So when one who is beloved by you removes in spirit from the earth to the eternal home beyond, do not grieve. It is selfish to do so, for he whom you have loved has but stepped into a higher plane.

"You rejoice when a child is born to the earth plane of sorrow and suffering; but grieve when that child is born into the land of peace and happiness and rest. Why? Because you do not understand that it is the fulfillment of the law.

"All nature will be kind to you if you will but realize that you are only here in obedience to the natural law,—that you are a part of the great scheme of life; and that you are a part in such a way that you can never step aside and escape your responsibility or your work. Your work is a part of yourelf. It was born into the world with you and you will not go forth from the world until you have accomplished that which you have been placed upon the earth to do.

"There are no two who require the same discipline, the same experiences; but all must learn according to his needs, and that is why one must follow one path and one another path.

"We bring to you all love, all encouragement and the message of the beloved Master on high,—the message of truth, of purity and kindness. These will bring you light and help. Live by these things.

"You are gathered here tonight to enjoy the harmony and the contact with the higher world. It helps us to give of our strength that those who are here may help one another. You help us even as we help you, and it is our work and our pleasure to bring to you unfoldment, calmness and joy.

"You, individually, here tonight, have some one specially interested in trying to give to each of you the strength which you need. Patience and devotion are required and sometimes sacrifices in order that you may unfold the highest within. To all of you tonight we can earnestly say that one and all are growing. You are growing in many ways, and it will not be long before you will have demonstrated this fact to yourselves and to others.

"Now, as I go, I leave with you that higher love, that greater purity, that divine sweetness which cometh from above, and we give unto you the blessing of the Father. May God's grace, peace and happiness rest with you all. Goodnight and Amen."

THE END

Messages similar to the foregoing reach me at the rate of two to five every week and could be recorded indefinitely. But the few I have selected will serve the purpose of the volume. My intimate friends who have loved ones on the other side, and for whom this book was prepared, will have no trouble recognizing the message from beyond, and those who think while they read will connect up many links of evidence that go to make a convincing chain.

To me the conviction is fixed that I have more to gain on "the other side" than I have on earth. It has divested me of every fear of death and I have long ago accepted as a proven fact the continuity of life without a break between this world and the next, and I accept with the same faith the evidence of spirit return and communication.

Just a suggestion to those who ask how they may become acquainted with a reliable medium: I believe your best chance is through visiting some well organized, well conducted spiritualist church and watching the work of the psychics there. In this way you will be more likely to find some one of integrity and talent than by following newspaper notices. Exercise care and judgment and you will in time meet the right sensititve. Then form a weekly circle under the direction of the psychic and cultivate results.

www.ingramcontent.com/pod-product-compliance
Lightning Source LLC
Chambersburg PA
CBHW020228170426
43201CB00007B/352